REMOTE LAN ACCESS

A guide for networkers and the rest of us

JEFFREY NEIL FRITZ

MANNING

Greenwich
(74° w. long.)

The publisher offers discounts on this book when ordered in quantity.
For more information please contact:

    Special Sales Department
    Manning Publications Co.
    3 Lewis Street
    Greenwich, CT 06830
    or
    lee@manning.com
    Fax: (203) 661-9018

Typesetting: Sheila Carlisle
Copy editor: Donna Brown-Wodaski
Design: Frank Cunningham
Cover: Paul Chevannes

Recognizing the importance of preserving what has been written, it is the policy of Manning Publications to have the books we publish printed on acid-free paper, and we exert our best efforts to that end.

The author and the publisher of this book make no warranties of any kind, expressed or implied, with regard to the information contained in this book. The author and publisher shall not be liable in any event for any loss or damages caused by, or arising out of, the use of information contained in this book.

All products mentioned in this book are trademarks or registered trademarks of their respective holders. Use of a term in this book should not be regarded as affecting the validity of any trademark or service mark.

Library of Congress Cataloging–in–Publication Data

Fritz, Jeffrey N., 1945–
    Remote LAN access: a guide for networkers
    and the rest of us / Jeffrey N. Fritz.
       p.   cm.
    Includes index.
    ISBN 1-884777-25-2 (softcover)
    1. Local area networks (Computer networks) 2. Integrated services
    digital networks. 3. Computer terminals--Remote terminals.
    I. Title.
    TK5105.7.F76 1996
    004.6'8--dc20   96-25891
                                                      CIP

96 97 98 99 CR 10 9 8 7 6 5 4 3 2 1

Printed in the United States of America

This book is dedicated with love to my teenage children, Nathan and Deborah. Both are active users of remote LAN access technology, and have been for some time.

I have learned a great deal about networking from my children. A network outage occurred not long after I had installed an ISDN line to connect my home LAN with the West Virginia University campus network. I came home from a long, hard day spent troubleshooting problems on the campus network. Instead of hearing the usual, "Hi, Dad!" as I arrived home, Nathan greeted me at the door with, "Dad, what's wrong with the network? I can't get to any Internet sites!"

May the benefits my children gather from the technology presented in these pages increase their knowledge of the world around them. May it also make up, in part, for the many times they were told that Dad was "writing the book" and could not be disturbed.

Contents

In his starring role as "Popeye," Robin Williams at one point is confronted with a particularly perplexing situation. Looking off-camera, he mutters under his breath, "I ain't no fizzy-kist, but I knows what matters." Jeff Fritz is no physicist either, but he knows what matters, particularly when it comes to remotely accessing Local Area Networks (LANs).

In his role as an early adopter and implementer of Integrated Services Digital Network (ISDN), Jeff has been there and done that. Since 1988, his goal has been to provide enhanced network access for students, faculty, and staff at West Virginia University. He has emphasized the deployment of ISDN and related technologies to achieve that end. That's why it is so helpful to read Jeff's book and benefit from his experiences and hardships. Adding Jeff's knowledge and experiences to our own, we find ourselves much more capable in our own attempts to provide remote access to or from those LANs and networks to which we have interest, and we do have interest in remotely accessing LANs.

High on the list for many readers is the desire to access commercial Internet service providers. Increasingly, Internet service providers furnish remote access to their networks, via strange-sounding protocols like PPP or Multilink PPP. They do this whether using ISDN or traditional modems.

Also high on the list for many of us is an interest in telecommuting. We are interested because we want, or need, to work from our homes. Telecommuting is a very liberating and addictive thing. Personally, I would not want to be without the ISDN line that connects my house to my workplace. Remotely accessing my corporate network allows me to get electronic mail, share files, and generally do nearly everything from home that I can do when I am at the office.

Even within our own enterprises, we find that both the organization and the supporting information technology systems have been reengineered from functional to process-oriented. This requires most of us to work in ad hoc teams with people of various disciplines that are at times unpredictable and often over widely scattered locations. Here again, remote LAN access becomes critical to productivity.

It is easy to see that remote LAN access does more than provide basic connectivity to the office. Through it, not only can we access corporate information services, but we can also exchange information with distant colleagues, attend international meetings, and generally stay abreast of whatever knowledge we need to do our jobs. Importantly, we have access to the information we want without ever leaving the comfort and convenience of our study or den.

As I said, telecommuting is a very enabling technology. However, it takes understanding and commitment from both the corporate and home-user sides to make telecommuting successful, or even possible. Ironically, better communications in the office often sets up dissonance when an individual is not able to access the corporate LAN. Perhaps that person is traveling, at home, or at a remote site that is not directly connected to the enterprise LAN. Although it might be extremely valuable for the remote worker to have network connectivity, the mysteries surrounding connection to remote networks often prevent the worker from connecting.

This book provides guidance and insight by focusing, in an understandable yet relaxed manner, on the things that matter in meeting the worker's connectivity needs. That is why *Remote LAN Access* is such a valuable resource. It provides solid remote LAN access guidance and insight to the network administrator, as well as to the interested telecommuter. Jeff's explanations help us understand what is happening, how to achieve success, and how to avoid problems. They also help networkers deal with the complex and often overwhelming issues involved in connecting their networks to remote locations.

Wisely, Jeff has avoided focusing on vendor-specific details. The reader will, of course, consult current technical journals, seminars, vendor literature, and other sources of vendor-equipment details. Instead, Jeff focuses on the practical aspects of remote LAN access. Having read this book, readers will be able to fit their need for network access into a specific framework of understanding. They will have the tools to apply what they have learned to particular implementations and equipment.

On a personal note, I have known and worked with Jeff for almost five years. He has led the group in the National ISDN Users' Forum dealing with the issue of remote access to LANs. He is one of the drivers in the process of promoting interoperability between different vendors' ISDN network devices. Jeff has worked at making the ISDN-industrial complex aware of the need to provide equipment and services to support remote access to LANs. Early on, his was a small voice steadfastly telling the telecommunications industry that ISDN was more than just a voice service. Somehow, miraculously, that tiny voice was heard. So, next time you connect remotely to a LAN, you might think about Jeff Fritz and others like him who worked long and hard to bring the enterprise network to your doorstep.

I hope you enjoy the book and profit from it, as I have.

GERRY HOPKINS, AUTHOR
THE ISDN LITERACY BOOK, 1995 (ADDISON-WESLEY)

Not very long ago, the prospect of connecting homes or offices to corporate information services was an intimidating process. Remote connectivity in any form was expensive, very difficult to achieve and, more often than not, less than reliable.

Remote communications could not be installed by just anyone. The equipment used for remote connection was sophisticated and complex. Installing and operating it required a level of technical expertise that was far beyond the knowledge of most business professionals. Typically, installations required a joint effort between corporate information services staff and the local telephone technicians. It simply was not an easy matter to design and install remote connection equipment and lines.

Only a few, very select homes had connections to corporate computing services. Those workers who did manage connections to corporate information services found that performance was low, and cost was high. Connectivity, where it did exist, was extremely limited. More often than not, remote connections were used to connect branch offices to corporate information services.

Today, things are different. New digital communications technologies have emerged to replace the limited-distance modems and copper connections of the past. Switched digital services, such as Integrated Services Digital Network (ISDN), are now commonly used for remote access. They make possible connections to corporate enterprise networks and the Internet that are viable and inexpensive. As a result, remote network access has taken off and is now growing at breakneck speeds.

As the number of remote network connections has spiraled upward, the focus on networking has shifted. The spotlight is now on Wide Area Networks (WANs) that give users access to corporate information services and the Internet. Remote LAN access has literally transformed the way users perform their daily work. Workers have learned that it is becoming increasingly possible for them to work no matter where they might be at the time. Now, more than ever before, it is becoming increasingly common for the office to come to the worker.

The Method Behind the Madness

Remote LAN Access is written for professionals looking to connect their corporate networks to remote locations anywhere in the world. It will be of special value to managers, engineers, technicians, and consultants who are responsible for providing remote connectivity to their networks from branch offices, telecommuters, corporate workers, and educators. This book will also be valuable for anyone who wants to separate fact from fiction when it comes digital remote access.

Remote LAN Access is designed to cut through the haze typically encountered when designing and installing remote LAN connections. The purpose of this book is to eliminate the mystery and frustration often associated with ordering, installing and supporting remote network connections. There is much misinformation, misrepresentation, and outright mumbo-jumbo when it comes to deploying and supporting remote network access. By exploring the many facets of remote LAN access, we will be able to debunk some of the common connectivity myths.

In working with remote LAN access and in teaching it to others, I have learned an important lesson: repetition is important to learning. Although some readers might dislike repetition, it is undeniably a valuable teaching aid. Therefore, you should not be surprised when you run into the same topic or ideas in several different places in this book. The repetition is deliberate. Reading the same ideas with changes in wording, or from different points of view, really does enhance learning.

Astute readers will notice a heavy emphasis on ISDN in this book. There are several reasons for this. ISDN is one of the most viable of all telecommunications technologies when it comes to remote LAN access. It is especially well suited to bringing enterprise networks and Internet access to remote users. Therefore, it demands a decent amount of attention.

As you begin reading, the reasons for the natural affinity between ISDN and LANs will soon become apparent. However, with all of its networking advantages, ISDN remains one of the most complicated technologies to order and deploy. Users are virtually forced to become systems integrators when they attempt to use the technology. They need to understand how ISDN works, how the telephone company has provisioned the service, and even how the telephone network is internally configured before they can effectively use the service.

The need for detailed and understandable information on ISDN has driven me to write several chapters on the technology, exploring it from a number of different angles. Do not let this cause you to assume that this is an ISDN book. It is not. It is a book about remote LAN access, written for networkers and the rest of us.

JEFFREY N. FRITZ
MORGANTOWN, WEST VIRGINIA

A book attempting to cover a subject as vast and all-encompassing as remote LAN access cannot be a solo effort. A number of researchers, telecommunications experts, educators, and authors helped with the content of this book. Many were kind enough not only to read drafts of the chapters in this book, but also to suggest what material should be included.

There are several people whose experience, advice and encouragement added directly to this work. Thanks must first go to Gerald Hopkins, of Bell Atlantic. Gerry is the author of *The ISDN Literacy Book* (Addison-Wesley, 1995) and co-editor and author of *The ISDN Solutions Guide* (Corporation for Open Systems, 1995). Gerry's many years of experience with ISDN standards made him a terrific sounding-board for ideas. Gerry checked the accuracy of many of the facts contained in the book. He even allowed me to rope him into reviewing most of the material in the book.

Don Radick, Senior Network Analyst for Holiday Inn Worldwide, contributed ideas for the section on voice and fax telecommuter services. Just as importantly, Don offered the benefit of his firsthand experience installing a corporate telecommunications program for Holiday Inn.

There are others to thank, as well. Salvadore Salamone is a good friend and, for several years, was my editor at *BYTE* magazine. Sal provided information on the integration of ISDN into the NetWare network operating system. Sal was also a great source of guidance. Having endured through a tome or two of his own, Sal was able to offer pointers that helped considerably in writing this book. Whether chatting in his Manhattan office or discussing the book over dinner in one of New York's finest Mexican restaurants, Sal was a great encouragement and inspiration.

This book could not have been written without a number of industry experts who helped provide accurate information on LAN and ISDN standards. Dr. Robert M. ("Bob") Metcalfe, Executive Correspondent of *InfoWorld* and Vice President of Technology for the International Data Group, supplied information on early networking. Most people in the networking business recognize Dr. Metcalfe as being the father of Ethernet, one of the world's most popular network topologies.

Jon Udell, Executive Editor at *BYTE*, reviewed the manuscript and proposed that a section on building enterprise networks be included. Jon has been dealing with remote LAN issues of his own at *BYTE*. Some of the problems and issues he has faced have shown up as examples in the book.

There were several people associated with the National Institute of Standards and Technology (NIST) who offered suggestions and contributions to this book. Special thanks go to Shukri Wakid, Director of the NIST Computer Systems Laboratory. When ISDN was born, Shukri Wakid was in the delivery room. He provided insight into a number of ISDN and remote LAN issues that appear in this book. The other individuals from NIST who took time to read the manuscript and offer suggestions include David Cypher; Leslie Collica, who chairs the North American ISDN Users' Forum; and Dawn McBrien. Thank you all!

Bell Atlantic's Patrick Donovan, Chairperson of the National ISDN Council (NIC), has been very active in the development of the National ISDN standards. Pat supplied much of the National ISDN information found in these pages. Microsoft's ISDN Product Manager, Bill Shaughnessy, provided information on ISDN integration into the operating system. William Miskovetz, Senior Engineer at Cisco Systems, provided background on Bandwidth Allocation Control Protocol. Finally, Dr. Frank Piepiorra, President of Data TeleMark L.C., furnished information on ISDN satellite and radio.

Credit is due to several individuals at Manning Publications who really made this book a pleasure to write. First and foremost, thanks go to Marjan Bace, Publisher and Partner of Manning Publications Company. Dr. Bace understood the need for a book on remote LAN access and took a personal interest in the book. His involvement in the details of the book, right down to the selection of the title, is deeply appreciated.

Len Dorfman, Editor, was the grandfather and cheerleader of this book. Whenever my doubts forced me to ask, "Why should I do this?" Len would always respond enthusiastically with, "Why not!"

Mary Piergies, Managing Editor, was superb at tracking all the important details that go into making a book like this. Mary masterfully handled the production of the book, always ensuring that all the pieces were in the right place at the right time.

Ted Kennedy, Review Editor, pulled all the reviews and reviewers together. His concern was always for the reader and the quality of the book.

Special thanks are due to Lee Fitzpatrick and Sheila Carlisle who did the production work on this book. Layout work can be tedious, but Sheila made working out the myriad details almost fun.

Finally, loving gratitude must go to my wife, Joanna. Joanna has read more books and technical journals than anyone I know. It was Joanna who insisted that this, my second book, could and should be written—even when I insisted it simply could not be done.

1

Introduction to Remote LAN Access

Not very long ago, remote access to enterprise networks was like caviar, luxury limousines, and upper class beach resorts—available only to a privileged few. The concept of working at home was virtually unknown. Connections to home offices, where they existed, were extremely limited in number and scope. They were mostly restricted to insurance offices, field sales offices, and a few well-to-do lawyers. For almost everyone else, work was synonymous with a daily commute to the office.

Even connections to corporate computing services from branch offices were far from pervasive. In fact, the very subject of remote connectivity was avoided as much as possible by network managers and their staffs. The topic simply raised too many thorny technical, financial and political issues. Almost without exception, every part of remote access presented a barrier of some sort to implementation. However, the two factors that worked the hardest against remote access were logistics and economics.

Logistics came into play because it was not a straightforward matter to provide connections to remote locations. Installations were almost always a logistical nightmare. In addition, installations involved a fair amount of work and coordination, both by the telephone company and by corporate information services.

Remote connectivity costs were as astronomical as installations were complex. Equipment was expensive, line costs were far from inexpensive, and the personnel required to support and service remote connections did not come cheaply.

Where remote connections did occur, the most common form of access was a slow-speed serial link to the infamous dumb terminal.[1] These terminals were rather large, intimidating devices that were usually connected to the corporate mainframe by coaxial cable. They also required a rather odd-looking device called a controller.

Figure 1.1 shows how remote connections were typically accomplished. The mainframe was channel-attached to a front end processor (FEP) in the computer room.[2] The FEP connected to a synchronous or limited-distance modem. A synchronous link was used to connect the FEP to the remote controller.

Sometimes a bank of synchronous modems or limited-distance modems connected a number of remote terminals to the FEP. In either case, a dedicated link connected the remote destination through the telephone company's central office. The link was channeled through the central office, but did not usually go through the telephone-switching equipment. At the destination was another synchronous or limited-distance modem. This modem connected to the controller with a serial cable. Finally, coax connected the terminal with the controller.

To the user the connection seemed quite ordinary. The terminal appeared to be channel-attached directly to the FEP. Anything that could ordinarily be done on a terminal in the corporate office could also be done on the remote terminal in the branch office.

To the information services staff, the connection did not appear to be ordinary at all. The word that a terminal had to be set up in a remote office location often sent chills down the corporate information systems manager's spine.

It was a job in every sense of the word. Terminals and controllers had to be shipped to the remote site, configured, and installed. A data line had to be run from the remote site to the corporate computing center. The telephone company had to dedicate wire pairs in their cables to the connection.

Once connections were in place, they were difficult to change. Moving the location of the terminal required changes that were neither cheap nor easy. Relocating remote circuits required the generation of telephone company work orders. This took weeks to accomplish and usually required several visits to the remote

---

1. I am not trying to denigrate these devices. *Dumb terminals,* like *dumb animals,* describes something that is capability limited. Dumb animals cannot speak (although they make us wonder sometimes). Similarly, despite being very large and intimidating, dumb terminals had very little processing power. They also had no disk capabilities and were totally dependent on the network host to control their operation. Therefore, dumb animals are really smarter than dumb terminals!

2. A channel has been considered, to some extent, as the mainframe equivalent of a network. It is a high-speed connection between the mainframe and its peripherals.

locations. The process was so costly and involved that relocating remote equipment was strongly discouraged. Eventually, additions and changes became nearly impossible to accommodate as open copper pairs in the telephone company's cable plants became scarce.

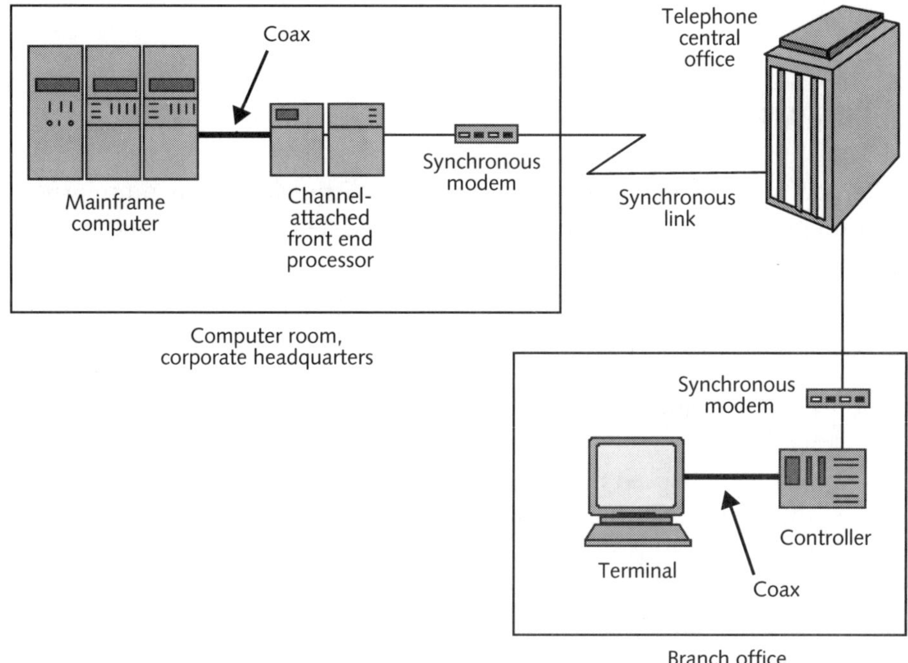

Figure 1.1   Branch office connections through dedicated links

The Transition to Local Area Networks

Today things have changed remarkably. Within a building or corporate site, communications capabilities have undergone a radical transformation. The prime mover for change was the deployment of Local Area Network (LAN) technology.

LANs have radically changed the corporate information infrastructure. They have led corporations to move away from terminal- and mainframe-based systems. These have been replaced with client/server-based information systems connected over LANs. Terminals were replaced by personal computers that could either emulate a terminal or become an intelligent part of the network in their own right. In many cases, mainframes became orphans and were replaced by network servers.

Where mainframes remain in service, their role has been often been relegated to handling large file or mail services. The mainframes themselves are, more often than not, accessed through LANs. All of this has given rise to new capabilities for information access.

Popular LANs

Few developments in technology have made such quick inroads into corporate computing environments as Local Area Networks. They have become extremely popular, and with very good reason.

LANs provided an overall level of connectivity that surpassed anything previously available. They offered throughput rates that were adequate for even the most bandwidth-hungry applications. LANs allowed users to transcend the limitations of their local computer, and to access local, regional, and worldwide information networks.

LANs provide high-speed multiple-user access to a wide variety of information sources residing on devices such as file servers, minicomputers, and mainframes. Peripheral devices such as printers, modems, and fax systems, can be connected via a LAN, making them accessible to multiple users. Today, virtually no one questions the statement that LANs were the most important technological advancement made during the last half of the eighties.

Limited LANs

However, with all their capabilities, Local Area Networks are far from perfect. They have limitations, sometimes significantly so, particularly in offering widespread connectivity. It is interesting that the very name given to LANs highlights their biggest limitation. Local Area Networks are just that—local. They are designed to provide network services only within a restricted area. This was not an oversight on the part of the LAN designers, it is exactly what the LAN designers intended.

Local Area Networks are local for a good reason. Early LAN designers never envisioned that their networks would someday be extended outside a fairly small radius. As a result, LAN technologies such as Ethernet and Token Ring deployed technology that has distance limitations. The intent was to use the LAN for network connections on the same floor or within the same building.

Distance causes erosion of the digital signal that is used to propagate information over the LAN. Besides signal loss issues, there are also delay problems with long connections. This is particularly true with Ethernet, since it uses a bus topology to connect workstations. Furthermore, the algorithm used to carry Ethernet causes the network to be even more limited when it comes to distance.

Devices on an Ethernet network use an algorithm called Carrier Sense Multiple Access with Collision Detection (CSMA/CD).[3] The CSMA/CD algorithm listens on the wire before it transmits in case another station happens to be transmitting at the exact same moment. Propagation delays along a lengthy backbone cable cause stations that are physically far apart to transmit at the exact same moment. The length of backbone cable masks the fact that more than one station is transmitting. This causes collisions to occur on the network. Therefore, Ethernet over thinnet or twisted-pair cable carries a distance limitation of 100 meters. This limits the propagation delay and helps prevent collisions from occurring on the network.

To get beyond the distance limitations required LAN segmentation and devices called repeaters. However, even this does not allow unlimited LAN distances. Therefore, LANs rarely traversed building boundaries. It was even less common for them to leave a corporate or university campus.

Winds of Change

As LANs became popular ways to interconnect various computer systems, things began to change for those who needed access to corporate information services.

For the user, the degree of information access has always had a direct impact on their productivity. In the office, a network is an extremely effective information

---

3. Ethernet was one of the earlier LANs. It was invented on May 22, 1973, primarily as a convenience for researchers working in the Xerox Palo Alto Research Center (PARC). The PARC scientists needed a method with which to exchange data locally. They developed the concept of Ethernet to support efficient data exchange. Little did the Xerox PARC researchers realize how their replacement for the "sneakernet" would change their lives and the world. Their convenience network grew and expanded into a network that eventually became known as the Internet. Is it estimated that as of 1996 there were in excess of 50 million computers operating over Ethernet networks. When this happened what PARC had developed as an internal, convenience network was no longer private or local.

access tool. Users directly on the LAN are given access to a variety of services. These include print, file, and fax servers. LANs also provide access to a number of network hosts. The problem is that off-site users have been unable to enjoy the same benefits and information access as a local LAN user. Users who worked on a LAN in the office and then tried to work from remote locations found themselves in an unenviable situation. They were extremely frustrated by the contrast in capability when they were off the network as compared to when they were on the network.

Connections for users who worked great distances from the LAN were the most problematic. Historically, network connectivity has been supported by communications programs and modems. This kind of access is radically inferior to what is available to a user in a LAN-connected office. At best, legacy remote services offered only a small subset of network capabilities. These reduced capabilities were only available with substantially slower transfer rates. This severely limited the ability for people to work from homes, remote offices, or other sites outside the corporate network.

On the one hand, LANs were extremely enabling technology. They let users accomplish things that were virtually impossible without them. On the other hand, due to their distance limitations, LANs accentuated the connectivity chasm between office and remote connectivity. This led to dissonance and dissatisfaction since some workers had much better connectivity than others.

Importance of Remote LAN Access

Remote users, as much as or maybe even more so than users directly on the office LAN, need decent connectivity. They desperately need, but seldom have, unrestricted access to information services. Their need for connectivity to common services is absolutely essential to their productivity because their resources are extremely limited. Typically, they work on a single workstation or, at best, an isolated cluster of machines. The remote user cannot, for example, cross the hall to get a file from another user or move to another computer in the office to print or fax a critical document.

There is a wide range of off-site users who require efficient access to the corporate resources that typically reside on LANs. This includes personnel who work on the corporate campus but are not physically located in the same building as the LAN. Personnel in the field and home office workers also need access to corporate computing services.

Take, for example, a typical university administrative department. Because they need to work with a number of different colleges on campus, administrative staff are often scattered among the departments or colleges. They may be located in the Engineering complex, in the Physics department, or in the Agricultural Sciences building. This creates a situation where, in their scattered environment, the department's administrative staff workers have to find ways to work together. Even though they are dispersed, administration staff still need to access common information services. More often than not, that information resides on network servers away from their locations.

If distance was not an issue, access to common information for the administrative staff would not be much of a problem. With staff located in a common facility, all that is required is enough network hardware and cabling to add them to the already existing Ethernet or Token Ring LAN. However, since the workers are physically scattered, information access becomes a significant problem.

West Virginia University faced just this situation with its Extension Education department. Extension Education interfaces students in each of West Virginia's 55 counties with all of the diverse colleges on campus. Because they need to work directly with the colleges, Extension Education staff are often located in the colleges themselves rather than centrally located. This means the staff is scattered across many departments and colleges, and throughout three separate campuses.

Without a better means of communication, the workers had no choice but to exchange information by campus mail. They would mail floppy disks back and forth. Obviously, this was far from an efficient way to communicate critical data. Disks frequently crossed in the mail. The latest versions of files were not always available, or even known. Most importantly, there was a time lag of several days to move the disks through the campus mail system.

The answer for the Extension Education department's dilemma was not very different from the solution for any worker who needs access to remote information resources. If it could be possible to provide each worker with remote LAN access to common campus network services, it would allow them to share essential information. They could even do this in real-time, if they wanted.

The Extension Education example illustrates an important point. If implemented properly, remote LAN access can result in a major increase in the department's productivity and accuracy.

Remote Access Applications

Remote access has become so important that a new acronym has been coined. SOHO, which stands for Small Office/Home Office, categorizes one of the largest groups that requires remote LAN connections to perform their daily work.

There are five applications that are considered to be important in terms of remote access for SOHOs.

• E-Mail

In terms of popularity, electronic mail is near the top of the mark. Many people check their e-mail long before they check their post office mail or even voice mail. Access to e-mail, of course, requires access to a network that offers e-mail services. For users directly on corporate networks, e-mail access rarely presents a problem. For remote users, there needs to be a method for connecting their computers to the network in order to receive their mail.

• Interactive Terminal Access

Users need access to host computers for information processing purposes. Sometimes this takes the form of a communications session with a remote host where the local computer does nothing more than echo the screen data to the user. This can be done with remote control software that allows users to control a network-connected computer. In other cases, it may require a Telnet or some other communications session where the user's computer becomes a remote terminal to a host computer.

• Connections to Remote Enterprise Networks

Often productivity demands that the user's computer becomes a client of a remote network. This is the most effective form of remote access. The remote user's computer functions exactly as it would on the remote network. This makes it feasible to do remotely the very same functions that are possible when directly connected to the office network. This includes accessing file and print servers.

• Internet Access

There is no question that the Internet has become an important information source for millions of people. Whenever users wish to "surf the net," access a newsgroup, or transmit files across the country or the world, the Internet is the vehicle they use. Until recently, Internet access has been available only to people on corporate or education networks. Now that the Internet has become important, people want to remotely access it from libraries, schools and even their homes.

- **File Sharing**

  The beauty of remote access is that it allows people to access files and applications from a common location. Several years ago, I had to transport floppy disks from my office, to my home, and back again to the office. This was necessary because I did a considerable amount of my daily work at home.

Like many others in a similar situation, I discovered that transporting floppy disks to and from work was less than a perfect system. If I was rushed and forgot my disks, or worse lost them, I was in serious shape. Additionally, I frequently became confused as to which disk and which computer had the current version of a file.

Today, remote access virtually guarantees that the files and applications that I need to do my work will be accessible whether I am in the office, at home, or even on the road. Since files are synchronized and readily available, I always know where the most current version is located. There is no doubt that file-sharing across a remotely accessible network is a much better way to do business.

Transparency of Access

As can be seen from the discussion of the top five remote access applications, network connectivity has become very important in getting work done. For many users, remote network connectivity is not a luxury. In today's "do more with less" business environment, users require instant access to their data. This is true no matter what the time of day (or night), where the user is located, or where their data resides.

The need is for remote access services that are transparent. In other words, the user should have access to information in exactly the same manner, no matter the location or the time. Just as importantly, the access method should be transparent, meaning that it is the same no matter what the physical location of the user or services might be. The ability to accomplish this equal access to network services is called "access transparency."

In years past, this was not at all the case. Workers in their offices accessed information in one way, typically through the corporate network. They had direct access to file servers and were able to use file transfer applications like FTP. When the same workers attempted to work from home, their access method changed dramatically. Now the worker typically was using a modem and a communications program to access their information. Direct access to file servers or network applications like FTP was impossible. Therefore, workers had to deal with two radically different methods of accessing information, depending on whether they were at home or at work.

Just about everyone whose business involves information of some sort can benefit from access transparency. Being able to access information whenever it is needed is a major contributor to productivity. Customers and associates prefer to hear, "Sure, let me look it up for you." What they do not want to hear is, "I'm on the road this week. Let me send you the information next week when I get back to my office."

Every company has its share of people whose work is of a critical nature, or whose work schedules are not tied to being in a specific location at any given time. Systems analysts, freelance writers, college professors, and research scientists rarely live by eight-to-five regimens. Often, their most creative times occur during what might be considered by most people as "off-hours." Ironically, since they generally spend their off-hours at home without decent remote network access, they have their least efficient connectivity during their most productive hours.

Mission-critical personnel are also good examples of those who can especially benefit from efficient, transparent remote network access. Essential personnel such as police or medical staff must have connectivity to critical information resources whenever they are needed, even if it is three in the morning or during a major winter snowstorm.

Sophisticated users are growing intolerant of the rather large disparity between their data communications capabilities at work and those at home or at a branch office. They have begun to demand transparent access to their information services. This has increased the pressure to find solutions that allow the remote user to connect to corporate information systems with the same capabilities as those in the corporate headquarters.

Clearly, user demand is a major factor driving the search for better remote access solutions. However, it is not the only reason. Several factors are combining to promote the growth of remote network access:

- Increased desire for Internet and World Wide Web access.
- Government air quality-control mandates.
- Municipal limits on the number of commuters permitted on local roads.
- Increased frustration with time-consuming daily commutes.

- Increased emphasis on educational capabilities in schools, libraries and homes.
- Promise of the National and Global Information Infrastructure.

Many of these pressures have preceded the creation and deployment of solutions for remote network access. As we will see in the next chapter, this fostered several early attempts to provide remote users with access to network services.

2

Early Attempts at Remote Access

Screen Sharing

Clearly, Local Area Networks are critical to corporate business; therefore, the need to connect to them from remote locations has become extremely important. As LANs progressed in stature, vendors began to realize that people needed to have connections to off-site networks. This caused them to develop techniques for providing remote LAN services.

Early on, a process called *screen sharing* was used for remote access. In some forms it still exists today. Programs like Carbon Copy, Timbuktu, and PC Anywhere are examples of screen-sharing applications. They allow users to operate remote computers when they are not near the machine.

The idea behind screen sharing is interesting. In its purest form, it is simply a method of input/output expansion. Screen sharing was derived from the belief that if keyboard input and video could be redirected outside the machine it would not matter where the CPU was physically located. If, for example, keyboard input could be redirected to another port, it would allow a remote PC user connected to that port to operate the keyboard of the machine. Redirecting the video out the same port would allow the remote user to see what was on the screen of the remote machine. Not a bad concept, except that the port that was chosen was the serial port. Therefore, all connectivity occurred through the PC com port, which is the most restrictive input/output system in a PC.

Figure 2.1 shows how screen sharing was usually handled. The serial ports of both computers were connected using either a modem or a null modem cable. An application or program ran on the primary machine and was controlled through the remote computer. Both monitors displayed the same screen image. Typing on either keyboard resulted in input that was reflected on the primary machine. Therefore, screen sharing required one machine to act as a host and the other machine to assume the role of a client. Actually, *client* may be too strong a term.

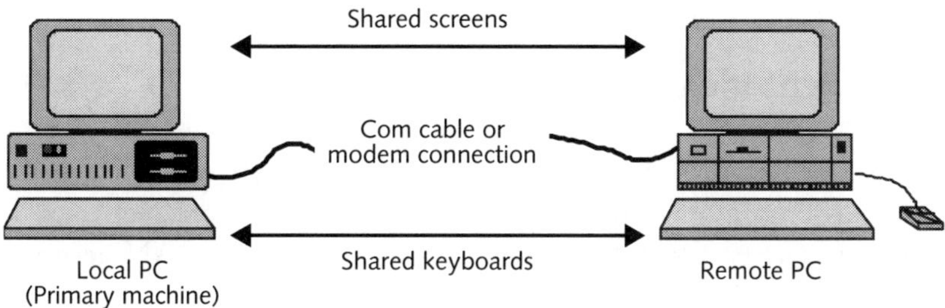

Figure 2.1   Screen sharing

With screen sharing, the remote PC takes on the role previously occupied by the dumb terminal. Its processing power is essentially bypassed during the screen-sharing process. With the exception of what is required to run the screen-sharing application, all the processing occurs on the primary machine. The remote user simply takes control of the host machine. This enables the user to do from the remote client whatever they could normally do if they were seated at the host. This includes accessing network applications, performing file transfers, assisting someone at the other side working on an unfamiliar task, or troubleshooting a problem. However, there are some major restrictions involved with screen sharing.

When screen-sharing applications first appeared, the 8250 Universal Asynchronous Receiver Transmitter (UART) chip was used in most PC com ports. This chip was restricted to 19.2 kilobits per second (kbps). In terms of data rates, this is very slow. It soon became a serious limitation to screen sharing, so much so that slow connections were blamed on the "UART bottleneck." When a modem connection was used to send information to and from primary and remote machines, the bottleneck became even more severe. At first, most modems were limited to 1200-baud, with only a few modems capable of the higher 2400-baud transmission rate. The low baud rates slowed screen-sharing updates down to a trickle.

For keyboard input, slow-speed connections worked very well. A keystroke or two could make it through without much trouble, even at the slowest modem rate. However, when it came to video output, the data due to the number of pixels (picture elements) that had to be transmitted became a significant factor. Video output associated with screen sharing caused a large amount of data to be squeezed through the slow com port, and the even slower modem connection. Screen painting, the process of drawing the screen on the remote side, slowed to a crawl. It was almost as if a tired, old painter was drawing the screen a few lines at a time. Nevertheless, because slow connectivity is often better than no connectivity, screen sharing did gain some popularity.

A Not-So-Bright Idea

One day, someone got a "bright idea" of networking remote machines. Now, users could operate a remote machine that was part of a Local Area Network. Placing the machine on a network did provide a limited degree of LAN access for the remote user. The problem was that overexcited product managers began referring to this limited remote control as "remote LAN connectivity." This was hardly the case.

The screen-shared network connection worked after a fashion, but was plagued by a series of serious shortcomings. The major drawback was that, marketing claims to the contrary, the user was not actually on the network. They were simply borrowing the keyboard and monitor of a remote machine that happened to be on a network. To the casual application or superficial user, the difference may have been relatively unimportant. However, this was a very big problem for crucial network applications, and for sophisticated users.

File transfers were slowed and complicated by screen-sharing applications. It was not always obvious to the user that files transferred over the network wound up at the primary machine. They were not on the hard drive of the machine where the user was located. Befuddled, confused users searched fruitlessly on their local drives for files that were not there.

Recognizing this flaw, screen-sharing vendors incorporated file transfer protocols into their products. This allowed users to move files over the network to the primary machine, and then to their machine.

Integrating file-transfer capability into screen-sharing applications enhanced users' networking capability. It allowed the user to upload or download files. However, it also meant that file transfers became a multi-step process. Obviously, this was a very different situation from what the user directly on the network experienced.

Network machines support a single copy or transfer operation to move the desired file. The user only had to find the file and transfer it with any one of a number of network file-transfer protocols. With screen sharing, the user had to first copy the file from the server to the remote machine that was sitting on the network. Next, the user had to invoke the screen-sharing application's transfer protocol and bring the transferred file to their local machine.

This two-step process had to be reversed for uploads to the server. If the user forgot one step or the other, the file would not arrive at the expected destination.

Since there were different processes involved in each stage of the file transfer, the user was forced to learn multiple file-transfer applications. The mechanism, and the commands, necessary for each transfer process were usually different. This caused great confusion and more than a little frustration among users.

Another drawback in screen-sharing file transfers was speed, particularly for large files. Large file size was not much of a problem for the primary machine sitting on a 4- or 10-Megabit-per-second (Mbps) LAN. However, when the user went to move a file to or from their local drive, the connection was not 10 Mbps, or even 4 Mbps, it was 1200 or 2400 bps, a drastic reduction in throughput. A one-megabyte file, which could be transferred in 8 seconds on the LAN, took almost 70 minutes to move across the slower link to a remote machine.[1]

Dueling Monitors

There were other problems with screen sharing. The earliest screen-sharing programs were monochrome (now called black-and-white). With the popularity of color monitors, it did not take long for screen-sharing programs to support color. After all, color is far more interesting to look at than a black-and-white image. Compounding this was the change from text-based to graphical screens. Graphical User Interfaces (or *GUIs*, as they are called) require much more information per screen than do character-based displays. Now, with GUIs, there was much more information that needed to be moved between the two machines.

---

1. The throughput difference between LAN and modem file transfers really is this drastic. Typical measured LAN throughput for a single workstation on a 10-Mbps Ethernet is close to 1 Mbps. Therefore, a one-megabyte file transferred over the LAN only takes about eight seconds. (1,000,000 bytes * 8 bits per byte/1,000,000 bits per second = 8 seconds). By contrast, a 2400-baud modem connection takes over an hour to transfer the same one-megabyte file. (1,000,000 bytes * 10 bits per byte/2,400 bits per second = 4,160 seconds, or approximately 70 minutes). In case you are wondering, ten bits-per-byte is used for modem transmission because asynchronous modems require two extra bits, a start and stop bit, for each byte. We will cover the reasons for this in more detail a little later in the book.

Additionally, color and graphical requirements led to conflicts between monitor resolution on remote and local machines. If the resolution differed on the two machines, the image became distorted and unreadable. To overcome this, some screen-sharing applications attempted to translate resolution between the two screens. Unfortunately, the extra processing required for translation slowed down the screen updates even more. However, the biggest reduction in screen-painting speed was due to the color image. It required far more pixel information to display a color screen because so much more data had to be transferred.

Depending on the color depth, the increase in data carried over the connection could be immense. The amount of data transmitted for color screens was multiplied by 4, 16, or 256 times compared to that required by monochrome screen sharing. Now, faced with moving so many pixels, the already slow modem connection bogged down even further. This was true even with increased modem speeds. When the newer 9600-baud modems came out, users hoped this would improve screen-sharing performance. In many cases, particularly for character-based screens and small file transfers, they did realize some improvement. However, the faster 9600-baud modems completely bogged down with color- or GUI-based screen sharing. Even top-of-the-line 28.8-kbps modems have difficulty with screen-sharing applications.

It did not take users long to figure out that screen sharing was not the same as remote LAN access. In terms of response and transparency of access, screen-sharing software was not at all the same as using a machine that was actually on a Local Area Network.

Remote Control Programs

Screen sharing has recently enjoyed something of a rebirth. It has reemerged with a new moniker: *Remote Control Programs.* Some examples of remote control programs include Citrix System's WinView, Ocean Isle's Reachout, and Tritron System's CO/Session.

Remote control programs allow users to access applications running on an applications server. Applications servers are usually personal computers that allow common applications on the server to be used by a number of users. For example, a word processing application can be installed on the server and then made accessible to several remote users.

Remote control software can also run on a user's computer, providing a communications path from a remote machine's keyboard and monitor to an applications server located on a network. The user dials into the network either through a serial link, or using a protocol such as TCP/IP or IPX. Once they have accessed the server, they are able to perform certain tasks on the network. This gives the users the impression that they are on the network, even though technically they are not.

While remote control programs have certain weaknesses, they also have some advantages. They can be run in computers that have multiple processors, allowing many users to share their resources at one time. They can also make the file-transfer issue a little less complex than earlier screen-sharing programs, although this usually requires the use of a file-transfer utility. Finally, users can redirect their print jobs through the server.

One special feature of remote control programs is increased application-launching speed. Since the applications are actually running on the server, not on the remote machine, they do not have to be launched across the network. Launching a large application like Microsoft Excel over a Wide Area Network (WAN) can take some time. Since most of the application's code must be moved to the remote computer, launching a large application is the equivalent of performing a multi-megabyte file-transfer. With remote control programs, this transfer does not occur because Excel, or whatever application is launched, is not actually running on the remote computer.

However, like the screen-sharing applications that remote control programs are based on, the user is not really on the remote network. Therefore all the network restrictions and limitations that apply to screen sharing also apply to remote control programs.

We will go into further detail on remote control programs when we consider analog remote network access in Chapter 5, "Technologies for Enterprise Network, LAN and Internet Connections."

Terminal Servers

Another remote network connection technology that became popular used terminal servers. A terminal server is a device that connects to a network and has one or more RS-232 serial ports. Users connected to the serial port had a form of dumb terminal network access through the terminal server.

Figure 2.2 illustrates two methods for gaining network access by connecting to terminal servers. In one method, a dumb terminal, or a PC running a communications program, is connected directly to the RS-232 port on the terminal server. Carrying the idea one step further, a second method made it possible to connect a

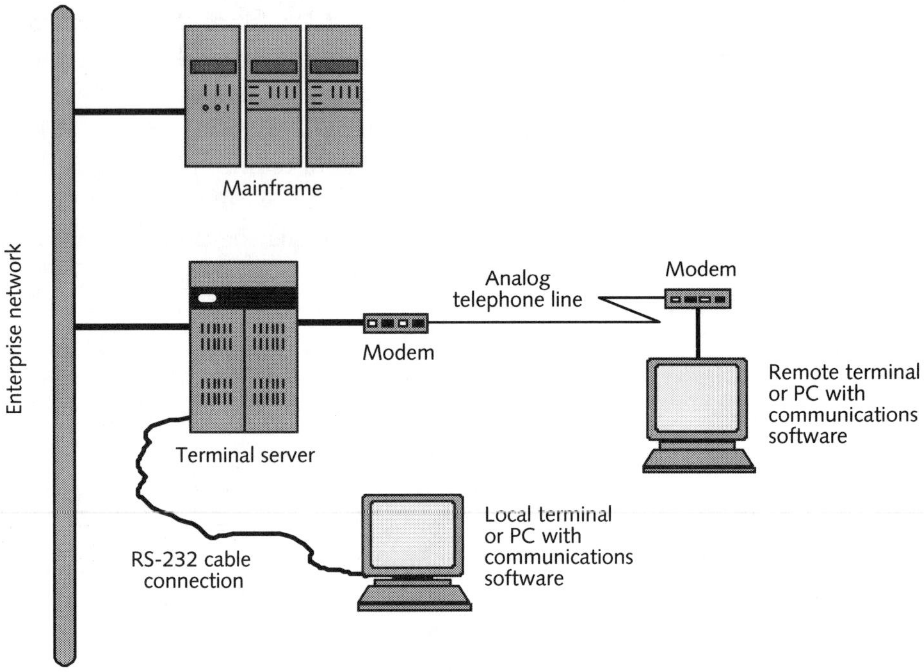

Figure 2.2   Terminal server connections

modem instead of a terminal to the terminal server's RS-232 port. Now, a remote PC could dial in through a modem connection, access the RS-232 port, and become a terminal on the network.

When dumb terminals were connected to mainframes, the FEP was frequently connected through a bank of synchronous, or limited-distance modems. This allowed multiple users to access the FEP and, therefore, the mainframe. The same technique can be used with terminal servers.

As Figure 2.3 indicates, instead of a single modem-to-modem connection, remote terminals and computers connected to a bank of modems, often called a modem pool. The modem pool was, in turn, connected to the terminal server. This allowed many users to access the terminal server and, therefore, the network, at the same time.

Generally, a limited suite of network communications protocols was available from the terminal server. The most common was Telnet, a protocol that allows establishment of a remote terminal session to a remote host. This allowed any connected machine access to any network host that supported Telnet logins.

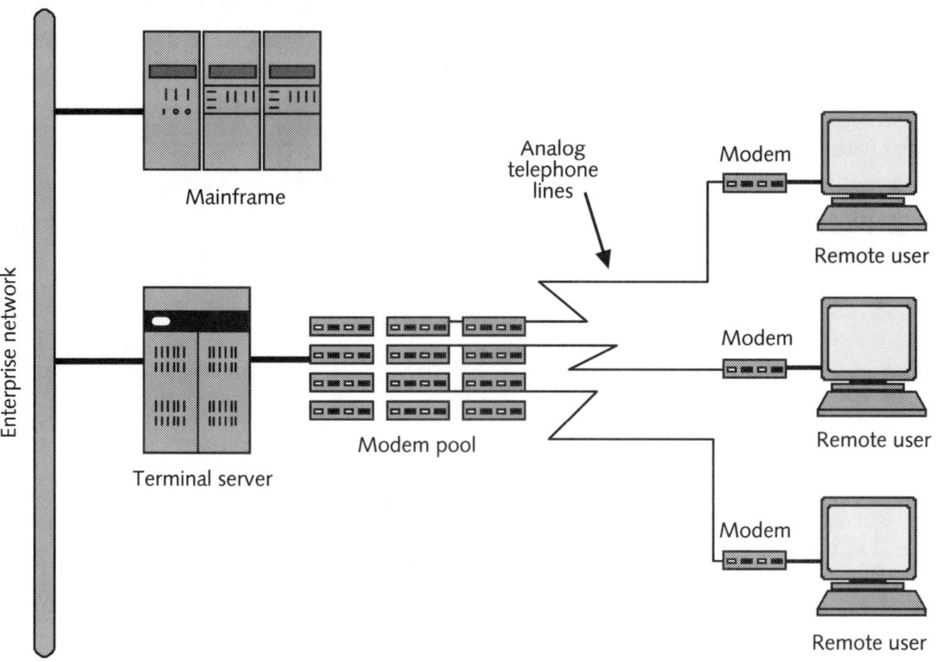

Figure 2.3 Terminal server connections using modem pools

Unfortunately, this solution did not offer significantly better network performance than screen sharing. Speeds were still limited, file transfers were far from effortless, and network access was restricted to a limited suite of protocols.

Moving Up the Curve

After LANs became more mature in the late 1980s, businesses tried to connect to sites using proprietary network connection solutions over asynchronous modem lines. Many of these proprietary attempts to interconnect networks were only marginally successful. Users could do remote e-mail, but not much more. While connections between LANs offered added capabilities, these were offset by other limitations. For example, Novell offered a product called NetWare Asynchronous Communications Server (NACS). NACS was designed to connect LANs together using asynchronous modems attached to Novell servers. Speed was limited to 9600-baud, which was not really useful for efficient inter-LAN connectivity.

Clearly, remote users needed better connectivity options than screen-sharing, terminal servers, or even proprietary remote access programs were able to provide. What users really desired was a universal connectivity medium that would provide them with "access transparency." As we mentioned earlier, access transparency means that the user sees the same interface and the same network services whether they are directly connected to the LAN, or whether they accessed the network using remote connections. None of the early remote network options fit this basic requirement.

3

The Beginning of Residential and Small Business Remote LAN Access

Evolving to LANs

As we have seen, screen sharing, proprietary remote access programs, and terminal server solutions were only partially successful in satisfying remote LAN access needs. Several vendors recognized that users needed much better access. Therefore, at the same time these methods were being tried, development was underway on a new method of remote network access.

This new method was radically different from either screen sharing or terminal service access to network services. Rather than trying to extend limited access to the network, this method used digital services to extend network protocols directly to remote users. This was done primarily over serial connections using digital services such as T1 and eventually, ISDN.[1]

There is little question that this kind of remote LAN access was successful. It is now one of the fastest growing applications. At the same time, it is also most one of the most perplexing data communications applications to design and implement. There are so many methods and variables for providing connectivity, that it becomes necessary to try and reduce some of the chaos. We can sort things out more clearly through the use of categorization.

---

1. A description of T1, ISDN, and other digital data transmission services can be found in Chapter 4, "Connectivity Services."

Connectivity Categories

We conveniently categorize remote network access into one of three types, depending on the number of workstations needing to be connected.

- **Single Workstation Remote LAN Access**

  This category is also known as residential or work-at-home. Telecommuters typically use a single workstation.

- **Small Office/Home Office Remote LAN Access**

  Typically, these are branch offices or small businesses needing to conduct business with other companies. Usually, remote offices operate with 2 to 50 workstations on a moderate-sized LAN. Sometimes home offices fit into this class, particularly if they use a small LAN in their homes to support operation of more than a single computer.

- **Large Multi-office Connections to Enterprise Networks**

  Connections between enterprise networks usually involve large networks in diverse locations. Sometimes this takes the form of corporate access to the Internet.

These three categories share several things in common. All seek access to corporate information services. Many users in all three groups also desire access to the Internet.

There are some differences in how each group is connected. To clarify the differences, the Enterprise Network Data Interconnectivity Family (ENDIF) sponsored by the North American ISDN Users' Forum (NIUF), has defined remote access in several categories.[2]

The ENDIF model defines remote LAN connections from Individual Workstations (IW), Group Workstations (GW), and Enterprise Data Networks (EDN). An IW is a single remote workstation or PC, typically used in a small office or in telecommuting. A GW is a small group of networked workstations like those

---

2. ENDIF has also been very successful in implementing multi-vendor agreements for remote LAN access. Although I chaired the group from 1992 to 1996, I cannot take much of the credit for this work. Major vendors such as Cisco, Digiboard, Combinet, and 3Com have played active roles within ENDIF. These vendors were primarily responsible for creating Implementation Agreements that allow interoperability of ISDN remote network products. It was wonderful to watch this process. However, as a user it is even more rewarding to see the fruits of this process. These agreements have directly led a wide selection of products that support interoperability between different vendor's ISDN-based networking products.

found in a branch office or department. The EDN is typically a large internetwork, such as the corporate enterprise network or the Internet. This leads us to the six remote LAN access configurations shown in Figure 3.1.

<table>
<tr><td>IW *</td><td>IW *</td></tr>
<tr><td>IW</td><td>GW</td></tr>
<tr><td>IW</td><td>EDN</td></tr>
<tr><td>GW</td><td>GW</td></tr>
<tr><td>GW</td><td>EDN</td></tr>
<tr><td>EDN **</td><td>EDN **</td></tr>
</table>

Where:

EDN is an Enterprise Data Network
(e.g., Internet, corporate data networks, etc.)

GW is a group of connected workstations
(e.g., a small- or medium-sized LAN)

IW is an individual workstation
(e.g., personal computer or workstation)

Notes:

* IW-to-IW typically refers to
peer-to-peer networking

** EDN-to-EDN is not recommended
with less than T1 connections.

Adapted from the Enterprise Network Data Interconnectivity Family Charter, North American ISDN User's Forum

Figure 3.1   Remote network categories

An example of an IW-to-IW connection would occur when peer-to-peer networking is in use. Computer operating systems with peer-to-peer capabilities, such as Windows 95 and the Macintosh operating system, allow users to provide file services from individual workstations to others on the network. Usually, users do not allow their workstations to remain as peer-to-peer file servers for extended periods of time. Therefore, access is usually transitory in nature.

Telecommuters and small branch offices with one workstation connected to the corporate enterprise are examples of an IW-to-EDN connection.[3] An individual workstation could also be logged into a network in a small branch or independent office. This would be an example of an IW-to-GW connection. Like IW-to-IW

---

3. When many people refer to *telecommuters,* they generally think of a single workstation located in a worker's home office. While this is often the case, it is, however, is a rather narrow definition of telecommuting. It is possible, even likely, to have a telecommuter whose home office has a number of computers networked. The connectivity needs of this kind of telecommuter are very similar to the connectivity needs of a small- to moderate-sized branch office. In fact, the same solutions apply to both groups. That us why they are often categorized together as a SOHO.

connections, IW-to-GW or IW-to-EDN connections are often transitory in nature, lasting anywhere from a few minutes to a few hours. Therefore, they usually do not need to be continuous.

The connectivity needs of businesses and larger branch offices are more demanding, and are often left up on an 8 by 5 basis.[4] These are examples of GW-to-GW and GW-to-EDN connections.

Finally, we have the case of an EDN connected to an EDN. A corporate enterprise connected to the Internet is an example of an EDN-to-EDN connection. This kind of connection frequently carries enough traffic to warrant higher speed connections and 24 by 7 connections.

Keep these three groups in mind as we continue our discussion of remote LAN access. Their unique requirements will have a direct bearing on the form of digital service that makes the most sense for their connectivity needs.

Work-at-Home

Work-at-home, where employees perform corporate work from their homes, is a growing trend today. This is the major group using IW-to-GW and IW-to-EDN connections.

The signs are everywhere that work-at-home's time has arrived. The ranks of telecommuters are increasing in response to cost-cutting measures and environmental initiatives. For the corporation, supporting telecommuting allows them to reclaim valuable space resources. For the employee, work-at-home is an appealing alternative to wasting otherwise productive hours each day in bumper-to-bumper traffic. Work-at-home also reduces work-related expenses such as day care.

It has long been believed that working at home results in higher worker productivity, and a decrease in work-related stress. According to recent studies conducted by the City of Los Angeles and Lawrence Livermore Labs, telecommuting makes a tremendous difference in both categories. From purely a time-management viewpoint, these studies seem to make sense.

We all know the drill. Wake up, shave (face or legs), shower, dress, get the kids ready for school, walk the dog, eat breakfast, and leave for work. It takes a chunk

---

4. Eight hours per day, five days per week is abbreviated 8 x 5 or 8 by 5. This is said as "eight by five." Similarly, 4 by 4 is four hours per day, four days per week. These wonderfully favorable work hours should not be confused with 4X4, which is an expensive truck. By the way, 24 by 7, which we will encounter shortly, is the same as all of the time.

out of our day just to get out of the house—and that is even before we begin the commute to the office.

Just consider the amount of time the typical worker spends getting ready for work and commuting:

- One hour per day spent showering and dressing. Considering a 50-week work year, that totals 250 hours per year.[5]
- One hour, 30 minutes per day spent commuting each way. Again, based on a 50-week work year, the typical commute gobbles up 750 hours per year.

That totals conveniently to 1,000 hours per year spent in the shower, in the bedroom, and in the car or train. I can think of many productive things I can do with 1,000 hours per year. I'll bet you can too.

Personal time resources are not the only things promoting telecommuting. Commuting in congested areas has become a critical problem. Air pollution, fuel conservation, and traffic congestion have all become major issues, particularly in large metropolitan areas. These factors have combined to encourage government and industry leaders to consider work-at-home as a reasonable alternative to the daily office commute. Forward-thinking companies have already made telecommuting an integral part of their organizational computing environment.

At least two states, California and New Jersey, have passed legislation requiring that companies allocate a percentage of their staff to work-at-home status. The penalties for noncompliance are stiff. Other states are in the process of considering similar legislation. So, if your home state has not yet joined the work-at-home revolution, it will—it is just a matter of time.

Environmental protection, energy conservation, horrendous traffic congestion in many urban areas, and the sanity of the work force have all mandated a change in today's commuting-based work style. Things have changed so dramatically that work-at-home is no longer considered a hope of tomorrow. Many companies, governmental agencies and workers see it as a solution for employment needs today. However, all the corporate intentions, state mandates and incentives added together could not promote telecommuting unless there was some means to provide telecommuting support.

---

5. Of course, this is not an attempt to claim that telecommuters do not shower or dress! However, the time required to casually dress for the home as opposed to the time required to dress more formally for the office is very different in many cases. Also, we must recognize that some telecommuters dress far more casually. Take, for example, the case of one telecommuter I know who lives in Seattle, Washington. He uses a desktop video system to meet with his clients. Since only the top part of his body is seen in the videoconference, this enterprising telecommuter dresses only from the waist up!

It took the arrival of affordable, reliable digital telecommunications services, coupled with inexpensive remote network devices, to make remote LAN access a reality. Although users did not realize it at the time, digital services would prove to be the key that unlocked the door to remote office connectivity.

The Arrival of the Digital Superhighway

Let's start with the following assumption: Any technology that successfully supports work-at-home applications must allow users access to corporate resources from remote locations, and do so as efficiently as if they were on the corporate network. It should make absolutely no difference where those resources reside, or where the user is located.

Once again, we are talking about access transparency. The important factor in successful remote LAN access is that users must be able to transparently connect to corporate information resources. On the basis of this requirement, it becomes obvious that work-at-home connections must be done over links that can emulate the connections found in the office. Of all the services that could potentially provide this service, an affordable high-speed digital network is especially well positioned. Using digital networks, transparent connections can be provided to homes or to branch offices.

It was a happy coincidence that, as the interest in telecommuting began to spiral upwards, telephone carriers began deploying digital networks. These new networks were capable of providing acceptable remote LAN access.

Unfortunately, the marriage between remote LAN access and digital telephone networks was very slow to evolve. Burdened by the weight of regulations, and slowed by their large size, telephone carriers have floundered in their digital network deployments. This was compounded by the startling fact that many telephone carriers completely overlooked the value of using their new digital networks for remote network access. This is ironic since it was the carriers themselves who stood to gain the most from the deployment of digital networks—particularly for remote LAN access.

A major reason for the slow deployment was the expense involved in upgrading telephone-switching offices with the equipment necessary to support digital services. Conversion from analog-based switching was, and still is, an expensive and time-consuming task. Generally, this conversion involves both hardware and software upgrades and, in many cases, requires that entire central office telephone switches be replaced.

The state Public Service Commissions in the United States were also largely responsible for the slow deployment that digital networks experienced. Obsessed with parity in telephone services, state regulatory agencies failed to make it easy for carriers to deploy their new digital technologies.[6]

Finally, the carriers themselves failed to understand the importance of their newer digital technologies for data networking applications. Largely due to their voice background, the carriers had great difficulty recognizing their unique role in supporting telecommuting, videoconferencing and remote LAN applications.

Vendors have been much faster in recognizing the importance of digital networks to telecommuting. To them, residential, work-at-home computing represents a potentially lucrative market. Companies like Cisco, 3Com and Microsoft have been quick to perceive this and to respond with products designed to support digital remote LAN access.

---

6. For those who are interested, here is Webster's and Fritz's definition of *parity:*

parity, *n.* 1. Equality, as in amount, status, or value. 2. Functional equivalence, as in the weaponry or military strength of adversaries. 3. The equivalent in value of a sum of money expressed in terms of a different currency at a fixed, official rate of exchange. 4. Equality of prices of goods or securities in two different markets. 5. The attempt to restrict someone or someone else so that all parties are equally disadvantaged and all new evolving technologies are equally delayed. (See also National Football League.)

4

Digital telephone networks are generally considered to be in one of two classes: leased services or switched services. The main difference centers on how the line connects from source to destination.

Leased services are considered to be permanent connections. In a sense, they are the functional equivalent of stretching a wire from point A to point B. That wire, however, usually offers excellent bandwidth. The problem with leased services is that they are not very flexible in handling multiple-destination connections. Usually, connectivity is strictly from point A to point B. If point A suddenly needs to be connected to point C, the connection must be changed. The change is not a simple process. It requires work orders and several days to be implemented. For the most part, leased lines are charged on a monthly basis and are mileage-sensitive. However, usage charges (charges per minute of usage) usually do not exist.

Switched services, on the other hand, support calls to a variety of destinations. Switched data services function like a typical voice telephone call. The user dials the connection to a specific destination number, accesses the network services, and then, when the session is complete, drops the call.

Like leased services, switched services usually carry a monthly charge. These charges, however, are typically mileage-independent and lower than leased lines. However, unlike leased lines, usage time-based fees usually apply. These fees may include long distance charges and, sometimes, a local data usage charge. Depending on how long the connection is maintained, long distance charges can be substantial. In some cases, they can be more than the monthly charge for the switched service.

Packet-based services use virtual connections between the source and destination. Charges are typically on a kilopacket basis. Frequently, a leased line is required to connect the packet service to the Public Data Network (PDN). When this is the case, there is also a monthly charge for the leased line.

There are a variety of telecommunications services available to support remote connections to enterprise networks. Each type of service has certain inherent advantages and disadvantages. Your choice of leased-, switched-, or packet-based services depends on your connectivity needs and budget. Among the most common digital services are Frame Relay, Integrated Services Digital Network, Digital 56-kbps service and T1 service. In addition, there is the ever-present analog service.

Leased Services

T1

Fixed T1 and its related service, Fractional T1, are digital data transmission services. They provide serialized connections over leased circuits. Digital T1 offers high-speed data transmission over a single-channel connection, while Fractional T1 breaks the single channel into a number of smaller, independent subchannels. Typical customers of T1 services are companies whose data transmission requirements exceed the speed and volume limits inherent in analog service. Leased T1 has become a mainstay of digital service in corporate networks. In North America, the service has a bandwidth of 1.544 Mbps. A related European version, called E1, has 2.048 Mbps bandwidth.

Digital T1 service is commonly used to connect various enterprise network sites. Because of the wide bandwidth, EDN-to-EDN connections are often supported over T1 circuits. Many corporate sites are connected to the Internet by a T1, or by a series of parallel T1 circuits.

Since T1 is a leased service, it is a dedicated service typically connected 24 hours a day, seven days a week. It is billed on a monthly basis, and is usually charged according to mileage.

There is a variant called Fractional T1. This service breaks the T1 pipe into multiple channels. Fractional T1 is very useful when several low-bandwidth services need to be connected from point A to point B. Unfortunately, Fractional T1 is not available in many locations.

The T1 termination equipment consists of a Channel Service Unit (CSU) and a Digital Service Unit (DSU). Often these functions are combined into a single unit called a Channel Service Unit/Digital Service Unit (CSU/DSU).

Leased T1 circuits are expensive to install, and carry monthly charges amounting to hundreds of dollars. Therefore, T1 services are most often used in large corporations, and are rarely run to home offices and small businesses.

T3

Leased T3 is similar in nature to T1. It is also a digital data transmission service. With a bandwidth of 45 Mbps, T3 is equivalent to 30 T1s. Like T1, T3 is a leased service.

Digital 56-kbps Service

Digital 56-kbps service was one of the earliest digital services. Even today it remains very popular. As its name implies, connections are made with 56-kbps bandwidth. Like T1 and T3, it is a digital data transmission service. It comes in two flavors, leased and switched. Therefore, it spans both the leased and switched digital service categories.

Digital 56-kbps service provides local, regional, national, and international connectivity. In many cases, 56-kbps service can be nearly as expensive as T1 service. Consequently, it is rarely used for SOHO connections.

Like T1, a 56-kbps line is usually terminated with a CSU/DSU.

Switched Services

Plain-old-telephone-service (POTS)

Analog is the oldest switched telephone service. It has been around since Alexander Graham Bell's days. When digital services first appeared, analog services were given a new moniker: plain-old-telephone-service (POTS). POTS devices include standard telephones, answering machines, fax machines, and the ever-present modem.

It is no secret that the vast majority of data connections have been supported by modems. This is still true today, and will probably remain true for some time to come. The reason for this popularity is that modems are cheap, relatively reliable, and plentiful. As long as an application is not very data-intensive, modems do their job well. They work with connections to terminal servers, to mainframe sites, to electronic bulletin board services, or to on-line service providers like Compu-Serve, Prodigy or America Online.

Although often marginal performers when it comes to networking, modems do provide their share of Internet and remote LAN access.

Switched 56

As we have already mentioned, 56 kbps spans both leased and switched categories. Switched 56 was one of the first switched digital services. It allowed digital calls to be placed on demand between various locations.

Although it has many appealing characteristics, some of which lend themselves to remote access, Switched 56 service does have some serious drawbacks. One, significant from a networking point of view, is an intolerably long call set-up time.

The signaling systems that telephone carriers use for Switched 56 set up a single switch node at a time. If there are a number of nodes required to connect the call, it can take some time to complete the connection. For example, Switched 56 can take more than thirteen seconds for a coast-to-coast call to be connected. Intrastate calls are not much faster. The long call set-up delay is deadly to some network applications because they time-out well before the connection has been completed.

Another disadvantage of Switched 56 is cost. In some regions, it can be nearly as expensive in installation and monthly charges as T1. In addition, Switched 56 often is tariffed at twice the ISDN monthly rate, yet it has less than half the bandwidth.

Integrated Services Digital Network

To provide truly cost-effective remote access, a flexible, far less expensive, digital service was needed. The most rapidly growing switched digital service is Integrated Services Digital Network. ISDN has been around since the early 1980s, but for a long time it was an extremely well-kept secret.

Most Regional Bell Operating Companies (RBOCs) consider ISDN, in one form or another, to be core to their telecommunications plans. Ironically, many of these companies never bothered to tell anyone. Keeping ISDN a secret delayed deployment and confused users as to its availability.

As Figure 4.1 illustrates, ISDN comes in two flavors, Basic Rate Interface (BRI) and Primary Rate Interface (PRI). Basic Rate ISDN is a 2B+D service. It has two

64-kbps B (Bearer) channels, and one 16-kbps D (Delta or Data) channel. PRI in North America has 23 B channels at 64 kbps each, and one 64-kbps D channel. Each B channel can support simultaneous, independent, voice, video, or data connections. Therefore, one BRI can support the user's choice of calls with a mix of voice, video or data.

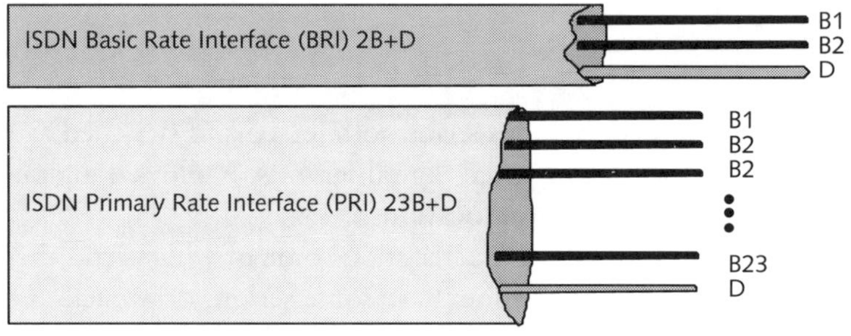

Figure 4.1   Basic Rate Interface and Primary Rate Interface ISDN

Basic Rate ISDN is usually very cost-effective. Monthly charges can be as low as 10 percent of what is typically charged for leased services like 56 kbps. Usage charges are generally reasonable, but there are exceptions. Some RBOCs see ISDN as a "value-added" service. Instead of setting rates that treat voice and data charges evenhandedly, they implement additional data usage charges, often referred to by users as an "ISDN data penalty." [1]

ISDN's biggest weakness is limited deployment. ISDN network devices are readily available from a number of vendors. Unfortunately, ISDN connections from the various Regional Bell Operating Companies are somewhat less plentiful.

This is particularly a problem in North America, where various telephone carriers have given different priorities to ISDN deployment. Deployment, however, is not the only problem associated with ISDN. It is also difficult to get accurate ISDN information from telephone company business offices. This leads to ordering problems, which is something we will spend considerable time discussing in Chapter 9, "Ordering Integrated Services Digital Network."

---

1. Depending on the carrier, local data usage charges may or may not apply. Some carriers charge voice and data local-usage charges. Others do not surcharge voice services, but place an extra fee for sending data over ISDN connections. This is rather amazing considering the fact that ISDN was designed from the ground up to be an integrated voice and data service.

Even with its disadvantages, ISDN is very appealing for remote LAN access. Leased T1 or Switched 56 kbps are often too expensive and too impractical for SOHO connectivity. It is very expensive to install these leased services in residential locations and small business offices. Analog connections, on the other hand, are often inexpensive, but much too slow. Network and Internet connectivity simply requires more speed than modems can supply.

For graphical web browsers, multimedia, and acceptable LAN connectivity, even 28.8-kbps modems have trouble coping. At 64 or 128 kbps and up, ISDN offers great network connectivity at a reasonable cost. An ISDN BRI, with one or two 64-kbps channels, provides a good mix of cost and throughput for most network applications.

Of all the remote LAN access alternatives available, ISDN is one of the most capable at supporting WAN applications. Because it is digital, ISDN is ideal for connection to network services like corporate LANs. Basic Rate ISDN supports two 64-kbps channels suitable for voice, data, or video.[2] This provides the user with a 64-kbps digital connectivity to the office with a simultaneous voice connection. If voice is not needed, ISDN can combine channels and be used as a 128-kbps data connection.

ISDN and networking, then, is potentially a very natural marriage. To the marriage ISDN brings enhanced services and the ability to provide nearly transparent LAN connectivity for the remote user. From the marriage, ISDN gains an important application that proves its worth as an important data communications medium. Because of its growing importance to remote LAN access, we will look at ISDN in considerable depth, starting in Chapter 7, "The World of ISDN."

Packet Services

Packet services, like X.25 and its older brother, Frame Relay, have many advantages for wide area networking. Since they are connectionless networks, they handle data in packet format, just as a Local Area Network does. This makes them

---

2. Why was 64 kbps selected? The digital-to-analog conversion required to support voice over digital networks uses 8-bit samples made 8,000 times per second. Multiplying 8 bits times 8,000 samples per second equals 64 kilobits per second. Higher sampling rates could be have been used for improved quality (as is done in audio CDs), but that would have required a greatly increased bandwidth from the telephone network. For voice purposes, the 8 * 8,000 sampling provides a bandwidth of approximately 300 to 4,300 Hz, which is plenty of range for voice services. It also results in a data rate for a single ISDN B channel of 64 kilobits per second.

very efficient with bursty, connectionless network applications. X.25 and Frame Relay are commonly used for WAN connections between corporate network segments, such as GWs and EDNs. For reasons that I will shortly explain, they are rarely used for SOHO connections.

X.25

The X.25 protocol has been around for quite a while. X.25 and its bigger brother, X.75, are popular because they support multiple virtual channels on a common link. This allows numerous users to share the bandwidth of a single, common pipe. Many of the Public Data Networks (PDN) use X.75 for their cloud interconnections, while X.25 over 56 kbps or T1 links is used to get the X.25 network to the end user.

Frame Relay

Frame Relay was initially designed as a bearer service for ISDN. In the blueprint, ISDN was to be the front-end access to metropolitan and wide area Frame Relay networks. However, Frame Relay soon won widespread acceptance and has recently emerged as an independent technology of its own.

Frame Relay is based on the X.25 protocol and its implementation in the ISDN Link Access Protocol (LAPB/LAPD) protocol. However, Frame Relay has an important advantage in its X.25 implementation. Assuming that it will be operating over reliable digital links, the creators of Frame Relay removed the extensive error-checking that was incorporated into X.25. Since error control is done at every node in an X.25 circuit, error-checking adds considerable overhead. While error-checking is necessary over less reliable services, it has dubious value with the more reliable digital services. Removing error-checking makes Frame Relay inherently more efficient than X.25.

Frame Relay is often offered with an option called Committed Information Rate (CIR). Not all carriers support CIR. However, where it is used, it represents the lowest guaranteed throughput over the Frame Relay. Frame Relay also can have a burst rate that is up to twice the CIR.

Integrated Services Digital Network

ISDN is considered to be both a switched and packet service. While many applications use circuit-switched ISDN services, ISDN also supports the X.25 packet protocol over both the B and D channels.

When provisioned for data, the ISDN D channel is always running X.25. Therefore, it can have multiple logical channels. That makes it possible for up to eight devices on the same ISDN BRI to simultaneously share the 9600-bps D channel. An even larger number of simultaneous users can be accommodated on B packet. Supporting multiple users through a single B channel using the X.25 protocol is something that we will discuss further in Chapter 10, "Network Connections using Terminal Adapters."

Cell-Switched Services

Cell-switched services, also known as cell-relay services, are a more recent development than switched or packet services. The most well-known and exciting cell-switched technology, by far, is Asynchronous Transfer Mode (ATM).

Broadband ISDN/Asynchronous Transfer Mode

Asynchronous Transfer Mode (ATM) is the darling of wide area services. It is an evolving service that promises very high speed connections. While ATM can be supported at T1 rates, its greatest advantage is found on multimode fiber at OC-3 (155 Mbps) rates. It also supports higher rates, such as OC-12 (622 Mbps) over single-mode fiber.

ATM is based on the Broadband ISDN specification (B-ISDN). Unlike narrowband ISDN, which is packet-switched or circuit-switched, ATM is a cell-switched technology. It uses fixed-sized 53-byte cells that are moved around the network through the modern equivalent of a crossbar switch.

Like ISDN, ATM excels at integration. ATM is equally adept at handling voice, video, and—with some magic called LANE (LAN Emulation)—at handling networking.

Aside from cost, the biggest disadvantage of ATM is deployment. Those who remember ISDN in the early days will experience déjà vu with ATM. As was the case with ISDN, there is little consensus on ATM deployment and interoperability. There is hope, however. Vendor and service providers, perhaps having learned from their miscues with narrowband ISDN, have been moving to solve the deployment issues. However, it will likely be some time before local service providers run an ATM line to your business or home.

For now, most ATM deployment is occurring locally to the enterprise. ATM is typically used as a backbone or, in some cases, peer-to-peer technology. This will change, of course, as ATM matures and its deployment gathers momentum.

There is almost no doubt that, in the future, ATM will be the network transport of choice. It is just too good at supporting voice, video and data connectivity to be ignored. It makes possible bandwidths that have, until recently, been mere dreams in the minds of futurists. Keep an eye on this emerging technology.

5

Technologies for Enterprise Network, LAN and Internet Connections

Remote LAN Applications

As we have seen, remote LAN access gives an enterprise network the ability to extend beyond the physical limitations of the LAN itself. Remote access enables users physically separated from the LAN to connect and use network resources as if they were locally attached. This includes access to all of the services normally offered on the network, including:

- Access to file servers
- Client-server databases
- E-mail
- Internet access
- Network applications
- Networked CD-ROM drives
- Shared files
- Web browsers

In short, remote access has one primary objective: It tries to make the physical distance from the network transparent to the user. With remote access technology, the remote user can utilize network resources as if they were directly on the LAN, even though they might be located many miles from that LAN.

There is more than one way to accomplish remote LAN access. There is also more than one technology that can be used to extend Local Area Networks to wide areas. In this chapter, we will look at some of the most common and viable technologies for accessing enterprise networks and the Internet.

Plain-old-telephone-service (POTS) and Analog Modems

Just about everyone with outside connections to their computer is familiar with modems. Modems form the core of data communications service for a majority of users. Although they are beginning to show their age, modems are still a viable technology. They are well established, ubiquitous, and inexpensive. As a result, analog modem technology is still a popular means of connecting to enterprise networks and the Internet.

Modem connections that are used for network access typically utilize one of two technologies. We mentioned one technique earlier, called Remote Control. The other technique is known as Remote Node. There are major differences between the two methods of accessing remote networks

Remote Node versus Remote Control

Remote control software was first introduced in Chapter 2, "Early Attempts at Remote Access." At that time, we referred to it as "screen sharing." You may recall that screen sharing permits a remote user to dial in and control a host PC physically located at another site. If the host PC is located on a network, it is referred to as an applications server. This is because network applications reside on the applications server, and are run from it. The application itself is not downloaded over the telephone line to the user's machine. Only screen images, keystrokes, and mouse clicks are passed over the telephone line between the host and client PCs.

Figure 5.1 illustrates how remote control software handles remote connections. Although the figure depicts a single PC accessing the application server, this is not always the case. Many remote control packages run on high-end, multiprocessor computers. In this case, there can be several remote control sessions running over a single applications server.

The process involved with remote control software is fairly straightforward. The remote user installs client software on their computer. The client software is responsible for handling connections over the modem connection to the

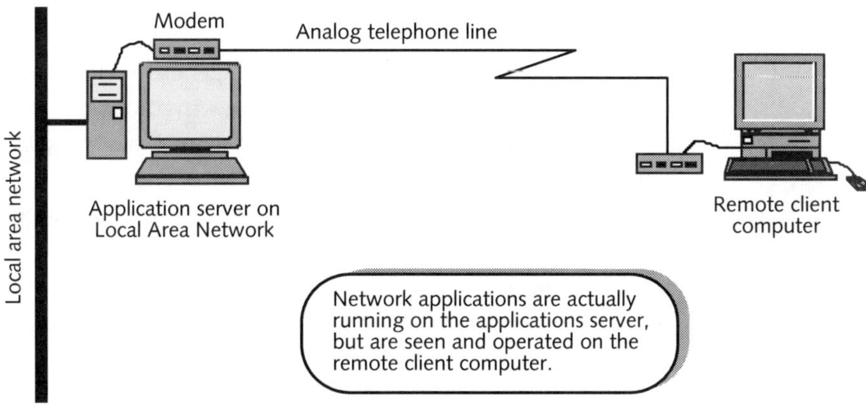

Figure 5.1   Application server access

application server. Networked applications can then be run from the application server, which, as we said, is essentially a PC operating in screen-sharing mode.

Since applications are operating remotely and not actually traveling over the modem connections, performance is often reasonable, particularly for DOS character-based applications. However, performance can be considerably slower for Windows, Macintosh, or any graphics-intensive applications.

Remote control software is most useful when applications need to be maintained on a common server and accessed through a common site license. Instead of providing a separate copy for each user, this arrangement allows a single application to be used by a number of users simultaneously. Keeping the application on the server instead of the client PC does help cut down on software piracy.

While piracy is minimized, other security problems can result from remote control software. Simply by loading the appropriate remote control software on their PC and calling the applications server, any user can create a remote access session. Thus, it is important that the remote control host be carefully password-protected. If it is not, virtually anyone can dial-in and gain access to the network.

There are two methods used by most remote control programs. The first method uses an address list. The purpose of the address list is to authenticate who can and cannot access the remote control host. The address list usually contains user names and passwords. The second method uses an access log. Although the access log cannot prevent users from accessing the remote control host, it does provide a record of who did what and when they did it.

It is important to note that the level of security provided by remote control software products is not as robust as that found in other remote access services, such as remote node connectivity. In Chapter 20, "The View from the Deck of the Enterprise," we will look into remote access security issues in more detail. You will notice that there is a whole arsenal of tools available to manage and secure remote node access. For the most part, these tools do not exist when it comes to remote control software. There is no device authentication or other method for adding additional layers of security, as there is in other remote access technologies.

Because the remote control host is typically not a file server, its file and directory protection is not very robust. This is a concern because applications, files, activity logs, and password files are maintained on the host. They can be accessed by others if not properly protected. On some remote control hosts, the user name and password files are not encrypted. While access privileges can be set to protect certain files and directories, it is not too hard to work around this protection.

As we pointed out earlier, the primary disadvantage with remote control software is that the user's machine is essentially a dumb terminal. All the action is occurring on the application server. Since applications operate on the server, if it should crash, a remote user is usually left out of commission and helpless. In addition, file transfers to or from network devices wind up on the applications server. To get them to or from the user's machine generally requires a two-step process. The file must first be transferred from its source to the application server. Then the file must be transferred from the application server to the destination machine.

From a management point of view, remote control programs can be rather difficult to administer. Very few programs incorporate any form of network management. Particularly for those remote control programs that support a number of users, this makes administration and monitoring of remote users tedious, to say the least.

Networking with Modems

Making a user's machine a remote node on the network overcomes many of the limitations of remote control software. To do this, however, we must first deal with the fact that modems are serial devices operating over circuit-switched connections. This contrasts with networks, which are packet-based connectionless topologies. Some method is required to move the connectionless network packets over the switched connection.

Fortunately, several protocols have been designed to carry network traffic over serial lines. Many of these do reasonably well over modern analog modems. Protocols like Serial Line IP (SLIP), or Point-To-Point Protocol (PPP) are specifically designed for remote network access. SLIP was one of the first protocols developed to connect network clients over serial lines. It is common to find terminal and communications servers that have been equipped with SLIP capability, and that support modem access.

SLIP dates from the early 1980s. It provides the basis for moving the IP packets over the modem link, by using a packet-framing algorithm that places network packets within frames. The SLIP protocol then transfers the frames over the serial connection to the destination. Once at the destination, the algorithm removes the packets from the frames and places them on the remote network.

Although SLIP works with almost any modem supporting transmission speeds between 1200 bps and 28.8 kbps, a faster modem yields significantly better network performance. Usually, SLIP connections are not recommended unless the modem connection is capable of 9.6 kbps or more.

Since it is IP-based, SLIP works particularly well for Internet connections. Standard IP packets are transmitted to and from the remote PC over phone lines. Therefore, the user's PC does not need to pretend to be an Internet node—it is an Internet node. This gives the user full TCP/IP client privileges. Internet Service Providers, and others offering Internet access, frequently support SLIP connections.

The main disadvantage of SLIP is that TCP/IP is the only protocol supported. The SLIP connection does nothing for users needing access to Novell, AppleTalk, or other non-IP services. This creates a communication gap for users who need to have full network access using a variety of protocols.

The Point-to-Point Protocol was written as a successor to SLIP. PPP can accommodate virtually any protocol over serial connections. Although it was primarily designed with ISDN in mind, PPP works well over modem connections as well. As was the case with SLIP, it is generally preferred that faster modems be used. For PPP, it is best that no less than a 14.4-kbps (V.32bis) modem be used on both ends of the connection. Higher-speed modems capable of 28.8-kbps (V.34) are highly recommended.

In function, the basic connection method is very much the same with PPP and SLIP. The main difference between the two is simply the protocol stack. Instead of running the SLIP protocol in the communications server and user's PC, a PPP stack is installed. The user can now access services as a remote network node using a variety of protocols.

Figure 5.2 shows how a SLIP or PPP connection is configured. A communications server at the network runs either the SLIP or PPP protocol. The user's PC is able to establish a network connection through client software that also supports either the SLIP or PPP protocol. Figure 5.2 also illustrates that the remote user can access file servers, mainframes and even remote printers. With SLIP, these devices would need to support the TCP/IP protocol to be accessible to the remote user. In the case of PPP, all devices are accessible to the remote PC.

It is possible for the PPP client to see all the hosts on the network no matter what protocol they may be running. The SLIP client, on the other hand, only sees hosts that are running TCP/IP. Therefore, by giving certain clients SLIP-only access, hosts running protocols other than TCP/IP are made invisible. In the case of Figure 5.2, the PPP clients can see and access the mainframe, the Novell file server, and the AppleTalk laser printer. However, the SLIP clients can only see and access the mainframe. The Novell file server and the AppleTalk laser printer are unseen.

More on Modem Pools

Notice in Figure 5.2 that a bank of dial-in modems, often called a modem pool, has been installed for analog access. We mentioned modem pools in Chapter 2, "Early Attempts at Remote Access." Modem pools are an efficient method of handling analog dial-in network access. They can be constructed from a number of individual modems connected to ports on the communications server. Some vendors sell integrated modem pools that combine the modems into a common chassis. Typically, the modems are constructed on cards instead of being standalone devices. Using cards makes it easy to slide modems in and out of the chassis. This allows for easy replace individual modem cards should they fail or need to be upgraded. In some cases, vendors offer integrated communications servers with built-in modem pools.

No matter which form is chosen, the modem pool serves a large number of analog dial-in users by simultaneously connecting them to the communications server. The physical connection between the modem pool and the communications server can be handled with a number of independent RS-232 cables. Each cable runs between a modem in the pool and a port in the communications server. This suggests a somewhat complex troubleshooting problem should one or more of the cables fail. To overcome this, some modem pools and communications servers support X.25 connections. As you may recall from our earlier discussion, X.25 supports multiple logical sessions over a single link. This results in a single connection between the modem pool and the communications server.

Even though we are discussing analog access to network services, you will notice that a series of Terminal Adapters is also shown in Figure 5.2. While we do not want to get too far ahead of ourselves, it is worth noting that SLIP and PPP work over both analog and digital services. Therefore, the communications server can also connect to Terminal Adapters for ISDN or a CSU/DSU for Switched 56 connections.

SLIP and PPP are not the only protocols available for remote network connections over serial lines. Some vendors are building modem-based remote network access protocols into their products. Apple Computer's AppleTalk Remote Access (ARA), for example, allows a remote Macintosh connected by modem to dial into an AppleTalk network. Network modems such as the Shiva NetModem allow modem-based remote access to AppleTalk and Novell Networks.

It is interesting that there is something of a trend in these proprietary products to migrate them to PPP support. Vendors are finding that PPP is relatively easy to incorporate into their products. They also realize that users prefer to use an interoperable, standardized solution as much as possible.

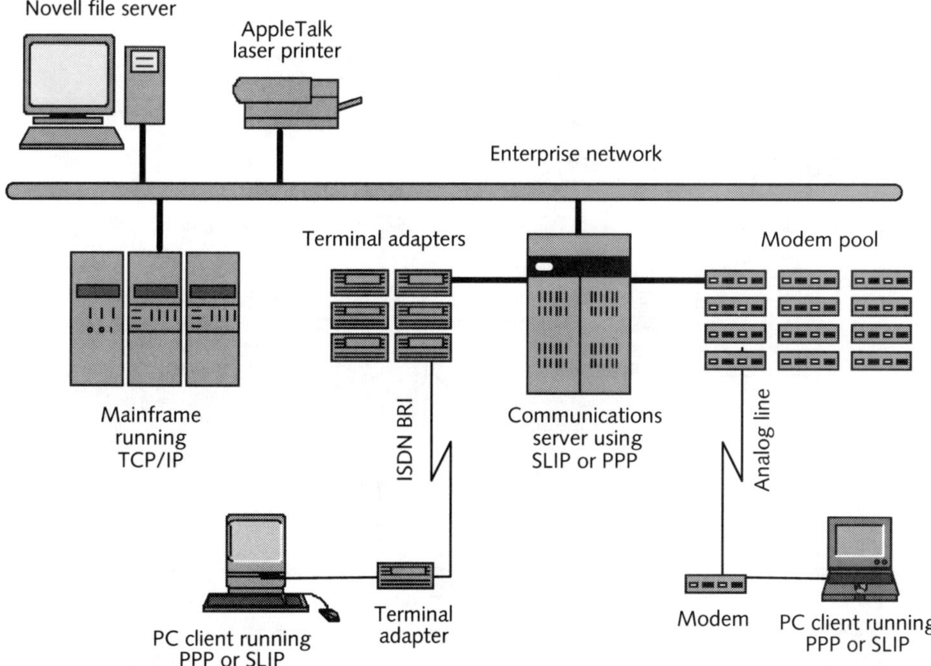

Figure 5.2   SLIP or PPP connection

Analog Dial-Out

Before we leave the subject of analog modem network access, it is worth briefly mentioning the use of dial-out modem pools. They are the reverse of analog-based remote LAN access.

Analog dial-out is the ability of a network attached user to connect to BBS hosts, fax machines, and on-line analog services directly from their LAN. As Figure 5.3 illustrates, this is typically done through the use of a bank of dial-out network fax modems. In some cases, the same facility functions as an incoming modem pool for remote LAN access and as an outgoing modem pool for network access to BBS and fax services. However, for reasons of security, flexibility, and performance, network dial-out is typically supported through the use of a separate outgoing modem pool. This consists of modems that can dial out, but cannot receive calls.

As Figure 5.3 shows, it is possible for all users to access the outgoing modem pool no matter what kind of network access they have from their computers. For

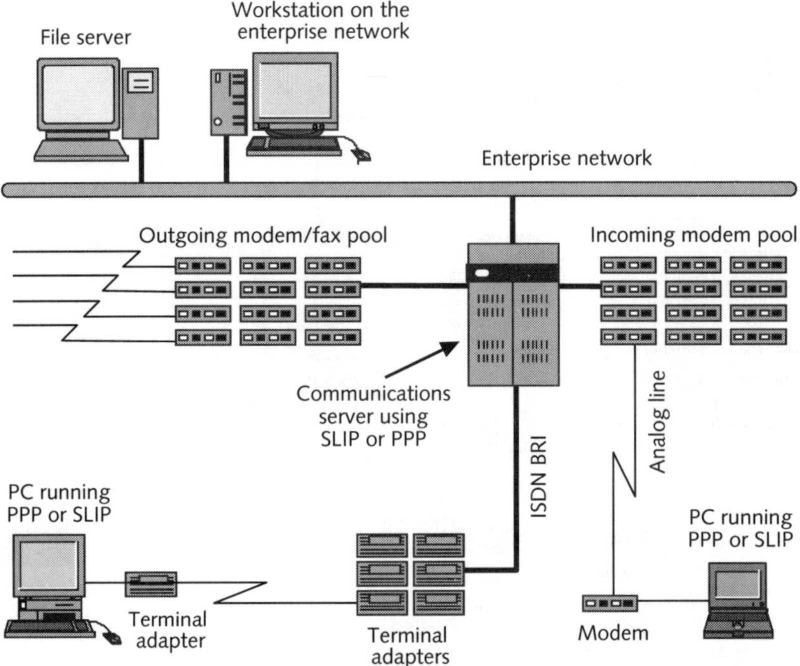

Figure 5.3   Analog dial-out

example, the outgoing analog line bank can be used by workstations on the enterprise, by the ISDN remote access users, or even by analog dial-in users. This gives common fax and outgoing modem capability to ISDN-connected users, as well as to users directly on the network.

Dial-out modems sometimes create billing problems. Unless restricted to local calling, users can access the dial-out modem pools to place long distance calls. Therefore, a charge-back mechanism is usually tied to access to the outgoing modem pool.

The Analog Ceiling

While a large number of modems are being used for remote network access, users are beginning to realize that the modem process has a serious handicap. Flaws are particularly evident when it comes to remote LAN access.

Computer data cannot be placed directly on analog telephone lines. Analog lines support analog frequencies, and computer data is digital. Therefore, a conversion process is necessary to put digital information on an analog network. This involves a modulation process that takes the computer's binary ones and zeros, and converts them to a series of tones that can traverse the analog network. On the receiving end, a reverse conversion takes place. Using a process called demodulation, the tones are converted back to their digital equivalents. From the modulation-demodulation process, we get the name of the device that handles this digital-analog-digital translation: modem (for MOdulate-DEModulate).

Unfortunately, the modulation process is susceptible to flaws in the telephone network. Poor line quality creates real problems for transmission of computer data over telephone lines. Data can become corrupted by line noise, echoes and spikes. Higher-speed modems depend on high-quality telephone lines and decent compression techniques to reach their top throughput. When line quality degrades, so does the speed of the connection. Even with high-quality analog lines, true 28.8-kbps connections are rare. There is very good evidence that 28.8-kbps modem connections seldom make it above 21 kbps, even on a good connection.

As a result, as data connectivity needs grow modems have a tough time keeping pace. It does not take much of an increase in connectivity needs for modem limitations to become painfully apparent. For example, modems can be excruciatingly slow for large file transfers. Additionally, current analog modem technology is only marginally fast enough to allow remote LAN access. Common network functions like downloading large files, viewing complex graphics or launching large network applications are often too much for modems. Even 28.8-kbps modems can be slow for large file transfers or downloading large World Wide Web images. They are simply not up to the task.

"The King is Dead. Long Live the King"

Although there are still a few trick cards left in the modem vendor's decks, it now seems that the upper limits of modem technology have finally been realized. By its very nature, the analog telephone network is bandwidth limited to around 4 KHz. This is an important point, because 4 KHz limits the base bandwidth and makes it difficult to support the higher speed connections necessary for network connectivity.

When it comes to networking, there is little hope for the future with modem connections. Modems cannot begin to support remote users with anything comparable to the kind of multimegabit bandwidth that LAN-based office workers enjoy. Therefore, it is now possible to make a blanket statement that modems have finally reached the top of their speed.[1]

Clearly, for network access this is a major problem. With the advent of the World Wide Web and its graphical capabilities, interest in higher speed Internet access has skyrocketed. Connectivity needs to the Internet and the enterprise network have begun to dramatically change remote LAN access requirements.

Obviously, vendors are not content to sit on the sidelines and allow this to happen without their involvement. Many modem vendors have been shifting their

---

1. That is a claim I would not have dared make either out loud, or especially in print, just a short while ago. Modem speed limits have been too much of a moving target to allow anyone to say that the they had reached their top speed. Just about every time some industry pundit came out with a statement that modem technology had gone about as far as it could, some enterprising modem vendor would design a newer, faster modem algorithm. This has made a liar out of more than one pundit.

Jumps in modem throughput from 300-baud to 1.2-, 9.6-, 14.4-, 28.8- and, finally, to 34.4-kbps are very well documented. Nearly every jump in throughput was preceded by a column stating that modem technology had reached the pinnacle of its speed capability.

What gives me the courage to finally say that modems are topping out is the physics of analog bandwidth. Analog bandwidth is fixed. It cannot support much more compressed throughput. This is also supported by the public statement of several key vendors, including Microsoft, that the end of throughput increases for modems are indeed near. Therefore, it can finally be said that analog modem technology does not offer enough throughput for LAN applications—and it probably never will.

emphasis to products that support the newer, faster digital network services. So it seems that the higher throughput switched digital services are well positioned to take over from modems. Clearly, a major transition in remote networking is underway.

However, there is one caution that must be observed. Just as it is tempting to declare modems to be dead and gone, it is tempting to end this section on analog network access and move on to other, more capable remote network technologies. There is a wrinkle that prevents me from doing that. It has to do with the ubiquity of analog and digital services.

There may be no argument that digital services are well positioned to take over remote network connections from analog devices and services. However, position and availability are two entirely different things. The newer digital services, like Integrated Services Digital Network, may be well endowed from a technological viewpoint to take over from modems, but that is not likely to happen any time soon. The reason is simple. Unlike analog services and modems, most digital services are far from ubiquitous.

Many telephone service providers, particularly the smaller independent companies, have no immediate plans to implement switched digital services. Even in the larger RBOC service areas, digital network deployment, while getting better by the day, is often spotty. This leads to an interesting paradox. While many people have access to modern, fast computers, not everyone has access to equally modern digital services. However, nearly everyone has at least one analog telephone line in their home or business. For this reason, fast computers and high-speed networks are frequently connected with very slow modems.

Nevertheless, even with all their shortcomings, modems can be and often are used for network access. This is true whether the network is the corporate enterprise or the Internet. As we will shortly see, many communications servers are designed specifically to offer network access to dial-in users accessing them over modems. This has resulted in an increase in network access capability which, combined with faster modems and slow digital services deployment, has given modems a brand new lease on life. Because slow access is usually better than no access, it is obvious that very few modems will find their way into the trash now or in the near future.

Asymmetric Digital Subscriber Line

Asymmetric Digital Subscriber Line (ADSL) is an attempt to provide more robust multimedia and network connections than are available through modems. It is no secret that the ADSL standard development (ANSI standard T1.413) was driven by the telephone carriers as a vehicle to compete with the cable industry. The carriers want to use ADSL for video-on-demand services. However, the technology also has potential as a remote LAN access service.

ADSL is part of a transport system called DSL, or Digital Subscriber Line. DSL circuits carry high-speed data over standard copper lines.[2] ADSL operates over the same unshielded twisted-pair cabling that brings telephone service into your home or office. Normally, standard copper cable pairs cannot support high bandwidths. Therefore, ADSL uses signal encoding, compression, and special modulation techniques to deliver its highspeed access over unshielded twisted-pair cables.

As its "asymmetric" moniker implies, ADSL offers different throughput rates. The ANSI standard T1.413 provides downstream speeds (network to home) from 1.544 to 6.144 Mbps, and upstream rates (home to network) ranging from 16 to 640 kbps. Typically, the upstream channel is 64 kbps, the same as an ISDN B channel.

Impressively, the 6.144-Mbps downstream bandwidth is 60 percent of the bandwidth found on 10-Mbps Ethernet networks. It is also more than 200 times the speed of a 28.8-kbps modem. This is sufficient to carry a real-time uncompressed video channel, or several channels of MPEG-2 compressed video.

Figure 5.4 shows how ADSL can be used for connecting remote users to the corporate enterprise. The ADSL standard calls for a specially designed modem to be connected at each end of the connection. One modem is installed at the user's location. The other is located at the telephone company's central office facility.

An awful-sounding device called an "ADSL Transmission Unit at the Central Office" (ATU-C) is at the service provider's location. The ATU-C transmits several high-speed simplex channels downstream, and receives the lower-speed upstream duplex channels. The ATU-C units may be standalone, or mounted with other telephone network devices in an equipment shelf. An "ADSL Transmis-

---

2. Integrated Services Digital Network, which we will discuss shortly, is also part of the DSL family. Many of the older telephone folks still refer to an ISDN Basic Rate Interface line as a DSL. Early on, PRI was called EDSL (Enhanced Digital Subscriber Line). One day, some alert marketeer realized that EDSL could be vocalized as "Edsel." Aside from being one of Henry Ford's sons, Edsel was the name of one of the most disastrous cars ever sold in the United States. Not wanting ISDN to be associated with that infamous car model, 2-channel ISDN was labeled BRI, and EDSL was relabeled PRI.

sion Unit at the Remote end" (ATU-R) is the mirror image of an ATU-C, receiving downstream data and duplex data. It is located at the user's end of the ADSL connection. It is expected that the ATU-C will be provided by the carriers and will not be purchased as a separate device by the user. This will limit purchase options, and may force prices to stay high. However, this should guarantee interoperability with other devices in the ADSL network.

ADSL is fine for broadcast video, which tends to be unidirectional. However, it has serious limitations when it comes to network applications that are typically bidirectional. A file downloaded from a remote server to the local PC would transfer well over the asymmetric link. In this case, the large packets containing the download would move easily over the 6-Mbps downstream channel. Small network acknowledgment packets would travel up the 64-kbps upstream channel without difficulty.

Now picture the reverse situation. We are attempting to upload a file from a local machine to a remote file server. Like salmon swimming upstream, large network packets containing the upload have to move over the relatively narrow 64-kbps upstream channel. The tiny ACK packets have the entire 6-Mbps downstream channel all to themselves. This is inefficient and a tremendous waste of bandwidth. In an attempt to deal with this problem, some ADSL uplinks have been developed to support rates up to 500 kbps.

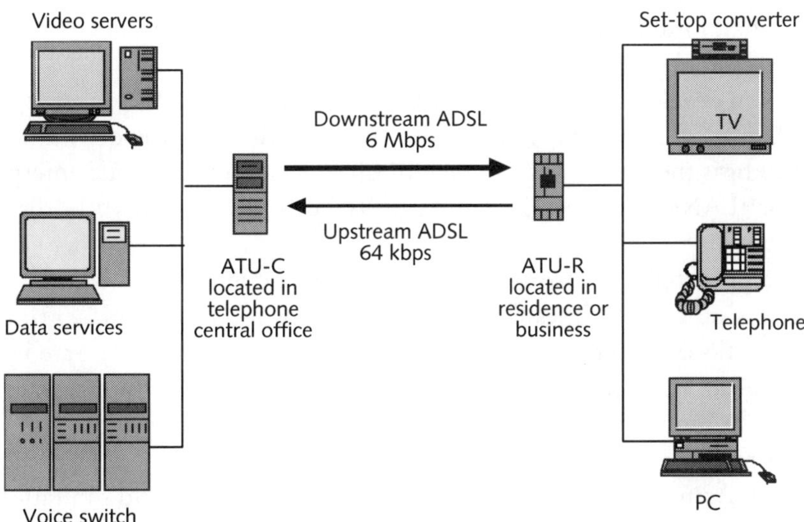

Figure 5.4 ADSL connections

High-Bit-Rate Digital Subscriber Line

High-Bit-Rate Digital Subscriber Line (HDSL) is related to ADSL. It is intended as a direct replacement for traditional T1 service. It promises transmission speeds ranging from 704 kbps to 6 Mbps. Since it delivers the same bandwidth both upstream and downstream, HDSL is better at handling network applications than ADSL.

Symmetric Digital Subscriber Line

In an attempt to even things up a bit, a related technology called Symmetric Digital Subscriber Line (SDSL) was developed. As you might expect, SDSL delivers the same bandwidth in both directions. The transmission rate ranges from 160 kbps to 2.048 Mbps. Like HDSL, this should make it favorable for remote LAN access and Internet connections.

Cable Modems

Cable modem technology was developed in an attempt to offer cable subscribers access to major information services like America Online, CompuServe, and Prodigy, and to the Internet.

The main developmental effort was focused on delivering IP packets over Cable TV (CATV) facilities. The early service offerings do not provide multi-protocol support, nor is the service provisioned for direct access to corporate enterprise networks or LANs. Figure 5.5 shows a typical CATV network distribution topology.

With a potential top throughput of 25 Mbps, cable modems can support network access up to 800 times faster than 28.8-kbps modems, and 2.5 times faster than a traditional Ethernet network. This impressive transmission rate is possible because the coaxial cable used by cable providers to bring television signals to your home has far more bandwidth than the wire used by telephone companies. However, before you get too excited, it is important to realize these rates are largely theoretical. Actual throughput must deal with several real-world limitations.

While cable modems are potentially fast, most users will see only a fraction of the theoretical throughput when they use the modems in real life. Cable modems are slowed considerably by congestion and delays in the cable network. They are

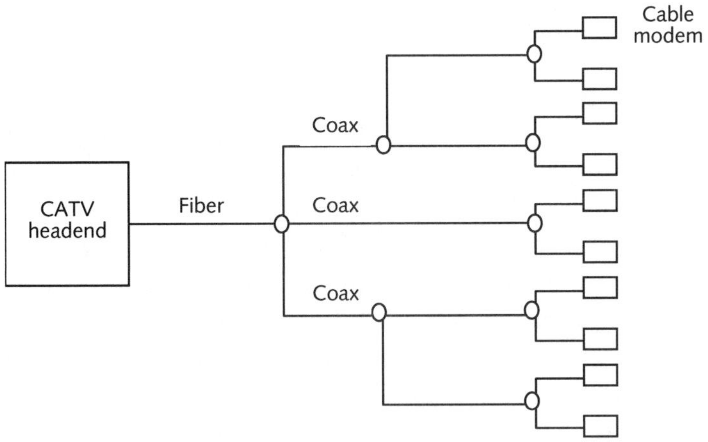

Figure 5.5   CATV network distribution topology

also notoriously sensitive to interference. Even common household items, such as hair dryers and vacuum cleaners, can give cable modems fits.

In addition, the cable technology itself has built-in limitations. Like Local Area Networks, the cable system is a shared network where all users on the same segment must compete for the network bandwidth. No matter how fast the bandwidth, all users must share it. Of course, this means that no single user gets all of the bandwidth all of the time. This is very different from ISDN, ADSL, and even analog modem connections. These services offer bandwidth that can be dedicated to the user.

Another limitation is that cable TV systems are inherently asymmetric. Like ADSL, cable offers more bandwidth for downstream traffic and less bandwidth for upstream traffic.

There is one more problem. The upstream channel is located in the middle of the amateur radio and shortwave broadcast range, from 5 MHz to 40 MHz. This makes it extremely sensitive to RF interference.

On the plus side, unlike switched services, cable modems are always connected. This difference works in favor of cable modem technology. Since cable modems are permanently on-line, they have no need to dial a connection to gain access to network services. This means that at any given moment the enterprise network or the Internet is instantaneously accessible to the user. This eliminates a whole series of connectivity issues that surround switched network connections such as ISDN and even analog modems. We will consider some of these issues, such as spoofing, later in this book. For now, suffice it to say that cable modems have the potential to make implementing remote LAN access somewhat less complex and much more immediate.

Perhaps the most troubling issue facing the deployment of cable modems has nothing to do with the technology itself, or even with equipment and service costs. It goes straight to the heart of how cable companies operate, or at least the public's perception of how cable franchises operate.

Many users feel, often with very real justification, that the cable industry has much to learn about networking before cable modems can become an acceptable technology. Many cable companies are totally ignorant of networks, networking issues and the Internet. Users question how cable operators can deliver a service they do not understand.

Of even greater concern for many users is how an industry, renowned for pathetic reliability, will be able to offer reliable network connectivity. Cable customers have become accustomed to frequent service outages from their cable providers, especially during critical moments in championship football games and during climatic sequences in feature films. Subscribers reason that if cable companies cannot provide reliability in their primary service, broadcast video, they are not likely to do so with network connections, which is a secondary service. Delivering network services requires a better understanding of network reliability than many cable companies have shown to date.

While it can be argued that telephone service providers are equally ignorant of networking, it has to be admitted that telephone companies have network reliability down pat. Telephone outages are so rare that when they do occur, they make headline news. Cable outages are so common that no one can remember the last time one made even the back page of the local newspaper.

Finally, in many users' minds there remains another reservation with cable provided network services. Over time, many cable companies have developed a reputation as being insensitive to community or user needs. Perhaps this is more of a public perception than a reality. Still, it is clearly an issue in the minds of many potential cable modem users. They are concerned that cable providers will prove unresponsive to their needs. They feel that this will make cable providers slow to offer new services and to improve current services. It is believed that this perception will make it difficult for cable providers to mold the service into a form that is viable for their customers.

Whether cable providers can bring themselves up to speed on networking, reliability and user responsiveness remains to be seen. One thing is clear, however.

Until these issues are made into priority goals and aggressively addressed by cable service providers, cable modems will have an uphill climb to successful deployment.

Digital Simultaneous Voice and Data

Digital Simultaneous Voice and Data (DSVD) is a modem technology that supports both voice and data over a single telephone line. It is commonly used for providing technical support and collaborative work, such as whiteboarding.

While DSVD is gaining some interest, it is not an entirely new technology. It is somewhat similar to an older technology known as Central Office Local Area Network (COLAN), which was developed by AT&T in the mid to late eighties.

Like COLAN, DSVD requires a specialized modem at both ends. With COLAN, the modem was called a Voice Data Multiplexer (VDM). The difference is that COLAN used an analog connection. The voice was handled in the normal frequency range. Data was frequency-multiplexed into a higher audio range. At the destination, a filtering system separated voice and data and directed them to two connectors, an RJ-11 for voice and an RS-232 connector for data.

DSVD uses a protocol that vendors add to V.34 modems. The protocol converts analog voice to digital format. Compression is then used to reduce the additional bandwidth required for the voice channel. This compression algorithm decreases the voice to about one-eighth the size of the original analog signal. The modem then mixes the digitized voice with communications data coming from the PC. Both are then converted to analog tones, and sent over the telephone network to their destination. At the destination, a DSVD modem breaks out the voice, decompresses it, converts it back to analog, and feeds it an analog voice set.

Figure 5.6 illustrates how DSVD supports voice and data connections to corporate resources.

The main advantage of DSVD is that it can easily offer both voice and data capabilities to telecommuters. It can do this without the cost of installing a second voice line. This increases the productivity of remote workers without significantly increasing costs.

Unfortunately, DSVD is not a perfect voice-over-data solution. Since we are dealing with finite bandwidth in an analog connection, the addition of voice significantly reduces the transmission rate of the modem. This is true even though the voice is compressed.

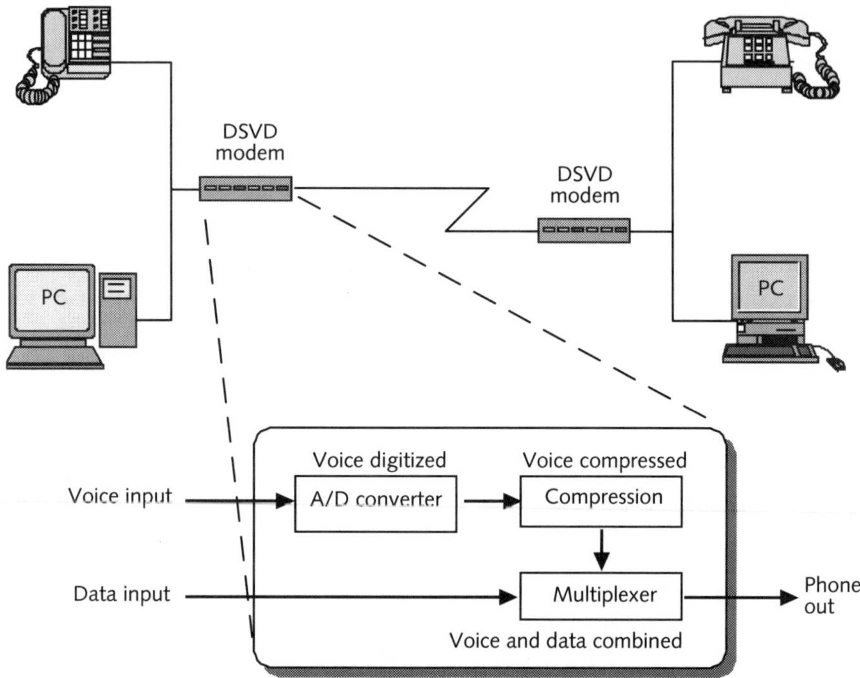

Figure 5.6   Digital Simultaneous Voice and Data

For example, when DSVD is operating over a 28.8-kbps modem, it can only deliver 19.2 kbps when a voice session is traveling over the line. This causes DSVD to be a very limited solution, particularly for remote network access. Remote LAN connections at throughputs below 28.8 kbps are extremely marginal.

Since it uses modem technology, DSVD carries the same disadvantages as traditional modem access in terms of connection time, line quality and throughput rate. As with traditional modems, DSVD does not support rapid connection times. Later, we will see how fast connections can make remote LAN access much more affordable and accessible.

Frame Relay

Frame Relay is a standard that is based on the X.25 protocol. It uses a multiplexed interface to a packet-switched network. Because it employs statistical multiplexing,

Frame Relay is able to define independent virtual circuits. The virtual circuits are really just data paths that are defined through the network cloud. Network bandwidth is not allocated to the paths until data needs to be transmitted. Therefore, within the network, bandwidth is dynamically allocated on a packet-by-packet basis.

Instead of modems or Terminal Adapters, Frame Relay uses devices called Frame Relay Access Devices (FRADs). FRADs can be standalone devices or they can be included as interfaces in bridges, routers, hosts, packet switches, or other network devices. Basically, the FRAD is responsible for delivering frames to the network. The network is responsible for switching or routing the frames to the proper destination.

Besides the FRAD, an access facility must be in place to connect the facility with the network. Although ISDN can be used for this purpose, front-end connections are more frequently handled using a 56-kbps or T1 link. A standard CSU/DSU is used in conjunction with the 56/64 kbps or T1 service.

Figure 5.7 shows a typical facility connection to the Frame Relay network.

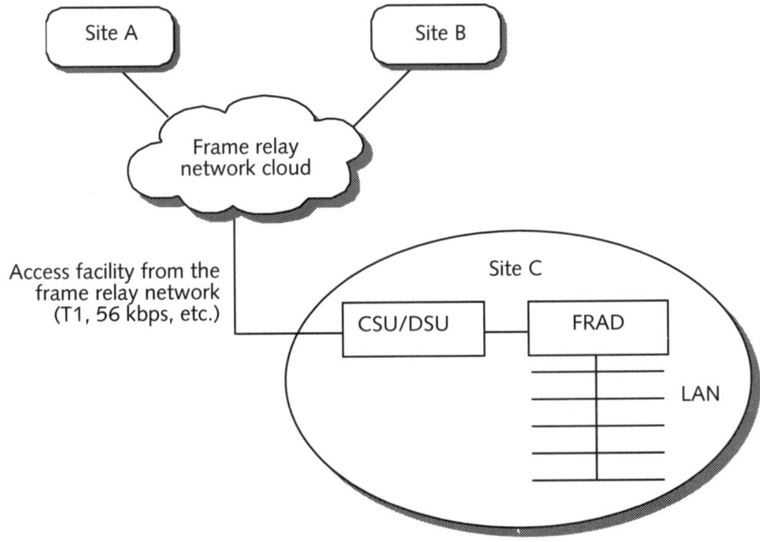

Figure 5.7   Frame relay

Because the access facility requirement is more expensive than analog or ISDN service, Frame Relay is rarely used for SOHO connections. For the most part, Frame Relay is used for connecting branch offices and remote facilities to the enterprise networks and, occasionally, to the Internet.

Integrated Services Digital Network

Because of its throughput and flexibility, Integrated Services Digital Network plays a major role in providing services for accessing enterprise networks and the Internet. There is much to be said on the subject of ISDN—and say it, we will. We have devoted a number of chapters in this book, beginning with Chapter 7, to ISDN. You will find information on how to order it, how to configure it, and how to use it in accessing remote networks. Although we only briefly mention ISDN here, we will discuss it in detail shortly. Stay tuned.

6

Service Comparisons

There are two aspects to service costing, the cost of the equipment and the cost of the telecommunications service. Most users are aware that equipment costs vary from vendor to vendor and are largely based on capability, features, and production costs. Telecommunications costs are determined in a much more complex manner that can be downright daunting.

Costs for telecommunications service are extremely convoluted and can change virtually overnight. It is extremely difficult to do any kind of straightforward comparison between various telecommunications services. Some have monthly charges, some have mileage charges, and some have usage charges. Some have a combination of the three. Even within the same service, ISDN for example, cost structures and charges vary widely between telephone service providers and from state to state. We will provide guidelines to help you sort out and clarify some of these issues.

Digital Service Cost Comparisons

Nearly all telecommunications services in the United States are regulated by the Federal Communications Commission (FCC) and by the state Public Service Commissions (PSC). Other governments have equivalent regulatory agencies or operate their own telecommunications services.

Each state has a Public Services or Public Utilities Commission (PSC or PUC) that is responsible for setting telephone rates in their state. The PSC or PUC has the authority to approve state tariffs that set rate structures for each telecommunication service. Usually, the tariffs are quite complex, having many options and conditions. These tariffs set the charges for all telephone services within the state.[1]

Because tariffs are so complex, sorting them out may require the assistance of a knowledgeable consultant. If you cannot afford to hire a consultant, you can ask your local telephone account representative to help you understand the local tariffs. If you do this, keep in mind that the account executive may have as much trouble understanding the tariff schedules as you do.

Once you review the tariffs for the telecommunications services that interest you, the next step is to select the service offering that makes the most sense for your environment.

Leased and Switched Service Cost Analysis

The first decision is whether to use switched or leased services. Since leased and switched services are billed on a different basis, take time to map out and convert the two so they can be reviewed equitably.

Leased T1 and 56-kbps services are charged on a basic monthly cost-plus-mileage basis. Switched 56 and ISDN services are typically charged on a monthly charge plus a per-minute per-channel connection cost when the call is in place. Table 6.1 shows a typical cost comparison of each of these services for a local link.

Each service in Table 6.1 is compared for one-time installation costs and recurring monthly charges for both sides of the connection. Recurring charges consist of the monthly line cost, and do not include mileage or usage fees. There is too much variation in mileage and usage fees, and they would tend to confuse the issue, so they have not been included in the figure.

To obtain the recurring cost per channel, simply divide the monthly cost by the number of channels. In this example, ISDN has the lowest installation and monthly cost per channel. Notice that the table is intended to find the lowest cost per channel. It does not take into account the bandwidth per channel or the effective bandwidth per service. If it did, the results would have been entirely different.

As you look over the table, keep in mind that rates vary widely on every service depending on state and local tariffs. It is impractical to list every possible state or local tariff in the table. Therefore, you should view this table as a model, not as an analysis. It illustrates a method you can use to determine the appropriate cost

---

1. You can order and read these tariffs if you like. Generally, your local telephone company or the PSC can supply you with tariff information.

	T1 Leased Service [c]	T1 Fractional Service [c]	56 kbps Digital Line [c]	ISDN Basic Rate Line [d]	ISDN Primary Rate Line [d]
FEATURE ANALYSIS					
Avail. user channels	1	24	1	3	23
Bandwidth	1.544 Mbps	1.544 Mbps	56 kbps	64/9.6 kbps	64 kbps
COST ANALYSIS [a]					
Recurring cost [b]					
Monthly line cost (both ends)	$ 613	$ 2,301	$ 421	$ 80	$ 2,300
Cost per channel	$ 613	$ 96	$ 421	$ 27	$ 100
One-time cost					
Installation	$ 1,087	$ 1,079	$ 480	$ 150	$ 2,000

[a] All costs are for illustration only. These are not to be taken as actual costs.
[b] Mileage and usage charges are not considered.
[c] Requires CSU/DSU lease or purchase @ approximately $2,500 per CSU/DSU.
[d] Requires ISDN device @ $400 to $12,000 per unit.

Table 6.1   Cost analysis comparison for T1, 56 kbps and ISDN services

comparisons. It is not intended to give any real cost data. For that information, you will need to call your local telephone business office. You may find that switched services, such as ISDN, may or may not be cheaper per channel than leased services. It all depends on applicable tariffs in your locations.

The table, however, only tells part of the story. To determine the most economical service, you must also take into consideration how much connection time your application needs. Do the locations need to be connected for just a few hours a week, as in the case of telecommuter network access? Perhaps they need to be connected all the time (nailed up), which would be the case with an enterprise's connection to the Internet. There needs to be a way of determining when to use leased, dedicated services and when to use switched services.

By the way, it is possible to force switched services to stay connected all the time (something that most telephone service providers do not appreciate because it eats up their switch resources). However, more often than not, switched services are more cost-effective for connections that do not need to be connected all the time. Dedicated or leased lines are usually cheaper if in use eight or more hours per day.

To determine whether leased lines or switched services are preferable, it is useful to create a second cost analysis table to compare the usage breakpoints between leased and switched services.

Table 6.2 charts the costs associated with a leased 56-kbps circuit and an ISDN line. This format can be used with any switched- and leased-circuit comparison.

Service	Monthly Service Charge	Usage Charge Per Hour	Hours Usage/ Per Month	Estimated Monthly Cost–ISDN	Estimated Monthly Difference
Leased 56 kbps	$850	0	N/A	N/A	N/A
ISDN	$43	2.4	50	$163	$687
			100	$283	$567
			150	$403	$447
			200	$523	$327
			250	$643	$207
			300	$763	$87
			350	$883	($33)
			400	$1,003	($153)
			450	$1,123	($273)

Table 6.2   Leased versus switched service break-even analysis

Unlike switched services, rarely, if ever, are there usage charges for leased services. Therefore, as the length of a call increases so does the overall cost of the switched connection. If a switched service, such as ISDN, incurs enough usage charges, at some point it becomes less economical than a leased line. Our task is to determine where the cost breakpoint occurs between the two services.

Notice that the analysis ignores mileage charges that are incurred with most leased links. You should include them if you know the distance charge, since they will provide a more accurate analysis.

In this example, the break-even point occurs between 300 and 350 hours per month. If usage is below this point, at least for this example, ISDN is the more economical choice. At 350 hours or above, leased service is a better choice.

The comparison chart in Table 6.2 is a useful tool for determining whether switched service or, conversely, leased service is the better buy.[2]

---

2. Once again, let me emphasize that this cost comparison is intended only as an example to show how comparisons between switched and lease services can be calculated. Please use it only as a guide. The break-even point is highly dependent on local tariffs that vary widely. Therefore, a word to the wise: Your mileage will vary greatly depending on your local rates.

If you decide that switched services are best, then you must next select the appropriate service from the various switched telecommunications services available in your area. If all services are available, this is usually based on a cost and feature analysis. Throughput capabilities and availability are always major parts of this decision.

An equation can be used to reduce analog and digital services to cost per kilobyte or maximum kilobits per second. The result can be mapped to the minimum acceptable throughput for your applications. This will disqualify certain services immediately, either as too slow or too expensive. The remaining services can then be evaluated on cost or other criteria, such as availability, connection time, etc.

The ISDN Service Smorgasbord

ISDN service offerings can really become a smorgasbord. A BRI can be delivered as a business service, a residential service, or as part of a service called Digital Centrex. Basic Rate is available from some service providers in a 1B + 0D, 2B + 0D, D, 1B+D, or 2B+D service configuration. Does this sound confusing? If so, you are beginning to understand just how complex telecommunications service costing can be. Fortunately, the major differences begin to become apparent when you examine the cost and features of the various offerings for ISDN services.

Usually, Digital Centrex offers more features, particularly for voice, than other types of ISDN. Centrex uses the telephone central office switch as a large and powerful PBX. It is intended for small- to mid-sized companies, although some universities and large corporations use it since it eliminates the need to install their own on-premise switch.

ISDN can also be purchased in Basic Rate or Primary Rate form. Many people automatically assume that a PRI carries the advantage of quantity cost scaling. For example, buying a case of florescent light bulbs is cheaper per bulb than purchasing one bulb at a time. Ironically, when it comes to telecommunications services, volume purchases are not always cheaper. Some telephone companies sell a PRI at more than twice the cost of twelve BRIs. Twelve BRIs, of course, offer an equivalent number of channels to a PRI.

It should be obvious by now that telecommunications tariffs can be perplexing matters. In some cases, tariffs are so complicated they make the most perplexing remote LAN technical issues look simple.

The best advice I can offer you on costing is to call on a knowledge consultant. A good consultant can sort out the various service options and tariffs in the locations in which you need service. If that is not possible, try contacting your local telephone business office. Hopefully, you will talk to knowledgeable sales people who can help you understand and equate costs for the services you want in the areas requiring connectivity. Then, use the methods described in this chapter to sort out which service makes the most sense for your locations and applications. Just be careful in your cost analysis. Be sure you know what hidden charges lurk in the shadows, and where the uncharted cost twists and turns are located.

Service Comparison

Table 6.3 shows a comparison of several remote LAN access technologies. This table gives you some idea about the comparative strengths and weaknesses of each service. Keep in mind that the table is a starting point, and is not intended to be all encompassing. You may want to place technologies that you are considering for remote access on a similar table and expand it.

Equipment Cost Comparisons

No telecommunications service focuses more attention on equipment costs than ISDN. In management meetings, in sales presentations and in Internet Usenet groups like comp.dcom.isdn, costing is the subject of much discussion. A little history shows why this is so.

When ISDN "desk sets" first appeared on the market, they started at several hundred dollars and went up to nearly one thousand dollars.[3] Inventory volumes were low, research and development costs had not yet been recovered, and support requirements were high. Therefore, vendors were required to set desk set costs very high compared to analog phones and business telephone systems.

---

3. For those new to ISDN lingo, an ISDN voice device is referred to as a "desk set," not a telephone. The reason is that more than just ordinary voice service is included in most ISDN telephones. Most have advanced voice features like built-in Caller ID, and integrated data capability. Unfortunately, desk set is not a particularly good term to describe an ISDN telephone. It brings to mind the combination calendars and pen sets we all receive at the office Christmas party. However, desk set is the only term we have that describes the additional functionality contained in ISDN telephones.

Service	Strengths	Weaknesses
POTS lines	High degree of interoperability Very low cost Easy to install Ubiquitously offered Dedicated bandwidth	Limited bandwidth Unsuitable for large data files Marginally suitable for remote LAN connections Subject to noises and signal interruptions Limited in terms of increased throughput
Leased lines	Supports WAN connections and continuous bit rate traffic Offers varying data rates to support high-speed connections Always connected source to destination No usage fees Dedicated bandwidth	Does not provide any inherent advantage in handling bursty traffic Single connections do not offer fully redundant interconnectivity Under-utilized. Often running at under 20% efficiency Typically has high monthly cost Has mileage charges
ISDN	Supports bandwidth-on-demand Supports networking-on-demand Connections to a variety of destinations on a per-call basis Reasonably inexpensive Very fast call set up Supports WAN connections and continuous bit rate traffic Dedicated bandwidth Supports packet- and circuit-switched connections	Widely varying tariffs Not as widely available as some other options listed here Very complex installations Has usage fees which can sometimes be costly
X.25 services	Both public and private service available Packet switching Efficient for bursty traffic Provides virtual circuits for any-to-any connectivity Embedded error detection and correction	Protocol requires error correction Protocol processing reduces efficiency
ADSL/ SDSL/ HDSL	Capable of very high bandwidths Dedicated bandwidth	Asymmetric bandwidth is not good for WAN solutions Very limited service deployment
Cable modem	Always connected from source to destination Potentially very high bandwidth Cable wiring already in place	Service reliability is questionable Shared bandwidth technology Very subject to interference Potential security problems Slowed considerably by congestion and delays in the cable network
DSVD	Offers telecommuters voice and data over one analog line	Marginal bandwidth for remote LAN access Voice reduces throughput of modem

Table 6.3 Remote access comparison table

Understandably, the high price of ISDN desk sets conditioned managers to think ISDN equipment was too expensive. After all, the only justification for purchasing a thousand-dollar telephone is if it is intended to sit on the Chief Executive's desk. It didn't take long for managers to inform their staff that ISDN equipment was out of the range of their departmental budgets.

To some extent, this misconception continues to this day. Although ISDN devices are dramatically dropping in cost, most managers still carry the perception that ISDN equipment is too expensive. This perception applies to a large range of ISDN devices, including those supporting remote LAN connections like Terminal Adapters, and ISDN bridges and routers.

Nevertheless, I have to admit there is some truth to this perception. ISDN equipment does tend to be relatively expensive, especially when compared to analog devices like modems. However, what is often overlooked is the fact that ISDN devices also tend to be rich in features. Anyone who has purchased a luxury automobile knows very well that features always translate into increased cost.

A fair cost comparison of ISDN equipment would equate features to price, and would set aside certain misconceptions that can otherwise skew the decision. For example, an ISDN desk set can make telephone calls, so it is commonly thought of as an "ISDN telephone." This analogy is unfair to the ISDN device. Comparing a desk set to a telephone is like comparing a race car to a bus simply because both have wheels and travel on roads.

A full-featured ISDN desk set provides extensive voice features, and built-in Caller ID. It typically has a built-in data module supporting one or two data ports. These additional services need to be accounted for when equating it to an analog or PBX telephone.

There is no way to fully emulate ISDN service in the analog world. However, a user requiring voice plus two data simultaneous connections could conceivably purchase an analog telephone, a 28.8-kbps highspeed modem and a 9600-baud modem. Since most ISDN service includes Caller ID, the user would also need to add Caller ID. Analog Caller ID frequently requires an extra device, which further increases the cost of this option.

Although the above configuration would imitate services offered by a single ISDN BRI line, it would probably result in considerably higher costs for equipment and line charges. Even then, the service would not be comparable. ISDN's unique voice and data features would still be missing.

Consider also that an ISDN desk set incorporates all services (one or two data devices, and a voice device) into a single integrated unit. Equivalent analog technology requires three separate devices, which take up valuable real estate on the user's desk. The added functionality and integration that ISDN provides are worth a great deal, and should be factored into any evaluation equation.

The comparison becomes even more complex if we take into account hidden charges for ISDN equipment in North America. The Federal Communications Commission (FCC) of the United States determined that the network terminator (NT1) required for ISDN service must be considered customer premise equipment (CPE). Phrased another way, the FCC has determined that the purchase and maintenance of the NT1 are the responsibility of the customer, not of the telephone operating company.

The FCC's judgment goes against the technical facts, and makes little operational sense. The NT1 is actually part of the telephone network. In fact, most countries consider the network terminator to be ahead of the central office demarcation point and, hence, the carrier's responsibility. The FCC refused to see it this way.[4]

The FCC's determination is unfortunate. Considering the network terminator to be customer equipment places a support burden on the customer. It also increases the cost of an ISDN installation by at least a hundred dollars per line.

---

4. There is no question that the FCC made an ill-advised decision in determining that the NT1 was CPE. It makes one wonder if the Commission really has the success of future technologies at heart. Perhaps the best that can be said is that the FCC's decision reveals how much the Commission failed to understand ISDN.

7

The World of ISDN

What ISDN Is and Is Not

In order to better understand how to access remote LANs using ISDN, we must know what ISDN is and, just as importantly, what ISDN is not.

Defining ISDN is simple. ISDN is a series of international standards created by the International Telecommunication Union–Telecommunications Sector (ITU-T, formerly CCITT) for a digital-based telecommunications service package.[1] We call this package Integrated Services Digital Network.

The significance of ISDN in communications is defined by its name. It is an entirely new telecommunications service that Integrates voice, video and data services into one cohesive Digital Network. Unlike the older plain-old-telephone-service (POTS), ISDN supports voice, video, and data with unprecedented integration. It is the integration of different services that is the hallmark of ISDN.

---

1. In case you are interested in the meaning of these acronyms, *CCITT* stands for International Telegraph and Telephone Consultative Committee. Perhaps you find yourself befuddled as to how that converts to *CCITT*. The name of the standards body is French and, literally, stands for "Consultative Committee International Telegraph and Telephone." However, in deference to English-speaking members, the organization refers to itself in the English form. Perhaps that explains in part why the organization recently changed its name to the International Telephone Union–Telecommunications Sector (ITU-T).

• ISDN is Integrated

In the past, corporations that deployed video, audio, voice, and data services had to employ up to four separate networks. Video was distributed on one network, typically over coaxial lines. Audio required yet another network composed of equalized, shielded wires. Voice services were handled over the traditional copper cable pairs. Finally, data services required coaxial or twisted-pair cables. These multiple infrastructures increased installation costs and maintenance complexity. ISDN simplifies and economizes these services by bringing all of them into a single integrated network infrastructure.

• ISDN is Services

ISDN is capable of supporting voice, video, audio, and data services over the same network with the same cable plant. Videoconferencing, real-time audio, data, voice services and even broadcast audio can be transmitted over ISDN with quality and reliability not available in previous switched services.

• ISDN is Digital

As its name implies, ISDN was designed from the ground up as a digital service. Even voice calls are digitized in ISDN telephones, and are passed over the telephone network as a digital data stream. Because the telephone network's infrastructure is very close to being entirely digital, ISDN can interface to it directly. This is good news for network connectivity.

Network devices like bridges or routers are digital devices just like computers. ISDN can output their digital signals directly to the telephone network without first converting them to analog tones. This end-to-end digital connectivity guarantees higher speed connections with significantly reduced error rates. This makes connections to Local Area Networks very efficient and reliable. In a very real sense, ISDN is the perfect Wide Area Network to support remote LAN access, since ISDN is a network, as well as digital in nature.

• ISDN is a Network

ISDN does not stop at building, campus, or even city boundaries. ISDN offers national and international network connectivity. ISDN makes it as easy to connect to an enterprise network half a continent or world away as it is to connect to a LAN across the hall. ISDN can connect diverse corporate networks across the world into a single, cohesive enterprise.

What ISDN Is Not

In many ways, defining what ISDN is not is just as important as knowing what ISDN is. ISDN has suffered from years of misinformation, both from proponents and opponents. We heard from naysayers that ISDN was too slow, too late in arriving, too hard to get, and too expensive to ever be successful. We heard from zealous proponents that ISDN could do it all. No matter what needed to be connected, they said, ISDN could do it, and do it better. The question they never answered was, "Better than what?"

Both its opponents and proponents often lacked any real experience with ISDN. Only those who worked regularly with ISDN knew the truth about its capabilities. They learned about ISDN's strengths, and under what circumstances it was the best tool to use. They also knew its weaknesses, and when it should not be used. Experienced users knew that in many (but not all) instances, ISDN could provide good connectivity in a sensible and productive manner. They were also well aware of its limitations. So, let's set the record straight as to what ISDN is not.

- **ISDN is not Just Another Telephone Service**

  Integrated Services Digital Network is not just another telephone service. It is an evolution of the telephone network to a new, higher level of service. It represents a transition from analog to fully digital switched telecommunications services. The ISDN evolution, or perhaps we should say revolution, offers enhanced services. These services have been, for the most part, previously unavailable in the telephone network.

- **ISDN is not a Voice-Only, or Data-Only Service**

  As we have already pointed out, if ISDN has one hallmark, it is that it is integrated. It seamlessly supports voice, data, and video. Voice and data integration were a large part of the original design of ISDN. Therefore, it is ironic that so many telephone companies completely overlooked ISDN's data capabilities. Because they failed to understand or appreciate ISDN's unique integrated nature, many telephone account executives attempted to sell ISDN primarily as a voice service.

  A sales phrase commonly heard in the early 1980s was, "Buy ISDN for voice, and data is a give-me." In other words, the sales pitch described ISDN primarily as a voice service with data thrown in for free. The implication, of course, is that data is nothing more than an afterthought to ISDN voice. This was very far from ISDN's design goal. It was also the first big lie told about ISDN. Unfortunately, even today many telephone company account executives have trouble understanding ISDN's data capabilities. These misinformed salespeople often tell potential customers to use ISDN primarily for voice. Worse, even today some of them urge their customers to avoid ISDN altogether.

The revelation for telephone companies occurred when users began to really embrace ISDN. Although tens of thousands of ISDN voice lines had been deployed, real acceptance of ISDN did not occur until its data capabilities became obvious to users. When users discovered the advantages of ISDN for holding video conferences, connecting to the Internet or to the corporate enterprise network, ISDN moved from "I Still Don't Know" to "Information Services Delivered Now."[2]

• ISDN is not a LAN

Because ISDN supports services that can be deployed in a LAN-like manner, some excited sales people have tried to selling it as LAN replacement technology. "Why bother wiring your building for Ethernet or Token Ring?" they ask. "Just use ISDN for all of your data needs."

This is the second big lie about ISDN. ISDN was never intended to function like a LAN. ISDN simply does not deliver the kind of throughput speeds, nor offer the degree of simultaneous multiuser services found on most LANs.

As Figure 7.1 illustrates, most LANs use a topology that is different from ISDN. ISDN is a point-to-point service. It connects a device at point A to another device at point B. That makes it ideal as a data link to connect two individual network devices. LANs based on Ethernet or Token Ring, on the other hand, use shared topologies that allow multiple devices at many locations simultaneous access to devices. All network topologies, including bus, daisy chain, and star, support simultaneous access of any device to any other device. In other words, unlike ISDN, LAN topologies are not dedicated point-to-point services.

Still, ISDN has a role to play in providing LAN access services. There are interesting and useful common applications, like printer sharing over the D channel, that ISDN handles relatively well. As we will soon see, ISDN can play an even more important role as means to provide remote LAN access.

---

2. The term "Information Services Delivered Now" has been largely credited to the inventor of Ethernet, Dr. Robert Metcalfe, who popularized it in his *InfoWorld* column. However, Gerry Hopkins of Bell Atlantic suggested it first in response to a query from Bob Metcalfe. Dr. Metcalfe was looking for a better catch phrase for ISDN than "I Still Don't Know." Soon afterwards, Gerry Hopkins introduced the phrase in his book, *The ISDN Literacy Book*.

• ISDN is not a High-Speed Network—Or is it?

In defining transmission rates, 64 kbps has been considered the demarcation point between low-speed and high-speed services. The problem is that saying that a given throughput is low or high speed is not an easy task. For one thing, the term *high speed* is a moving target. As newer, faster, technologies have been deployed, the demarcation between low speed and high speed has consistently increased.

For example, a few years ago many people considered 2400-baud modems to be "high speed." That changed when 9600-baud modems arrived on the scene. Modems operating below 9600 baud were no longer considered high-speed devices. This changed again with the advent of 14.4-kbps "high-speed"

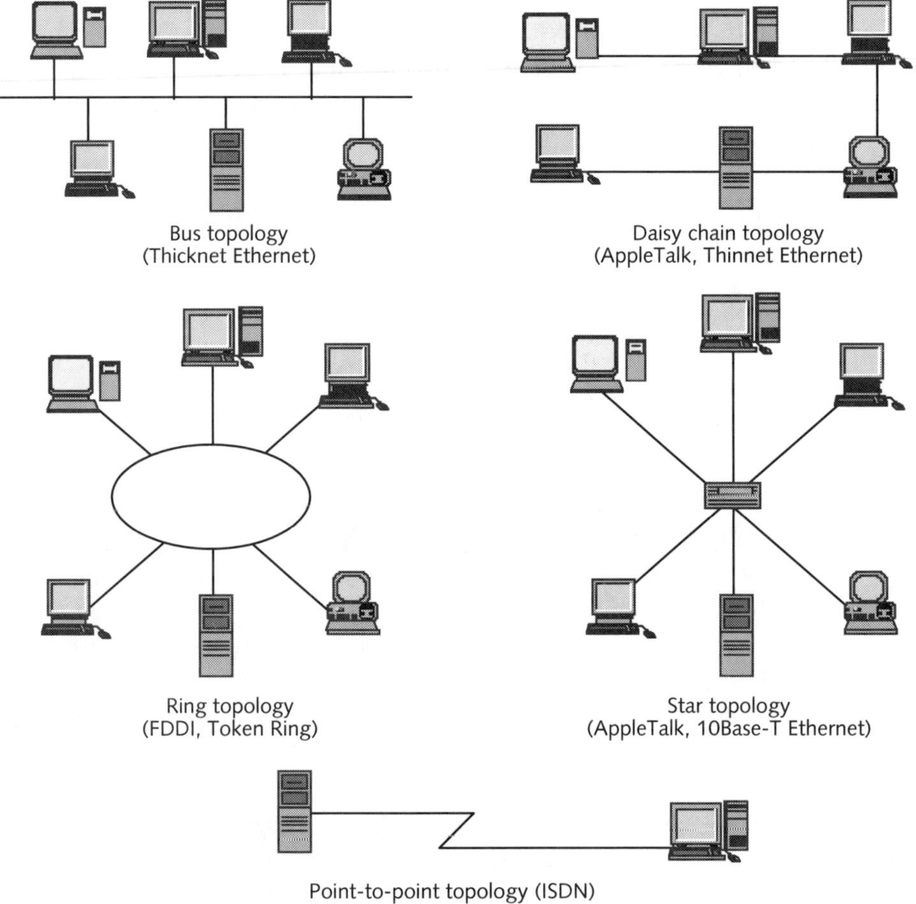

Figure 7.1   Network topologies

modems. The ante went up once again when 28.8 modems appeared. When that happened, 9600 baud was referred to as "low speed." Then ISDN arrived with its 64-kbps and 128-kbps bandwidth. Once again, the high-speed bar was raised. There is no indication this will end anytime soon.

If modem speed demarcations were not confusing enough, ISDN itself is a moving target. Is it a low-speed or a high-speed service? The answer is, "It depends." Packet data operating over an ISDN D channel at 9.6 kbps can probably be considered low speed. Similarly, an asynchronous connection over a B channel at 38.4 kbps also falls in the low-speed category. However, is a B channel connection at 64 kbps high speed or low speed? Again, it depends.

Many people would describe 64 kbps as a moderate speed. As we will see shortly, some ISDN devices and services can increase the user bandwidth by aggregating B channels into one faster virtual channel. Therefore, ISDN can be a slow-, moderate- or high-speed connection, depending on how it is configured and utilized.

ISDN Alphabet Soup

Like any new technology, ISDN has a myriad of strange new terms associated with it. We will try to make sense of some of the more common terms.

B Channel

The basic building block of ISDN is the B (or Bearer) channel, a 64-kbps digital channel designed to support voice, video or data.

The B channel is somewhat unique, since a single B channel can support synchronous, asynchronous, and isochronous services. Video and audio applications are often considered to be isochronous, or Constant Bit Rate (CBR) services.[3] They need connections that provide continuous and dependable bandwidth.

---

3. Most technical people are familiar with the terms synchronous and asynchronous. Isochronous, also known as Constant Bit Rate, may be new to many readers. Simply put, isochronous is defined as those applications that are time sensitive. Audio and video are two good examples of isochronous applications. While a delay in data transmission over a data network is barely noticeable, similar delays in audio or video transmissions can be very disruptive. Delays may cause video frames to jump, and audio frames to become choppy and unintelligible. Therefore, audio and video are time critical, or isochronous, applications. The ISDN B channel has very little latency, and is especially well equipped to support time-critical isochronous applications.

LANs usually are connected by synchronous devices. LANs tend to be classified as Variable Bit Rate (VBR) applications. Their connectivity needs change literally moment by moment. Therefore, they benefit greatly from communications services that can change bandwidth as needed.

Personal computer serial port communications programs and modems are asynchronous. Often, communications programs get along fine with Available Bit Rate (ABR). ABR applications are reasonably content with whatever bandwidth they can get.

Happily, the ISDN B channel supports synchronous, asynchronous or isochronous services with equal aplomb. Depending on how it is set up, the B channel can provide service for CBR-, VBR-, and ABR-based applications. Therefore it is extremely flexible.

The B channel can be set up in either a circuit-switched (a dedicated connection) mode or in a connectionless packet mode.

D Channel

The D (Data or Delta) channel is a 16-kbps channel whose primary function is signaling between the central office telephone switch and the Customer Premise Equipment (CPE).[4]

ISDN devices use an HDLC protocol that is characterized by a series of status checks. A continuous stream of signaling information—between the central office telephone switch and the ISDN device occurs over the D channel—even when the device is not being used. These "how are you doing" messages are primarily used for internal network call control and device maintenance.

Call control comes into play when a user event occurs. For example, removing the handset from the phone's cradle to place a call causes a call-control event to occur. When the caller picks up the handset on an ISDN phone, a flurry of internal signaling information is transmitted between the CPE and the central-office telephone switch. The information to the telephone switch says, in effect, "The user has just picked up the handset." The response returns from the switch saying, "Fine. Turn on the dial tone signal in the device."

As busy as it can be at times, the signaling channel does not need the entire 16-kbps bandwidth to do its job. Therefore, some of the channel's bandwidth can be used for X.25 user packet data. Therefore, the D channel functions as two totally

---

4. CPE is another telephone company acronym. Simply put, it describes the equipment that you, the customer, buy to operate in your location (premises). Telephones, modems, fax machines and ISDN Terminal Adapters are all considered CPE.

separate, independent data paths. One is for user data and the other is for network signaling. Data on one path does not affect data on the other path. The D channel supports asynchronous (as commonly used in PC serial ports) packet data at rates up to 9.6 kbps.

BRI

The beauty of ISDN is that it can be built in various sizes. The single-size portion, called Basic Rate Interface (BRI), has two 64-kbps B channels and one 16-kbps D channel. Basic Rate Interface (BRI) is familiar to most ISDN users. It is typically used for ISDN service in homes, schools and small businesses.

PRI

Primary Rate Interface (PRI) is the economy size version of ISDN. One flavor is used in Europe, and another in North America. For the most part, the two inter-operate. The main difference consists in the number of channels used.

In North America and Japan, a PRI runs over the same 1.544-Mbps bandwidth as T1. The North American Primary Rate Interface consists of 24 channels, divided into 23 B channels and 1 D channel. Each channel is 64 kbps. In Europe, the PRI is based on the 2.048-Mbps E1 interface. It has 31 user channels, usually divided into 30 B channels and 1 D channel. As in North American PRI service, each channel is 64 kbps.

PRI is typically used for voice and data connections between a PBX and the telephone company's central office.[5] Sometimes a PRI connects from the PBX directly to the IXC (Interexchange Carrier).[6]

PRI has significant advantages for data. When used on the hub site of a remote LAN access telecommuting application, one PRI can replace twelve BRIs. This simplifies the installation and maintenance of communication hubs. Instead of a maze of wires running multiple BRIs to a centralized hub, a few PRIs lines can provide a better solution at lower cost with much less wiring.

---

5. PBX is an acronym for Private Branch Exchange. A PBX is a telephone switch operated by the customer, rather than the telephone company. A PBX may or may not support ISDN. If it does, it may or may not support B or D channel data.

6. The Interexchange Carrier is typically the interLATA, or long distance telephone company. The best known IXCs are AT&T, MCI, and Sprint. I am sure you have heard of them and maybe even seen an occasional TV commercial for their services.

B-ISDN

BRI and PRI services are considered part of narrowband ISDN. There is also a broadband version of ISDN that supports connectivity at rates up to, and exceeding, 155 Mbps. Broadband ISDN, or B-ISDN as it is called, forms the basis for an up and coming communications technology called Asynchronous Transfer Mode (ATM).

H Channel

The ISDN H channel offers a high-bandwidth connection ranging from 384 kbps (H0) through 135.168 Mbps (H4). It bridges the gap between narrow and broadband ISDN by amalgamating a number of B channels to provide higher bandwidths. H4, at the top end of service, is equivalent to 2,112 channels. That is a lot of B channels!

ICLID

Called by various names such as Calling Line ID, Caller ID, and ANI (Automatic Number Identification), Incoming Calling Line Identification (ICLID), provides the number of the calling party to the called party. Not only is this a convenience, it can be very useful for dial-in authentication for network access. The calling device's phone number is passed to the network and can be used to validate network access for the caller.

NI-x

For a "standards-based service," ISDN can be very unstandardized at times. The National ISDN (NI) specification is an attempt to unify ISDN services. NI-x is based on the Bellcore technical specifications.[7] Currently there are three NI specifications, NI-1, NI-2, and NI-3, also known as NI-95. Each one builds on the previous specification. ISDN switches and devices that are NI-x compatible tend to have a higher degree of interoperability.

---

7. National ISDN-1 is covered in Bellcore Special Report NWT-001937, dated February 1991. Similarly, NI-2 is covered in Bellcore Special Report NWT-002120, dated May 1992.

NT1

ISDN requires a little box with a bunch of lights called a network terminator, or NT1. Other than paying for it and plugging the box in, the user has very little to do with the NT1. It primarily functions as part of the telephone network's central office telephone switch. It converts the 2-wire U interface from the central office telephone switch to the 8-wire S/T interface, which most ISDN devices use. The NT1 can also perform some maintenance functions, usually under central office control. In addition, the NT1 provides limited information on the status of the ISDN lower layer connection to the user.

The NT1 is often thought of as a standalone device. However, there are also chips that implement the entire NT1 functionality. These ICs have had a big effect on reducing both the size and cost of CPE. It is now possible, even common, for the NT1 to be incorporated into ISDN equipment. This reduces the cost and simplifies the installation of ISDN equipment.

SPID

One of the most confusing parts of ISDN is the Service Profile Identifier, or SPID. The SPID identifies an ISDN device to the network, much like an Ethernet address identifies a Network Interface Card.

The concept behind the SPID is to associate a series of features, called service profiles, with an individual ISDN device. This is done with the SPID, an identification number for the device. The SPID allows the ISDN telephone switch to associate the service profile with a specific ISDN device or line.

The SPID usually looks like a standard telephone number with a bunch of extra digits thrown in before and after the number. Without a SPID, the ISDN device will not work on most lines.

The SPID is downright confusing. Some ISDN switches require only one SPID for both channels. Other switches require one SPID for each channel. The format of the SPID changes, depending on which ISDN switch and telephone company are used for service. There are enough variations and permutations to make a grown man cry. Your telephone service provider should be able to tell you what your SPID is and how many SPIDs you need to enter into your ISDN device.

SS7

ISDN is based on a signaling system called Signaling System 7 (SS7). This system is responsible for an advancement in the telephone network called *out-of-band signaling*.

In many ways, out-of-band signaling broke new ground. Prior to SS7, the telephone network handled call management (call set-up, call maintenance and call tear-down) using *in-band signaling*. In-band signaling works by stealing some of the channel's bandwidth and redirecting it to call-control services. This limits the available bandwidth for user data, cuts down on redundancy and slows connection time.

The SS7 system handles call control in a completely separate network, resulting in higher user throughput and, even more importantly, very rapid call set-up times. Under SS7, connections are measured in a handful of seconds even with long distance calls.

S/T Interface

Just to keep users a bit off balance, ISDN has several interfaces, or connection points. As Figure 7.2 illustrates, one of the interfaces is labeled *U*. The other is labeled *S* or *T*. The S/T interface, as defined by ISDN Standards, is an eight-wire interface. One pair is for transmitted data, one pair is for received data, one pair supplies power from the user to the network, and one pair is power from the network to the user.[8] Some installations use only one power pair. In this case, only six wires (three-pair) are used.

The S/T interface is on the customer (user) side of the NT1. Many ISDN devices come with built-in NT1s that allow direct connection of the U interface to the device. However, they may or may not provide an external S/T interface.

TEI

The Terminal End Point Identifier (TEI) is used with the SPID to identify individual devices on the ISDN line. The TEI may be set using either automatic assignment or nonautomatic assignment. Unlike the SPID, which is confusing, to say the least, and must be set by the user, the selection of the TEI is far simpler with automatic assignment. In many installations, the user simply selects the auto configuration option. The switch takes care of assigning the TEI for the device. Oh, that more of ISDN was this simple!

---

8. "Power from the network" means power supplied from the NT1 to the ISDN device, not power from the telephone network. Unlike POTS, ISDN is not powered by the telephone network.

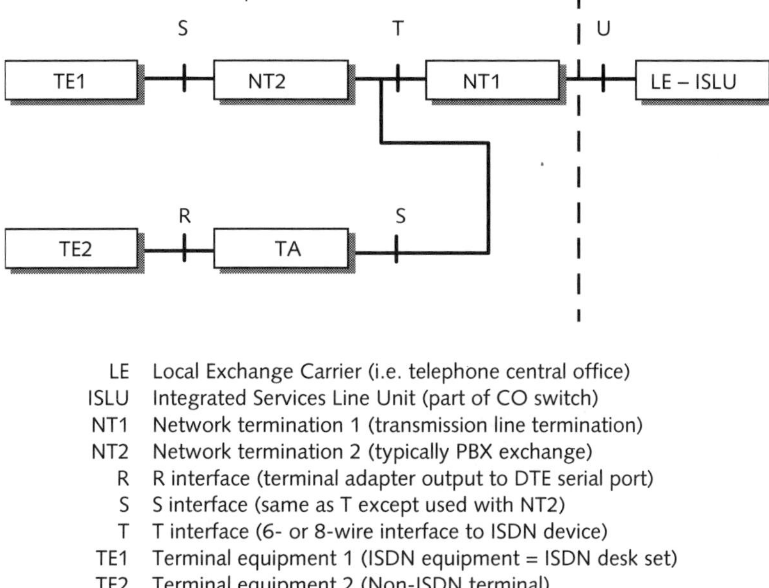

LE   Local Exchange Carrier (i.e. telephone central office)
ISLU   Integrated Services Line Unit (part of CO switch)
NT1   Network termination 1 (transmission line termination)
NT2   Network termination 2 (typically PBX exchange)
R   R interface (terminal adapter output to DTE serial port)
S   S interface (same as T except used with NT2)
T   T interface (6- or 8-wire interface to ISDN device)
TE1   Terminal equipment 1 (ISDN equipment = ISDN desk set)
TE2   Terminal equipment 2 (Non-ISDN terminal)
TA   Terminal Adapter (adapts TE2 for use on ISDN)

Figure 7.2   ISDN interfaces

U Interface

The U interface is a two-wire (single-pair) connection from the central office. It is on the far (switch) side of the NT1. Devices that have an internal NT1 allow direct connection from the telephone line to the U Interface.

The Future Implications of ISDN

ISDN's potential is virtually unlimited. It is an evolving technology. Today's narrowband ISDN will lead to tomorrow's broadband ISDN networks such as ATM. ISDN already operates over copper, fiber, and wireless services. It offers scalable bandwidth for data, voice, or video. Aggregate throughput ranges from 64 kbps all the way into the gigabit-per-second range.

Very few people dispute the fact that ISDN will be a major on-ramp to the National and Global Information Infrastructure's Information Superhighway. ISDN is the first bold step in a digital communications future that promises more than today's mind can comprehend.

8

ISDN Advantages and Disadvantages

ISDN Advantages

Low Error Rates

Clearly, ISDN's biggest advantage is that it is entirely digital. It is far less error-prone than analog connections. Therefore, ISDN lends itself well to supporting data services.

POTS connections have a typical error rate of 10^{-4} (one error in ten thousand bits transmitted). ISDN typically supports an error rate of 10^{-6} (one error in one million bits transmitted). This is a factor of one hundred times lower than the best error rates encountered in POTS. For digital services over fiber links, error rates have been measured as low as 10^{-12}.

Bit Error Rate Tests (BERT) run on an ISDN B channel by West Virginia University were impressive. They revealed no errors in a 21-hour period.[1] Considering the continuous 64-kbps throughput over a 21-hour period, our BERT test did not show any errors when sending 5×109 bits. This worked out to be far less than the often-quoted digital service error rate. This kind of very low error rate is good in anybody's book.

---

1. For more information on ISDN error rate testing, I heartily recommend my first book, *Sensible ISDN Data Applications* (1992, West Virginia University Press). The book discusses ISDN data applications in detail. For the reader, it also offers the chance to learn firsthand how West Virginia University pioneered ISDN data applications. For me, it offers the potential to earn more royalties!

Keep in mind that error rates are rarely, if ever, guaranteed. Under poor conditions, error rates on ISDN connections can exceed 10^{-4}. In fact, such high error rates can be used as an early warning system that there is trouble in the ISDN network. By the same token, it is possible that local POTS connections can experience lower error rates than 10^{-4}. Keep in mind that the built-in error correction found in modems and many ISDN devices tends to mask errors.

Fast Call Set-Up Time

Besides lower error rates, ISDN has another important capability. ISDN has very fast call set-up time. Although not always given very much prominence in sales literature, call set-up time is very important, particularly for network applications.

We have all become accustomed to the unnerving sequence of squeals and squawks that come out of a modem as it attempts to negotiate a connection. This negotiation process is called *modem training,* and is downright irritating.

Besides having an annoying sound, the modem's training process is very time-consuming. It can take 15 seconds, or more, for a pair of modems to negotiate a connection before a single byte of user data is transmitted. Meanwhile, the user has no alternative but to sit and wait for the training process to be completed.

When it comes to connecting data calls, ISDN is a major improvement. Not only is it silent while setting up connections, but ISDN's connection speed is lightning fast.

In every case, ISDN devices are much faster than modems in setting up call connections. Calls within the same switch set up in about 600 milliseconds (0.6 seconds). Intercontinental calls set up in less than five seconds. Three seconds is fairly common. While the actual call set-up times for analog and ISDN connections are almost the same, the negotiation procedures of the modems themselves take considerably longer. Therefore, compared to modems, ISDN set-up time is very short indeed.

Because connections can be made and dropped so quickly, ISDN is well suited to a configuration called "on-demand networking." On-demand networking establishes calls only when information has to be transmitted over the Wide Area Network. When there is no traffic, the connection can be dropped. This greatly reduces usage charges.

We will discuss on-demand networking in more detail in Chapter 12, "Call Control."

ISDN Disadvantages

There is no denying ISDN is a great technology. It is exceptionally well suited to remote LAN access. However, the ISDN picture is not all rosy.

ISDN has some real drawbacks. Some are relatively minor. Some are much more serious. Anyone planning to deploy remote LAN connections over ISDN should be aware of the issues that come in to play when ISDN is used to connect WANs.

Lack of Ubiquity

I mentioned this point before, but it bears repeating: The biggest disadvantage by far is that ISDN is not ubiquitous. Particularly in North America, ISDN deployment has been very spotty. Deployment varies all the way from very good, to mediocre, to just plain lousy.

Some regions have "ISDN Anywhere" programs which promise ISDN services to virtually anyone.[2] Other regions have only limited ISDN deployment. Finally, and to the consternation of many users, some regions have service that can only be called "ISDN Nowhere." In these places, ISDN is not available at any cost, anytime now or in the foreseeable future.

On the bright side, the situation is improving. Half way through the 1990s, ISDN deployment in the United States topped the 50 percent mark. This means it was available to more than half of the customers of the U.S. public telephone network. By the end of 1995, it was estimated that global deployment of ISDN lines exceeded two million lines. Perhaps this is still a drop in the bucket when compared to the total number of global subscriber lines. Still, it shows a definite upswing in the deployment of ISDN service.

---

2. "ISDN Anywhere" is an offering from several RBOCs that promises to provide ISDN to virtually any customer throughout the region. Bell Atlantic was one of the first RBOCs to offer an ISDN Anywhere program. Pacific Bell and several other RBOCs soon followed suit. While ISDN Anywhere is a good start towards ubiquitous deployment of ISDN services, users are cautioned to read the fine print of these programs. They are usually somewhat less than anywhere and contain certain restrictions. For example, users must sometimes be within 18,000 feet of a central office to qualify for ISDN Anywhere service.

Irregular ISDN Charges

The second disadvantage of ISDN is varying prices. While ISDN tends to be the least expensive digital service option, charges for ISDN are heavily dependent on the location and the serving company.

More often than not, ISDN tariff rates offer little parity. The options and charges may or may not make sense. Monthly rates vary from under $20 per month to well over $100 per month for exactly the same service. Usage fees for ISDN data range from nothing to several cents per minute for local calls. For some users, ISDN can be so inexpensive it becomes a "no brainer," while for others it can become so expensive that it is totally out of the question.

In some regions, ISDN rates can be illusory, particularly if the telephone company considers ISDN a "premium" or value-added service. When a carrier builds ISDN charges in this manner, they publicize what, at first, appears to be a low ISDN rate. However, not all is always as it seems. These attractive ISDN rates often omit essential items, such as basic telephone service charges.

When gathering ISDN rate information, be sure you have the whole picture. Ask the telephone sales office for an estimate of charges you can expect to see on your monthly bill. When ordering service, be sure the telephone office includes installation and any other added (hidden) charges.

Throughput Limitations

Another disadvantage is that narrowband ISDN is simply not fast enough for some applications. Let us not fool ourselves. Compared to modem throughput, ISDN is fast. However, compared to T1, T3, or ATM, ISDN is slow.

There are real throughput considerations that come into play when designing ISDN WAN connections. The application should determine whether ISDN, or any other telecommunications service, has reasonable throughput at an acceptable cost. It is just as wasteful to use a T1 to connect computers through their com ports as it is to connect large enterprise networks with narrowband ISDN.

Complex Installations

Installing ISDN is very complex and prone to errors. More often that it should, ISDN installations approach nightmarish proportions.

Sometimes, ISDN lines are not installed in the promised time frame, are incorrectly installed, or are improperly configured. Every ISDN installation involves switch translations. Switch translations set up the ISDN line for specific devices. Generally, translations are tricky business and they can become extremely fouled. Since installation is by far the most complex part of ISDN, we will devote an entire section of this chapter to ISDN installation issues.

ISDN Complexities

POTS connections are simple. Plug in, power up, and connect. Unfortunately, ISDN is not as straightforward. Several steps are required for interfacing any device to the ISDN network.

Before you can use ISDN, you need to know how it is to be configured. Careful thought must be given to the differences between channel capabilities, since some channels are better suited than others for particular applications. For example, D channels offer 9600-baud packet services for data communications. This is fine for asynchronous data (PC serial port) through communications programs. However, it is typically too slow for remote LAN connections. Furthermore, the D channel cannot handle voice or video services.

Voice, video and higher-speed data typically use B channels. However, a single B channel is not enough bandwidth for some video and high-speed data applications. In these cases, multiple B channels must be combined for additional bandwidth. High-speed video and enterprise-to-enterprise network connections are best supported on the H channel.

Therefore, it is important that you associate the application with the required ISDN bandwidth. This takes some foresight and careful planning. Never throw ISDN, or any other service, at an application. Doing so is a waste of resources and will likely doom the application to failure.

Physical Plant Limitations

Although ISDN is superior to POTS in many ways, POTS has an important advantage over ISDN. POTS lines can be installed just about anywhere. All that is needed to carry POTS is a pair of copper wires, and they do not have to be a particularly good pair at that. ISDN is far more fastidious. Because it is a digital service, ISDN is subject to a number of plant limitations.[3]

Loading coils, bridge taps, old cable trunks, and water-filled manholes all conspire against ISDN. These are of far less concern with POTS. In fact, loading coils and bridge taps are an advantage with POTS. Loading coils improve the network's voice frequency response and reduce frequency loss. Bridge taps allow more rapid and less expensive service provisioning.

Before ISDN can be offered, all loading coils must be removed since they degrade the digital signal. Bridge taps (used for the interconnection of cables) must also be removed. The process of checking the physical plant for ISDN capability is called "line qualification." It tells the service provider whether the cable plant between the CO and your location can support ISDN service.

Sometimes, telephone cables are so old, or in such poor shape, they cannot support ISDN—even if the bridge taps and loading coils are removed. If this is the case, cleaning up the telephone company's plant is a major undertaking. Removing bridge taps and loading coils is both labor- and time-intensive. It can easily become a major project for customer engineering department of the telephone service provider.

There are locations where there is not enough potential ISDN sales to warrant the expense of converting the cable plant. If this is the case, the telephone service provider may have a difficult time justifying an investment in plant renovation. This is especially true for an individual, or a small number of potential ISDN customers. It is not unusual for a service provider to decline offering ISDN services in such cases. Once in a while, customer engineering can be talked into gleaning a good pair out of an otherwise bad cable trunk.

Ironically, if the telephone service provider has completed a citywide qualification for ISDN, the cable plant is generally in pretty good shape. This means that POTS connections, particularly for modems, improve drastically. Line noise is minimal and connection reliability is very high. So in places where ISDN has been installed, users frequently see an immediate improvement in analog modem connectivity.

---

3.   When a telephone installer uses the word *plant,* it is not in reference to the green thing that grows under the window in your living room. Plant refers to the telephone cable network, including cross-connects, interconnects, and all the trappings that go into wiring your telephone services to the central office.

Configuring ISDN Hardware

Just as ISDN lines need to be configured for the specific device, the equipment must be configured for the line. Besides being set up so that it can make the physical connections, ISDN equipment needs to be configured for the specific switch type used in the local central office. There are a number of ISDN switches and switch vendors. The most common switches found in North American ISDN central offices include the AT&T 5ESS, the Northern Telecom DMS, and the Siemens EWSD.

Additionally, the SPID, TEI, and any operating parameters must be properly configured in the device. Usually this is done either through the front panel of the device or through a serial port on the device. ISDN network equipment can frequently be configured through the network itself. Over the network, this can be done by using Telnet or Simple Network Management Protocol.

Most vendors supply configuration information with the device's documentation, similar to Figure 8.1.

Configuration parameters can vary widely between different devices and between different vendors. However, there are common elements in most configurations. For example, in Figure 8.1 the device configuration specifies the type of switch and ISDN type. Just about every ISDN device needs to know what switch it is operating from, and what ISDN type (National ISDN or Custom) is being used.

The next section of the configuration deals with call-control parameters. Call control can be done in many different ways. This is where an installer tells the device which method to use. We will discuss call control in further detail in Chapter 12, "Call Control."

For now, be aware that many network devices can use manual (the user dials the device) or automatic (the device calls by itself) call connection. The configuration in Figure 8.1 shows "Auto On" as the connection type. This means the device is programmed to automatically call a network site device at 293-5555. If the call fails, the device will take action. Just like a faithful dog, the device, as programmed in the retry delay field, will attempt to call the remote side every 30 seconds. It will call for forever if that is necessary. (These are very persistent devices!)

There are additional call control parameters, such as call back. Call back is a form of security that verifies an incoming call and calls back the remote site device. In this case, the ringback number field is blank. Therefore, this configuration does not make use of the call-back feature.

It is possible to set up a device to be called but prevent it from calling anyone. This type of configuration is typical with enterprise side network devices. Network administrators usually do not want to pay for calls to remote users. The device can be prevented from placing calls simply by turning the auto-call parameter off or by removing the called number. Auto off will tell it not to call on its own. Without a phone number, the device would not have a clue who to call even if auto-calling was turned on.

The third section in the configuration shown in Figure 8.1 deals with security. We will discuss security in Chapter 20, "The View from the Deck of the Enterprise." For now, realize that, by nature, any dial-in access device presents security risks to itself and to the network. As we will see in Chapter 20, using the proper network configuration parameters can help protect the device and the network from unauthorized access.

CONFIGURATION PARAMETERS

Switch type	5ESS	*Set up for an AT&T 5ESS custom switch*
ISDN type	Custom	
Callback	Off	*Call back of remote user is off*
Line speed	64K/line	
Protocol	COMPRESSED	*Compression is turned on*
Address age time	1000	*Toss out addresses older than 1000 seconds*
Connection type	Auto On	*Automatically call the remote device*
Packet timeout	OFF	
Retry delay	30	*If call is unsuccessful, try calling the remote every 30 seconds*
Called number	2935555	*Remote bridge phone number*
Ringback number		

SECURITY PARAMETERS

Access status	ON	*Remote access of device for configuration is on*
System password	Exists	
Client password	None	
Callback security	OFF	
Remote configuration	PROTECTED	*Device configuration is password-protected*

PROTOCOL FILTERING

0806 ACCEPT	*Pass these Ethernet protocol types to the WAN filter all other protocols*
809b ACCEPT	
80f3 ACCEPT	
Type forwarding mode is ONLY	
Type demand mode is ANY	
Number of Ethernet addresses: 20	*Bridge has learned 20 Ethernet addresses*

Figure 8.1   Typical configuration of an ISDN bridge

Other parameters, like compression, filtering, and forwarding, are included in the device configuration. These will be discussed in Chapter 15, "Optimizing WAN Connections," and in Chapter 16, "Network Filtering."

Looking over the list of parameters may seem a bit daunting. There is no question that device configuration can be somewhat difficult to master. However, there is no need to worry. As the various options and configurations are explained, they will become more obvious and somewhat less intimidating.

Fortunately, many network devices allow the device to load a custom-tailored common parameter set. This set becomes the default for every newly installed device. In that case, the general configurations will be automatically set before the device is installed. All the installer has to do is customize the specific parameters, such as the SPID and calling number, that are required for the individual device. That makes the task of configuring and installing these devices a little easier and much more reassuring.

Testing ISDN Lines for Successful Installation

When it comes to ISDN data installations, we have to face the fact that most telephone companies are geared to voice service. Although data has been part of the telephone network for years, voice services have traditionally been the bread and butter for service providers. It should come as no surprise, therefore, that the telephone carriers are much better at supporting voice services than they are at supporting data services. This becomes particularly evident when a user encounters data problems over the telephone network.

Many technicians employed by the telephone company are caught completely off guard by data problems. They do not know how to troubleshoot or repair data circuits. Sometimes, they will even go so far as to report there is nothing wrong with the line when there is clearly a problem.

For self protection, it is up to the user to develop troubleshooting procedures that reliably point to the location of the problem. If the problem seems to be centered in the telephone network, it is essential that you not let the telephone service provider convince you otherwise.

Never assume that a new ISDN line is working simply because the telephone installer tells you the installation has been successfully completed. All too often, installers do not thoroughly check ISDN connections after installation. Even if they do check the line operation, it may not be enough. Unless your equipment is properly configured and connected to the line, there is no guarantee that the line will perform properly. After the installer leaves, the new line may or may not work properly when it comes time to plug in your gear.

The best way to assure yourself of the proper installation of any ISDN line is to be at the location with your equipment when the installer arrives. That way, you can test your ISDN device before the installer leaves the premises. If trouble occurs, you can ask the installer to work on the problem right there and then. This is much better than having to place a service call and wait days or even weeks for a return visit.

Sometimes it simply is not possible for you to be on-site when the installer arrives. In this case, installation testing becomes a multistep process. First (you hope) the installer will check the installation with an ISDN line tester or, at the very least, examine the NT1's lights for normal operation.

Using an ISDN line tester is the best way to check an ISDN line. It provides superior information to the installer. It is much better than just looking at the status lights on an NT1. However, sometimes installers will do no more than observe the NT1 LEDs for what they consider to be normal operation. Even worse, some installers do not even bother to look at the NT1 LEDs when they complete the installation. Instead, they merely check an ISDN installation by listening for line hiss with their analog butt sets. Frankly, this is really not a test at all. Hearing noise on an ISDN line does not mean the line works. Far from it, actually. More than one botched ISDN installation has been declared "operational" by an installer who did not bother to adequately test the line. Telephone company installers should know better.

Most telephone service providers charge for trouble calls if they do not find a problem in their network. In addition, sometimes the telephone company will tell you there is nothing wrong with their network, even when there is a problem. Therefore, it is best to check out the situation yourself before placing a service call. If the ISDN connection fails to work, you may not know if the problem is in the line, the translations or the ISDN equipment. A test procedure should be developed to assist in isolating the problem. The following three-step process may be helpful to use as a model.

Step One: Check the ISDN line yourself

When you arrive on the scene, you can simply plug in the ISDN device and see if it works normally. If it does not, you can check the line by examining the NT1 LEDs or by testing the line with an ISDN line test. Try swapping NT1s if you have a working second unit. Alternately, you can check the line with equipment known to be functioning. You will need a device that works with the line's current translations. If you have access to one, use an ISDN protocol analyzer to determine if the problem is in the line or in the device.

Remember that a line problem can be physical (a wiring problem in the central office, on the poles, or in the premises) or it can be logical (translation problems).

Step Two: Check the ISDN equipment

You can check the ISDN equipment on a known good line, if you have one with appropriate translations. Use the process of elimination to narrow down exactly where the problem occurred. If the device works properly on another ISDN line but not on the recently installed line, that is a very good indication that you have line problems.

It also helps to double-check the equipment configuration to see if the device is set up correctly. Make sure it is configured for the proper switch type and ISDN line (National or Custom). Check the SPID to verify that it is correct. In fact, you may want to check and double-check the "big five." The big five are the most common device configurations required by most ISDN equipment. In order, they are:

1. The ISDN switch type: This is typically a selection of National ISDN, Custom ISDN, and the appropriate switch vendor.
2. Channel #1 telephone number: This is typically the local directory number. Sometimes ISDN equipment requires a Directory Number (DN) before it will accept or make calls.
3. SPID #1: This is the Service Profile ID for the first B channel. Without the correct SPID, in many instances the ISDN switch will not recognize the device. When this happens, the device cannot make or receive calls.
4. Channel #2 telephone number: This may or may not be the same as the channel #1 local Directory Number.
5. SPID #2: Like the channel #2 number, this may or may not be the same as SPID #1.

Step Three: Place a trouble call and pray

Finally, as a last resort, call in the failure to the telephone service provider and pray that it really is a telephone network problem.

Data Service Support

All of this leads to the issue of support for WAN services and devices. Data service support is far too important a matter to work out during your first data outage. Be sure to have a data support understanding in place with your telephone service provider. Otherwise, you may find out during an emergency that you have much more to deal with than just the loss of service.

The telephone companies do not always understand data services. Even so, account executives at some telephone companies will aggressively sell their accounts on making the phone company the company's data service provider. Who can blame them? There is big money to be made in providing and supporting data services on an outsourced basis.

Ironically, having sold themselves as a data outsource firm, the telephone company then reacts to data troubles with the exact same standard they apply to voice troubles. As a result, they will tend to treat the data outage with the same urgency (or lack of urgency) that they deal with any trouble call. In data outages, this can be disastrous.

If a service provider really wants to be a company's data provider, it is important for them to understand corporate needs during data outages. For many companies, the difference a voice and a data outage have on business functions and on the corporate bottom line can be substantial. Very often, while a voice service disruption can be troublesome, it can be tolerated. Voice service interruptions can adversely affect corporate activities, but seldom does a voice outage completely cripple the company.

Data carries with it a completely different set of operational and support criteria. A data disruption can be potentially disastrous to a company's business. Therefore, unless your WAN connections have a high degree of redundancy or survivability, you should seek agreement from your service provider as to their minimum trouble response time.

It is amazing how many companies have technical support response time guarantees built into their equipment service agreements, but have no such clause in their contracts with telecommunications service providers. Trying to negotiate a response time for data line troubles is very worthwhile—even if you have to compromise in other areas. Once a response time has been agreed upon, you should take it seriously and make sure that the carrier does as well. Measure the actual response time and, if necessary, hold the service provider to the agreed time.

Remember that a thousand promises of rapid response are not worth one quick response during a data communications outage. Get it in writing and let the telephone service provider know that you are serious about response time and expect them to be as well.

People who have never installed ISDN services may wonder why I have chosen to devote an entire chapter to ordering ISDN service. Those who have attempted to order ISDN will understand and grin. Spotting this chapter in the table of contents, they likely turned here immediately.

My City Has It But Yours Doesn't

The first step in ordering ISDN is to understand that in numerous places you cannot order it. In many countries, including the United States, ISDN is far from ubiquitous. ISDN deployment is often spotty, even within the same telephone service provider and within the same Local Access and Transport Area (LATA). Therefore, the first thing that must be done before ordering is to verify whether ISDN is available in the locations that you want to install it. There are several ways of getting this information.

A call to the local business office will sometimes produce information on the availability of ISDN. However, contacting business offices is usually a crap shoot. Some business offices understand ISDN fairly well and can provide up-to-date deployment information. However, other business offices will not have a clue what you are talking about when you mention the four-letter "I" word.

A classic example, which actually happened, was when a customer called a sales office in a RBOC that actively promotes ISDN. He asked to talk to someone about ISDN rates. The response, was, "ISDN? What's that? Do we have that?"

Another, perhaps more effective, approach is to contact the service provider's ISDN information center. Many service providers have created ISDN service centers that are just a phone call away. RBOC ISDN centers are generally well equipped to answer questions about ISDN availability and charges in their regions. Sometimes the centers also have information about selected ISDN equipment. Use them as a resource for your installations.

Unfortunately, not every carrier has an ISDN center. If that is the case, Bellcore or the North American ISDN Users' Forum (NIUF) can generally be of help in determining whether ISDN is available in the local area of interest. A discussion of resources can be found in Appendix A in the back of this book.

There are other sources that also offer ISDN information. One of the best is the Internet. The Internet features ISDN discussion groups and World Wide Web home pages dedicated to ISDN. Ameritech, Bellcore, Bell Atlantic, Bell South, and Pacific Bell are among a few of the Regional Bell Operating Companies who maintain information pages on the Internet. Many ISDN vendors, service providers, user groups and users have ISDN products and services listed on the World Wide Web.

Dan Kegel's ISDN Web page is one of the best sources of ISDN information on a variety of ISDN equipment. Dan has included pointers to a large number of vendors and ISDN information resources. You can find his page at: http://alumni.caltech.edu/~dank/isdn/.

The Hardest Part

Without question, the hardest part of ISDN is ordering it. To give credit where credit is due, the telephone companies have done a simply horrible job in this area.

Even when the RBOC sales office answers, "Sure, how many ISDN lines to do you want?" there still can be problems. Ordering ISDN service is complex. There is simply no other way to put it. Each ISDN line requires very specific switch translations that are usually, but not always, available from the ISDN equipment vendor.[1] The translations vary between different ISDN products, different ISDN central office switches, and even different forms of ISDN within the same switch, such as Custom or National ISDN.

---

1. Translations are similar to configuration statements used in network routers, only they tend to be far more convoluted. If you are unfamiliar with translations (or routers), there is no need to worry. We cover both in detail later.

Adding to the confusion, not all equipment works with every ISDN switch. Some equipment is manufactured for a specific vendor's ISDN switch. Using it on another switch may require an upgrade to the device, which may not even be possible. Furthermore, while some devices can operate on multiple switches, the same equipment may need to be configured in different ways depending on which switch is in the telephone central office. What a mess!

Device Certification

Device certification means that a particular device has been tested and certified to work on a specific vendor's ISDN switch. Therefore, before you buy, you should ask if the vendor's equipment has been certified on the particular switch you will using. Be aware that even though some vendors may tell you that their equipment operates on a particular switch, there is a very big difference between this pledge and device certification.

Saying that their devices "operate on a switch" simply means the vendor thinks that some of their devices are being used by customers in locations using that switch. This is not the same thing as a vendor receiving certification by the switch vendor. Many switch vendors operate labs where vendors can bring their equipment for compatibility testing. If a device interoperates properly in the switch vendor's lab, it is considered to be certified for operation with that switch.[2]

Before proceeding with any ISDN installation, protect yourself by calling the local business office to find out what kind of switch is being used in your local exchange. Then, armed with that information, make the vendor verify that their equipment is certified to work on that particular switch. If you think this process is putting too much responsibility on the user, you are absolutely right!

---

2. Certification can be a deceptive term. The certification is usually done informally. It is often left up to the device vendor and the switch vendor to specify what compatibility tests will be performed. Therefore, the depth of testing varies depending on the particular switch vendor and the capabilities of their lab. It would have been a good idea if some form of standardized certification testing had been developed. Unfortunately, this has not happened and it probably never will. At one point, some user groups pressed for an Underwriter's Laboratory type of sticker on certified ISDN devices. For obvious reasons, the vendors objected.

Switch Translations

You have your new ISDN WAN products in hand, your remote sites are ready, and you need to connect. However, there is the matter of switch translations to be handled before the connection can be made.

To properly order ISDN service, you must supply the appropriate translations for the device and ISDN switch to the telephone company. Translations define the device to the switch. They are very device-specific. Rarely can a device be used on a line that was previously translated for a different device.

Switch translations can be nasty business. ISDN translations are similar to configurations used by network devices such as routers. Just as a router configuration deals with port assignments and protocol parameters, ISDN translations describe how each port (line) on the switch is to be configured.

Translations encompass many things, including the terminal type, the kind of service (voice or data) required on each channel, D or B packet services, and the determination and function of each button if the device supports voice services.

ISDN equipment vendors expect users to know what switch their local operating company uses in the local exchange—information that is available, but not well publicized by local carriers. To make matters worse, each ISDN switch vendor has different translation requirements. This makes translations very technical and complex matters. If even one translation entry is wrong, it is entirely possible the ISDN line will fail to function.

In spite of this, telephone carriers expect users to provide translations for every ISDN line they order on whatever switch is being used in their area. End users are expected to tell the telephone service providers exactly how to translate the central office telephone switch for the ISDN device. Take a moment to think about that. It is a little like being asked to pilot a Boeing 747 simply because you were once a passenger on one.[3]

---

3. Actually, in many ways it is easier to fly a 747 than to translate an ISDN line. This is not to take away from the expertise required by airline pilots. However, on a recent flight from San Francisco to Hong Kong, I was invited up front to sit in the cockpit of a 747-400. It was an interesting experience; I learned that the aircraft virtually flies itself. In normal flight, it is operated entirely under computer control. Because of this, there is very little for the crew to do during those long transcontinental flights. Their job is essentially monitoring the aircraft's performance and communicating with ground control. If you doubt that ISDN translations are more difficult than operating a 747, try asking an experienced airline pilot to look over your ISDN configuration sheet, and see what happens!

Most people do not spend an appreciable amount of time worrying about which type of telephone switch is in their local central office. With ISDN, you not only need to wonder, you must know! When it comes to this part of ISDN deployment, telephone companies need to do whatever it takes to simplify the process.

It is truly a shame that technical matters like switch translations are being left up to the customer, rather than vendors and telephone service providers. It seems only right that telephone companies supply every customer with the correct ISDN device information for the type of switch used in their Central Office. They should also supply users with the type of ISDN (National or Custom) being supplied to the site.

Besides being complex, translations are intolerant of errors. Switch translations must be entered perfectly. Even one error in an otherwise correct translation can stop the ISDN line dead in its tracks. This means that the user must pass the translations correctly to the service provider and, just as importantly, the service provider must input them perfectly into the switch.

This multistep process is extremely error-prone. To keep mistakes to a minimum, fax the ISDN configuration page from the device's operating manual directly to the telephone carrier. However, even this does not guarantee success. While they are improving, telephone service order takers are notorious for incorrectly entering the translations.

This all leads to one inescapable conclusion. You can expect your new ISDN line not to work the first time you try it.

It is ironic that translations have become the most complicated part of ISDN. They should be the easiest. In a perfect world, the user would not even be bothered with switch translations. Translations would be uploaded from the equipment to the switch the first time that the device was connected to a new line. Unfortunately, this is not a perfect world, and complex translation parameters have to be supplied to the telephone company by a user who generally does not have a clue about their meaning.

ISDN Ordering Codes

Clearly, users need a way to simplify the ISDN service ordering process, which is currently akin to having to give McDonald's a list of ingredients every time you order a Big Mac.[4] Order simplification, which would reduce the complexity of ordering, has been discussed for a long time. There has been ongoing work in this area in the North American ISDN Users' Forum, and in the Corporation For Open Systems (COS). Both organizations have proposed ISDN Ordering Codes (IOCs), which are standardized phrases that can be used when ordering common translation schemes.

IOCs are an attempt to simplify the ISDN service ordering process by creating a series of translation shortcuts or codes for ISDN equipment. Instead of having to read or fax a laundry list of translation fields to the telephone service providers, participating vendors give their translation sets nicknames like *Intel Blue* or *Combinet A.* [5]

There are two classes of IOCs. One class is known as *Generic,* and the other as *Non-Generic.* Generic IOCs are based on the Capability packages created by the North American ISDN Users' Forum. Capability packages are feature and capability menus for particular sets of ISDN devices. Therefore, they are more-or-less standardized translation sets. Non-Generic IOCs, on the other hand, contain deviations from the generic packages, which are often requested by specific vendors.

According to the IOC plan, the vendor supplies the telephone carriers with complete translation specifications for each of its devices. When the user calls the phone company's business office and orders an ISDN line set to "Capability Package R," the carrier is supposed to know exactly how to translate the line. By using the ISDN Ordering Codes, it is hoped that users will be spared the arduous task of detailing their device translations to the service provider.

Conformity to IOC procedures requires that each participating vendor test their equipment with the telephone network equipment. This is supposed to provide a degree of confidence that the IOC will work, and that the translations are correct. Vendors are not required to test their equipment, however.

---

4. The choice of McDonald's in this example is deliberate. McDonald's was one of the first users of ISDN service. Starting as early as 1987, they wanted to connect their restaurants directly to their Chicago-area headquarters using ISDN. Their goal was to receive up-to-the-minute information on sales and inventory from thousands of stores. In a carefully guarded trial with Ameritech and AT&T, McDonald's proved that ISDN was a good data technology. They also proved that the lack of ISDN interoperability prevented them from getting any useful real-time information from their restaurants.

5. When IOCs first appeared, they had colorful names such as *Intel Blue* or *Combinet Purple.* As they became more institutionalized, IOC names changed to alphanumeric codes such as *Capability S1.* Somehow, it was more fun when the IOCs were imaginative and colorful. Such is the price of progress, I suppose.

Therefore, the consumer has to rely on the equipment vendor for assurance that the IOC really does work. Similarly, the user must rely on the ISDN service provider for assurance that the IOC is recognized and implemented properly. It really takes a whole lot of faith.

It is unclear at this point how helpful IOCs really will be. Although there is little question that the IOC process is a step in the right direction, it is far from perfect. Unless the terms are imparted to every local telephone carrier and the telephone business office personnel understand what they mean, the IOCs will not work.

The problem is that not every vendor subscribes to the IOC system, nor do many service providers support it. Those service providers who do subscribe to IOCs do not always do a good job of getting the word to the people accepting customer orders. When the user asks the business office for "Capability Package R," there is often a long silence on the other end of the line. The order takers are often clueless about what the customer is requesting. In order for IOCs to work, they must be ubiquitously adopted. There are no signs this will happen anytime soon.

Even where IOCs are supported, there are problems. Telephone services providers often complain about the difficulty of dealing with large numbers of IOCs from multiple vendors. Therefore, the carriers strongly prefer a small set of Generic IOCs that vendors adopt for multiple devices. Vendors, on the other hand, want IOCs that are specific to their equipment, and often favor Non-Generic IOCs that are very device-specific.

Simplified ordering codes are still in a state of flux. New developments are still unfolding, so the matter of simplified ordering codes is far from settled. Although things may change at any time, the concepts and goals that form IOCs should remain the same.

Auto Configuration

A better method of ISDN line configuration would be to let computers do what they do best, and avoid the translation process altogether. In computer networking, it is common practice for devices to bootstrap themselves into operation.

A new router, for example, may come out of the box with a basic configuration that allows a minimal amount of communication with a configuration server. The server has the image file that contains the final configuration the router will use when it is in full service. Once basic communications have started, the configuration server downloads the specific configuration parameters into the flash

EPROM in the router. After the download has been completed, the router loads the final configuration into its memory and reboots.

Automatic device configuration is so common in network devices that it is astounding that vendors have not implemented similar capabilities into their WAN products. With the cooperation of ISDN equipment vendors and switch providers, it is entirely plausible that similar magic can be done with ISDN equipment. If vendors were to implement auto configuration into ISDN devices, it would greatly simplify the entire ISDN process.

Imagine the following scenario: You are about to install a new ISDN Ethernet bridge. Inside the bridge is a flash EPROM containing the ISDN line translations specific to that device. The bridge is connected to the ISDN line and comes up in a low-level signaling mode that allows D channel communications between the Central Office ISDN switch and the bridge. Once the communications link is established, the bridge begins to send translation information to the switch. The switch uses this information to reconfigure the ISDN line to the specific translation parameters the device requires. Similarly, the device derives its ISDN configuration from the switch.

Other than plugging the bridge into the ISDN line, the user and the local carrier have little or no involvement in the translation process. Such a scenario would certainly be helpful—and it is entirely possible today. Some switch vendors have already built some of this capability into their ISDN switches. However, it is unlikely you will be able to take advantage of this to bypass the translation process any time in the near future.

Vendors are not aggressively incorporating automatic configuration into their devices. Also, do not expect your local carrier to tell you about this feature. They have to pay an extra charge to use the feature, and they stand to lose some installation dollars from the user if they support it. To date they have been quiet, keeping users in the dark and ISDN configuration complex.

Service Profile Identifier

Of all the ISDN configuration issues, ranging from bothersome to a royal pain, at the head of just about everyone's list is configuring the Service Profile Identifier (SPID). SPIDs are tricky because they are complex numbers that vary by switch and telephone carrier.

For example, some switches require a single SPID for each channel in a BRI. Other switches want different numbers assigned to each channel. The SPID format itself can vary depending on what the switch expects. Some switches, such as the AT&T 5ESS running single-point Custom ISDN, do not even require a SPID. It is all very confusing business.

Unfortunately, SPIDs cannot be ignored since, without the correct SPID, the ISDN device will fail to work.

An example of how messy the SPID situation can become recently occurred while I was in New York City teaching an ISDN class. Nynex, New York's telephone service provider, had installed an ISDN line in the classroom. The line was put in several weeks in advance of the class. The installer said the line was fully operational.

When I entered the room, I looked at the ISDN jack. The SPID was neither indicated on the jack, nor was it mentioned in any of the installation information left by the installer. I was left to guess what the SPID might be since it was not reflected in any information provided by Nynex. All I had to work with was the line's telephone number.

My attempts at guessing the SPID were an exercise in futility. Because I am familiar with their format, I started with the SPID configuration used by Bell Atlantic. Typically, Bell Atlantic switches use the SPID format of 01-NXX-XXXX-001. For example, if the number of the ISDN line is (304) 555-1234, the SPID resembles 015551234001.

Of course, that applies to SPIDs in the Bell Atlantic region. This was New York City and Nynex territory. Attempts at using the SPID in Bell Atlantic format failed miserably. Obviously, there were more differences in the Nynex SPID than just the area code. I tried a number of variations, hoping to stumble on the correct SPID. Unfortunately, the Nynex switch was not impressed by any SPID I sent it.

It took several phone calls and a couple of hours to learn that Nynex includes the area code and four zeros at the end of their SPID. It turned out that the SPID on this line was in the format of 21255512340000. Go figure!

The lesson to be learned from this experience is that there is no way to guess and get the SPID right. It is up to you, the user, to make sure the service provider provides the exact SPID configuration their switch requires. Do not leave this to guesswork; make sure the service provider gives you the SPID, and verifies that it is correct.

In some cases a protocol analyzer with ISDN capability is helpful in seeing if the switch accepted the SPID you entered. Unfortunately, the switch keeps the SPID a deep, dark secret. Therefore, the protocol analyzer cannot tell you what the SPID should be. It will only indicate whether the SPID you entered in the ISDN device was accepted by the switch or not.

Automated SPID Selection

Several groups have been working on methods that enable a process called Automatic SPID Selection. Once this capability is included in ISDN devices, it will reduce the terminal initialization procedures by having the switch send the SPID to the terminal, rather than having the user enter it. The goal, of course, is to completely remove the user from the SPID process. This is clearly a noble objective.

The process, as proposed, would require that a service provider assign the SPID, as is the case now. However, instead of sending the SPID to the user, the service provider would let the ISDN switch send the SPID directly to the device. This, as they say, eliminates the middleman. The user is no longer involved in the process.

In a little more technical detail, here is how the process would work. The ISDN device initiates the Auto SPID Selection process by sending an initialization request to the switch with the fixed SPID. In a sense, this is similar to the process where a workstation comes up with an initial IP address, such as 1.1.1.1. A network device, such as a BootP server, can then communicate with the workstation and assign it a real, working TCP/IP address. In a similar fashion, this can be accomplished with ISDN SPIDs. The ISDN switch determines which service profile is associated with the terminal's interface, and sends the corresponding SPID or SPIDs to the terminal.

When the device receives its SPID, it is expected to store the SPID and use it to request full initialization from the switch. If a device is operating on a National ISDN or multipoint line, it may require more than one SPID. Typically, there is a SPID for each channel in the device. Therefore, when the device receives multiple SPIDs from the switch, it is expected to present this information in a format that is understandable to the user. For example, it must indicate the SPID assignment in a manner that allows the user to associate the correct SPID for each channel.

Generic SPID Specification

The problem with automatic SPID assignment is that it requires switch and CPE development work. Today's ISDN switches and devices are not able to accommodate Auto SPID without modification. Obviously, incorporating Auto SPID into ISDN switches and devices will take some time. In the interim, a number of switch vendors, including AT&T (Lucent Technologies), Nortel, Siemens and Ericcson, have proposed an alternative system called Generic SPID Specification. Many of the RBOCs have also endorsed the proposal.

Basically, the Generic SPID specification creates a common SPID format for use on all new ISDN line installation. It replaces the horrendously wide variation in SPID format. The Generic SPID format uses 14 digits, which are composed of three elements. The elements are the 10-digit telephone number, a sharing terminal ID and the Terminal Identifier (TID).

The sharing terminal ID is used to differentiate the various terminals (devices) using the same Directory Number (DN). It is a 2-digit number ranging from 01 to 32. The TID differentiates terminals having the same main DN and Sharing Terminal Identifier. It is also a 2-digit number, but it ranges from 01 to 08.

Putting this together, the Generic SPID format looks like:

[NPA NXX XXXX] [01] [01]

where NPA is the 3-digit Numbering Plan Area (also known as area code), NXX is the 3-digit number prefix, and XXXX is the number. So if your ISDN number is 304-555-1234, your SPID for a single device would be:

30455512340101

Although the NPA, NXX and the number would change, the format for the SPID would be exactly the same, regardless of who installed your line or where it was installed.

Support for the Generic SPID format has been strong. It has been backed by Bellcore, the North American ISDN Users' Forum and several RBOCs. Impressively, unlike Auto SPID, Generic SPID can be instituted today.

10

Network Connections Using Terminal Adapters

Without question, the most common device used for data connections in the world is the analog modem. Modems are ubiquitous. They are used everywhere for all kinds of data connectivity. Nearly everyone who uses a computer either owns a modem or, at least, understands what modems do.

Unfortunately, modems have several disadvantages. They are relatively slow at transferring large files. As we have seen, they are extremely subject to line quality variations. Finally, modems do not work directly on the newer digital services such as ISDN.

With digital services, it is not necessary to modulate or demodulate the computer's digital data. All that is necessary is to "adapt" it in terms of throughput and data format. To support modem-like connections over ISDN, a device called a Terminal Adapter (TA) is required. A Terminal Adapter connects the PC com port to the outside world by adapting ISDN B channels to existing terminal equipment serial port standards such as RS-232, RS-422, and V.35.

Terminal Adapters are typically packaged in a similar fashion to modems. They are available either as standalone units or as interface cards that plug into a computer. Like modems, the TAs plug into the com port on the PC, or other serial interface. The ISDN line plugs into the S/T or U interface jack on the TA. Sometimes ISDN Terminal Adapters also have an RJ-11 jack for an analog device.

Figure 10.1 shows how a typical TA can be connected to both analog and digital devices.

Terminal Adapter Features

Capabilities and features vary among different TAs. Some TAs offer only a single communications port. Some offer two serial ports. Some Terminal Adapter ports operate at slow speeds, typically 19.2 kbps or less. Others operate at 64 kbps or higher. Some TAs can join B channels to support even higher throughput connections.

Certain TAs offer an RJ-11 jack frequently labeled as either *phone* or *phone out*. The jack is intended for analog devices. This makes it possible to connect a telephone, modem or fax directly to the ISDN line. The ISDN device uses one of the B channels to support the analog device, leaving the other B channel free for digital data or other ISDN services. Since analog devices require ringing voltage, sometimes the TA has enough internal or external power to support this.

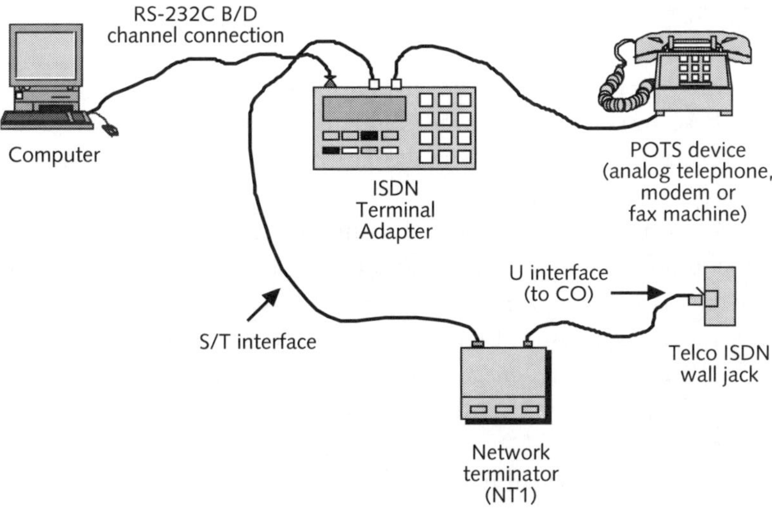

Figure 10.1   Typical connection using an ISDN Terminal Adapter

Accessing Networks with Terminal Adapters

Terminal Adapters can be used for network access in two methods. In the first method, the TA is used with standard communications software. In this configuration, the Terminal Adapter serves simply as a high-speed modem replacement. The resulting network connection is used to access on-line services, bulletin board services or terminal servers.

If the destination supports ISDN, connections can be made at 19.2, 38.4, 57.6, 64, or 128 kbps. This gives access to on-line services at decent throughput rates.

The second method provides more robust network access. Using software specifically designed for serial ports, the TA can support direct network connections. This allows support for common network protocols such as TCP/IP, IPX/SPX and AppleTalk. The Terminal Adapter is used to extend these network protocols to the remote client. This is the core of remote LAN access, and is a topic we will explore in some detail in Chapter 13, "Making a Successful Remote LAN Access Connection."

ISDN Modems

Some product literature refers to TAs as *ISDN modems* or *digital modems*. Although these terms have become popular and are in common usage, strictly speaking they are inaccurate. Terminal Adapters generally do not interoperate with modems; they replace them.

As we mentioned in Chapter 5, "Technologies for Enterprise Network, LAN and Internet Connections," the process used to pass digital computer data over the analog voice network involves modulation and demodulation of a carrier signal. This creates a series of tones that are transmitted as audio over the analog voice connection. ISDN, being an all-digital service, has nothing to modulate or demodulate. Thus, in a real sense, there is no such thing as an ISDN or digital modem. However, some ISDN devices do have characteristics that allow them to be classified as "ISDN hybrid modems."

Certain ISDN TAs can be operated in one of two modes. They can be used as a straight Terminal Adapter, or put in a mode where the TA emulates a modem. In the latter mode, the device grabs a B channel, requests voice-bearer services and uses a Digital Signal Processor (DSP) that emulates a modem. Since the B channel supports voice-bearer services, it can handle the modem carrier tones and pass them to an analog modem on the far side of the connection. The modem on the other side thinks it is talking to another analog modem.

The ISDN network makes the connection possible because it interoperates, when using voice-bearer services, with any voice telephone device. That is why it is possible to use an ISDN phone to call any voice phone in the world. This interoperability makes modem emulation possible over an ISDN line.

Once modem emulation is implemented in the ISDN TA device, it is relatively easy to incorporate fax emulation into the same device. This makes it possible to include ISDN data, modem support and Group III (analog) fax capability—all in the same device. Devices that incorporate this capability can be legitimately called *ISDN modems.*

Figure 10.2 shows how an ISDN modem can access both analog and ISDN networks. If the switch sees a call coming in with a data bearer request in the set-up message, it directs the call to the ISDN network. The device can then call another TA attached to a PC, or gain digital access to a service provider's network. If, on the other hand, a call comes in with a voice-bearer request, it will be switched to the analog network. Therefore, it can call any modem or fax machine.[1] Why would anyone want a device that pretends to be a modem when they can have faster, more reliable connections through the "real thing" with ISDN? The answer is simple.

As we have already seen, ISDN services are not available everywhere. Its deployment is limited. In addition, there are hundreds of on-line services that have no ISDN access. Similarly, there are thousands of bulletin board services (BBS) that only support modem dial-up connections. Furthermore, Group III fax is unavailable under ISDN, since ISDN uses the digital Group IV fax standard. Group III fax has become a world-wide standard, supporting well over 90 percent of the fax machines in operation.

To access ISDN services, an on-line or BBS service, or to send a fax, requires that a user purchase up to three separate communications devices. They would need an ISDN TA, a fax device and an analog modem. The ISDN modem decreases costs and space by bundling all three products into one device. This is a good solution until that far-off day when the world becomes entirely digital.

---

1. The distinction between analog and digital networks is much less marked than it used to be. At one time, voice and modem calls were entirely analog-based. ISDN data calls, on the other hand, can only be made over digital networks. As the telephone network becomes entirely digital things have begun to change. Now both voice and data can, and frequently do, travel over the same network. However, for illustrative purposes, Figure 10.2 preserves the analog and digital network separation.

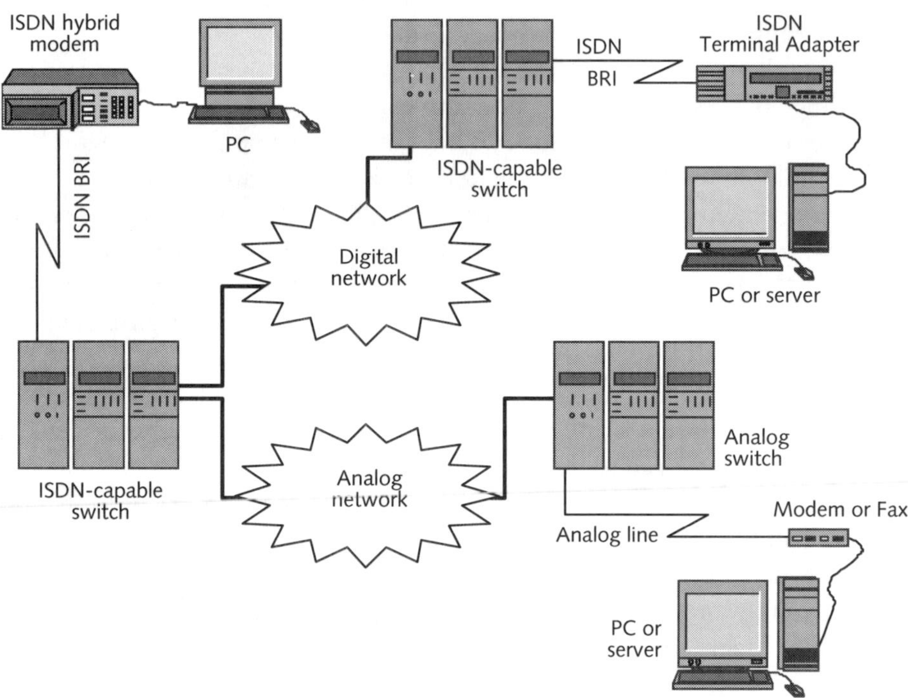

Figure 10.2   Connections to analog and digital networks

Synchronous versus Asynchronous Connections

All communications devices share one thing in common. Since data is usually made up of packets of information, the devices need to know when a section of data has begun and when it has ended. To do this, communications devices require the transmission of some sort of indicator delineating the beginning and end of a data packet.

This delineation is accomplished in synchronous devices by either an internal or external clock signal. The purpose of the synchronous clock signal is to coordinate transmission of data between the sending and receiving devices. Synchronous clocking is very similar to the role a baton plays for an orchestra leader. The conductor uses the baton to make sure all the players stay in time. In a comparable fashion, the sending and receiving devices are coordinated by the synchronous clocking.

Asynchronous devices do not use a clock signal. Therefore, they must rely on flags to coordinate the data flow. These flags require additional data bits, referred to as *start* and *stop* bits. Typically, there is a start bit, eight bits of user data, and then a stop bit.

Since start and stop bits must be transmitted over the link just like user information, they add overhead and slow down transmission of actual data. The performance penalty is two bits out of ten, or 20% of the overall throughput. Therefore, synchronous devices generally deliver better performance than asynchronous devices. For that reason, a modem operating at 14.4 kbps, and a synchronous TA operating at 19.2 kbps, are much further apart in transfer rates than might be assumed from their throughput figures.

To illustrate this more clearly, we will do a comparison between a synchronous and asynchronous device transferring the same file. We will assume we are attempting to transfer a one-megabyte (MB) file over a 28.8-kbps modem and a 28.8-kbps synchronous ISDN device.[2]

Analog modems use 10 bits per byte, while synchronous devices use only 8. The difference, of course, is due to the asynchronous overhead of the start and stop bits (2 bits per byte). Therefore, it is necessary to multiply by 10 when calculating throughput for the modem, and by 8 when calculating throughput for the TA.

The time to transmit a one-megabyte file over the 28.8 modem would be:

$$\frac{1,000,000 * 10}{28,800} = 347.22 \text{ sec} \approx 6 \text{ min.}$$

The time to transmit the same one-megabyte file over the 28.8 synchronous Terminal Adapter would be:

$$\frac{1,000,000 * 8}{28,800} = 277.77 \text{ sec} \approx 5 \text{ min.}$$

It is easy to see the result. Simply by eliminating the asynchronous start and stop bits, we decreased the time to transfer a one-megabyte file by 69 seconds. This is a significant time reduction. It is all attributable to using a synchronous, rather than an asynchronous, device to transfer the file.

Later on, we will discuss ISDN network devices such as bridges and routers. It is important to know that, with the exception of some Terminal Adapters, ISDN

---

2. For some reason, there are virtually no ISDN devices that support 28.8 kbps. The throughput range for ISDN devices is typically 19.2, 38.4, and 64 kbps. However, to keep the example as simple and clear as possible we will make some adjustments. For this example we will pretend that we have a modem that actually can do a full 28.8 kbps (most cannot) and that we are using that rare Terminal Adapter which operates at 28.8 kbps.

network devices are synchronous devices. This, coupled with higher throughputs, gives them a significant advantage in throughput, a point often overlooked when comparing a 28.8-kbps modem with a 64-kbps ISDN PC card. There is a much bigger difference between the devices than a roughly two-fold increase in data rate.

The same holds true for comparisons between modems and Terminal Adapters. The TA operating in synchronous mode at 64 or 128 kbps has an inherent advantage over high-speed modems, both in raw speed and overhead efficiency.

Rate Adaption

Most ISDN Terminal Adapters share a nice property. They can adjust the speed of the B channel to support connectivity at less than 64 kbps.

We have seen that the Terminal Adapter's B channel obtains its clocking from the central office telephone switch. The switch supplies each B channel with a 64-kbps clock and, therefore, the B channel carries a 64-kbps throughput. However, not every communications device can support 64 kbps.

Devices such as PC AT serial ports, synchronous controllers, and other older devices, are capable of supporting slower throughput rates, typically 9.6 or 19.2 kbps. If ISDN Terminal Adapters were unable to slow down the B channel rate, they would be useless with much of the older equipment already in operation, a limitation most users do not want to have in their communications equipment.

In support of slower equipment, ISDN Terminal Adapters use a technique called rate adaption to adjust the speed of their connections. Rate adaption uses a bit-stuffing process to slow down the 64-kbps ISDN connection. It does this by putting extra bits in the empty time slots unused by the slower devices. The device clocking still runs at 64 kbps, as does the bit-stuffed data. However, the effective speed is lowered to whatever the device expects.

Figure 10.3 shows how a simplified version of rate adaption works. Since the incoming data is slower than the clocking of the link, there are empty packet slots. Bit-stuffing fills these slots. In places where a data bit might normally be located, the bit-stuffing scheme has simply stuffed a placeholder. In the diagram, user data is denoted by the letter *d*. The stuffed bits are denoted by the letter *s*. The slower the user data, the more slots are stuffed.

The Terminal Adapter on the other side uses the same bit-stuffing algorithm, so it is able to detect and ignore the placeholders. When the data is reconstructed, the bit stuffing is removed and the data remains. It comes out of the destination TA at the very same rate it entered the originating TA. Therefore, a 9.6-kbps connection enters the TA at 9600 bps, and leaves at the same speed. The fact that the actual communications connection is running at 64 kbps makes no difference.

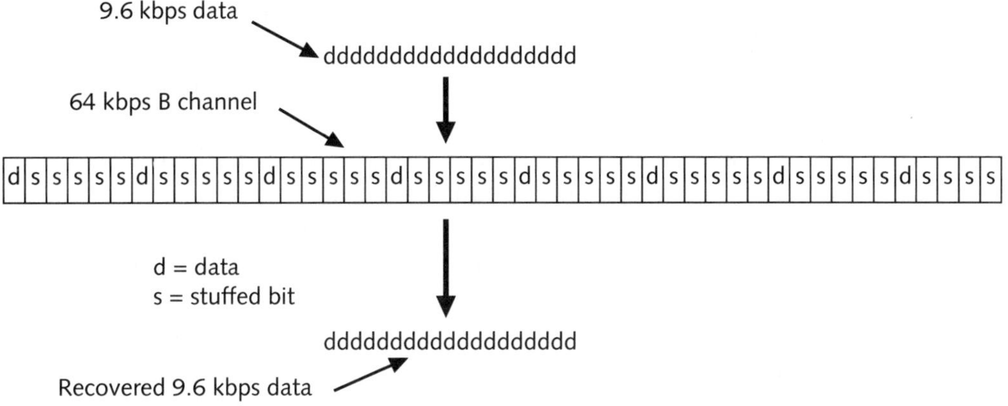

Figure 10.3   Bit stuffing

For rate adaption to work, the same rate adaption protocol must be used on both sides. This is because different rate adaption protocols use different schemes. Usually one protocol cannot interpret another protocol's bit-stuffing scheme. As a result, it is necessary to use the same vendor's Terminal Adapters on both sides of the connection, or to use devices that support standards-based rate adaption.

Both V.120 and V.110 are standardized protocols that are commonly used for rate adaption by Terminal Adapters. Proprietary rate adaption schemes, such as T-Link, DMI Mode 2, exist, but they are used less often. Initially, V.110 was the first protocol commonly accepted as a standard. The newer V.120 protocol is the more robust successor to V.110, although both are still widely used.

Terminal Adapters and Terminal Servers

Earlier, I mentioned that limited connections to network services can be accomplished through terminal servers. However using a terminal server is not the same thing as actually being a client on the network. It's like the difference between watching a football game on TV and actually being present in the stadium.

Network clients are full participants in the network. They can use network applications like File Transfer Protocol (FTP), Telnet, and Gopher. They can also use graphical World Wide Web browsers such as Mosaic or Netscape.

Network clients can fully participate in LAN activities in a free and unrestricted manner. This is possible because the user's computer is directly attached to the LAN. This is accomplished by installing a Network Interface Card (NIC) in the computer, and by using a coax or twisted-pair connection to the network segment or backbone.

As we discussed earlier, terminal servers typically provide only restricted access to LAN services. Many common network applications are either unavailable through terminal server connections or, if accessible, they are extremely limited. Usually the best a user can expect is to Telnet into the remote hosts on the network. However, for many users even reduced network access is good enough.

We have seen how terminal servers can be connected to terminals by serial cables or by modems attached to the RS-232 ports. Connections can also be made to terminal servers through ISDN Terminal Adapters. Using TA connections allows higher speeds than are usually associated with modems.

Terminal server configurations are fairly standard. On the network side, there is usually a bank of ISDN Terminal Adapters or modems connected to multiple terminal server ports. There can be as many modem or Terminal Adapter connections as there are ports on the terminal server. This method provides inexpensive connectivity for multiple users.

X.25 Terminal Servers

An ISDN B channel can operate either in circuit-switched or packet mode. When in packet mode, the B channel can support multiple individual connections called Logical Channel Numbers (LCNs). Each of the LCNs serves as a virtual independent channel for up to 127 individual users. Terminal servers that support the X.25 protocol can take advantage of ISDN running on B packet mode to set up multiple simultaneous LCNs for user access to network services.

A nice feature of most ISDN switches is the ability of the B channel and D channel packet handlers in the switch to transfer packets between themselves. This forms a link between a single B packet channel and a number of individual D channels. Thus, one 64-kbps B channel can be used to connect a large number of 9.6-kbps D channel users.

The concept is really quite straightforward. Figure 10.4 shows how this is accomplished. A BRI is set up so it uses the X.25 protocol to communicate with a Packet Assembler Dissembler (PAD) at the network site. The Terminal Adapter connects to the PAD, which, in turn, is connected to the terminal server.

Users connect to the PAD through a D channel Terminal Adapter. The D channel TA can be a standalone unit, or can be incorporated in their desk set (ISDN telephone). The ISDN switch gathers the individual D channel calls and places them on the common B channel. The PAD then breaks the users apart and routes each to their individual destination. Thus, each user simply dials a common ISDN number from their D channel ISDN terminal. A logical channel number is assigned by the ISDN switch for each user and is maintained for the duration of the session.

Although this may sound somewhat complex, it is all very transparent to the user. They just dial a common number and are connected to the network over their D channels at 9600 bps. For the network side, the X.25 connection leads to a very nice cost utilization factor in terms of lines and communications equipment. What

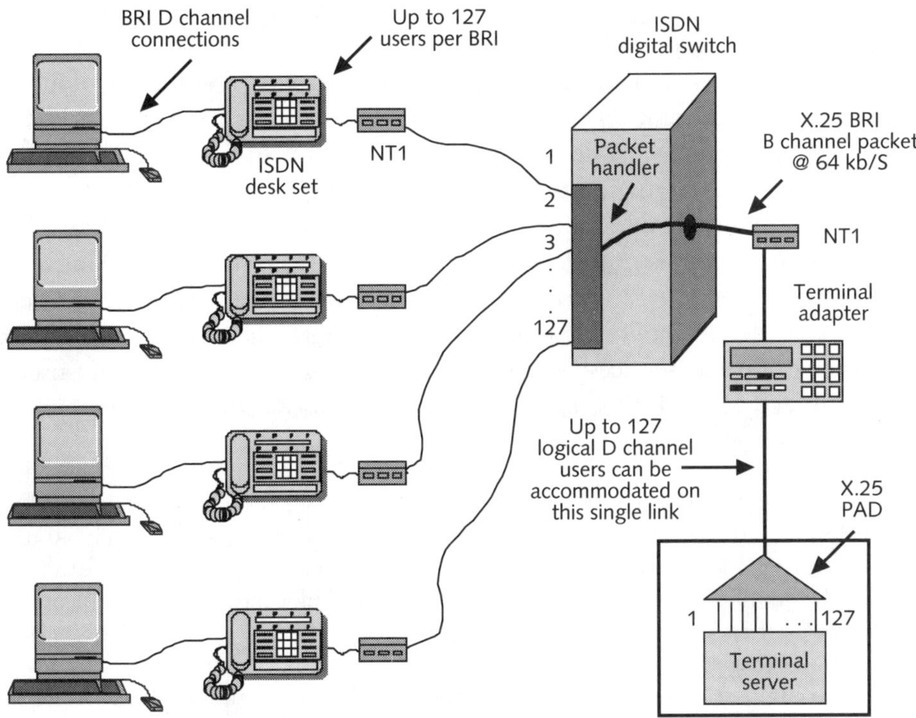

Figure 10.4 ISDN X.25 multi-user access

previously required up to 127 modems and analog lines at the network site can now be accomplished with a single ISDN line and just one TA.[3]

As can be seen, the benefits of ISDN X.25 networking are enormous. However, setting up this kind of connection can be challenging, particularly when coordinating the myriad of parameters between the packet handler in the ISDN switch and the PAD in the gateway. These devices use complex parameters that are not intended for the fainthearted or inexperienced. It is necessary to go through the same laborious process with each terminal server vendor. The network technicians have to align each and every PAD parameter to agree with the telephone company's central office telephone switch. The good news is that once the configurations are made, they rarely, if ever, need to be changed.

Communications Hubs

Terminal server capability can be expanded into what is known as communications hub. Figure 10.5 shows this configuration.

With a communications hub, multiple LAN services can be made accessible through a common interconnection point. The hub can support ISDN Terminal Adapters and analog modems, as well as LAN connectivity. This leads to a multiple-access LAN service solution, and to cost-effective network connections. Users on analog, ISDN, or LAN services can have direct access to mainframes, minicomputers and servers residing on the LAN.

Although remote LAN access is an important element of this application, the communications hub is not limited to inbound LAN connectivity. Using a communications hub as a gateway service allows true interconnectivity between a number of different services. As Figure 10.5 illustrates, gateway service hubs can interconnect diverse services. In the configuration shown, an Ethernet user can connect directly to an ISDN user, or to an analog-based service via a modem pool.

---

3. In theory, an ISDN B channel running the X.25 protocol has support for up to 127 users. In practice, the number of users is usually set to a much lower number, typically 40 or less. This is because a single B channel, regardless of the number of users allowed to access it, has a total bandwidth of 64 kbps. The X.25 protocol increases link bandwidth requirements as the number of users transferring data over the link increases. Once the total 64-kbps aggregate bandwidth is exceeded, X.25 link saturation occurs. When this happens, all users are adversely affected because X.25 does not degrade gracefully. Packets from all users become damaged, causing substantial communications problems. You may, therefore, want to take steps to limit the number of users who can simultaneously access the X.25 B channel.

Similarly, an analog user can use the modem pool to access the hub gateway and connect to an ISDN user. The process is pretty straightforward. The analog user dials the number associated with the hub's modem pool. Once connected, the user selects the ISDN prompt and then simply dials the ISDN data number. In a similar manner, any ISDN user can dial the common X.25 link number, gain access to the communications hub, and select the modem pool service. At this point the user is connected to an available modem, and can issue standard modem AT commands.

The hub gateway configuration takes this connectivity capability far beyond the original concept of terminal server bounded LAN access. However, this is exactly the point that network designers are trying to work towards—enabling diverse services to interoperate with each other. With a communications hub gateway configuration, ISDN and analog services become integrated as part of a much larger network fabric. The ability to connect from any service to any other service forms the basis for true interconnectivity. While the ISDN-inspired communications hub does not completely fulfill this goal, it is a credible step in the right direction.

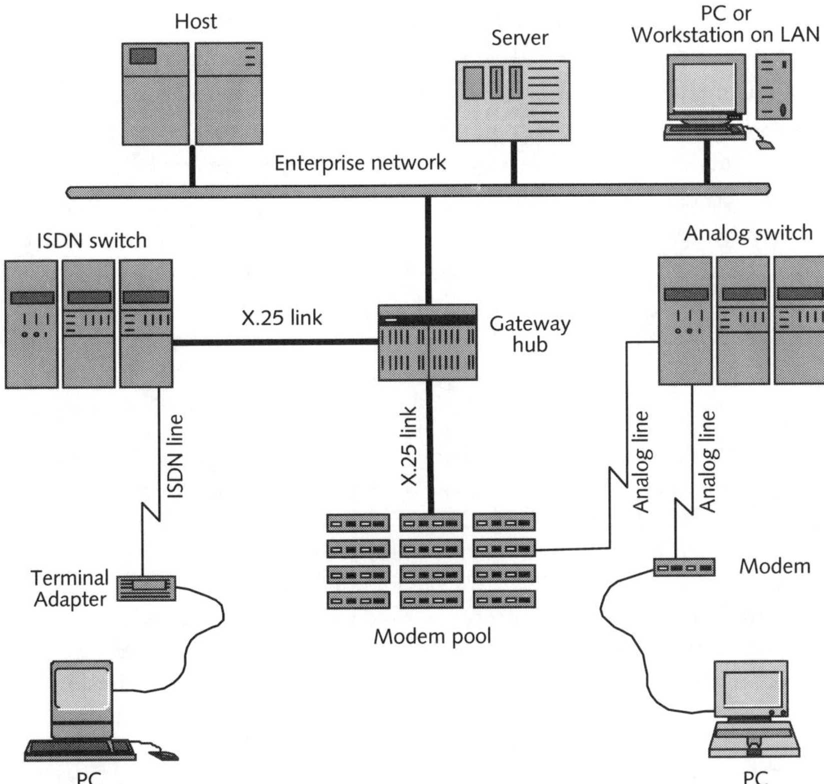

Figure 10.5   Gateway hub configuration

Communications Servers

Usually, terminal servers provide access to network services through communications programs running on the local PC. In effect, a virtual Telnet host session is set up in the communications server. The remote user uses something related to screen sharing where the output of the Telnet session is directed to the remote computer's monitor, and the input comes from the computer's keyboard. This is the basis for network access in most terminal servers.

Communications servers are the second generation of terminal servers. They give an entirely different level of service. Instead of providing terminal-only access, communications servers support network protocols over serial connections.

The communications server makes it possible for a remote user to dial in to the network as a true client. This means the user can access files on the department file and print servers, have Internet access and share files with other networked computers. In short, the remote user has the ability to participate on the network in a manner very similar to directly connected users.

Communications servers typically connect users with Serial Line IP (SLIP) or Point-to-Point Protocol (PPP). We introduced SLIP and PPP in Chapter 5, "Technologies for Enterprise Network, LAN and Internet Connections."

By way of a refresher, Serial Line IP allows dial-in users to access TCP/IP network services across serial lines (analog or digital). Point-to-Point Protocol (PPP) is the new kid on the block. Both get the job done; however, PPP offers many more features and capabilities than SLIP.

PPP was created by the Internet Engineering Task Force (IETF) as a dial-in network access standard. The IETF sets de facto standards for networking, called Request For Comments (RFC).[4] PPP is described in RFC 1134, "The Point-to-Point Protocol: A Proposal for Multi-Protocol Transmission of Datagrams Over Point-to-Point Links," and in RFC 1661, "The Point-to-Point Protocol (PPP)."[5]

---

4. The Internet is a very de facto place. Internet folks have very strong and diverse opinions on how things should be done. Therefore, any attempt to introduce a new standard nearly always creates a firestorm. Despite this, the IETF realized the need for certain conventions to be accepted for use over the Internet. Without standards, de facto or not, communications over the Internet would be nearly impossible. To avoid unnecessary problems, rather than call their output "standards," the IETF refers to them as "Requests For Comments." These RFCs go though many drafts and comment periods. Many, like PPP, eventually become de facto standards. However, to avoid the inevitable firestorm, Internet standards are still called RFCs, even well after the comment period has been closed.

5. D. Perkins, "Point-to-Point Protocol: A Proposal for Multi-Protocol Transmission of Datagrams Over Point-to-Point Links," RFC 1134. W. Simpson, "The Point-to-Point Protocol (PPP)," RFC 1661.

Unlike SLIP, which only supports the TCP/IP protocol, PPP supports any network protocol. PPP is usually a little simpler to configure and use than SLIP. Importantly, PPP also supports authentication and compression. Both are very important to remote network access.

SLIP is almost always used for network access through the PC com port. PPP, on the other hand, can be used in one of two ways. It can handle network sessions over the PC com port, or it can be coded into an ISDN bridge or router. Stand-alone network devices and ISDN PC cards are also able to take advantage of PPP supported connections.

The difference between com port and ISDN device implementations of PPP is typically speed and convenience. On most PCs, the UART chip limits the com port's throughput to about 115 kbps.

ISDN PC cards, on the other hand, can operate at higher throughput rates. They are only limited by the PC bus speed and how many B channels are used by the ISDN PC card. PC cards usually support 128 kbps or higher throughput with compression.

The UART chip is crippled even more by being an asynchronous device. As we have already seen, synchronous devices, such as ISDN PC cards and standalone network devices, are inherently more efficient than asynchronous devices.

Digital technologies such as ISDN are capable of transmitting data faster than many PC com ports can support. This is particularly true if a communications session occurs under Windows 3.1, or if the PC uses an older UART. For example, the 8250 or 16450 UART chips used in many 286 and 386 PCs cannot keep up with the 57.6- or 115.2-kbps rates possible over ISDN. Transfers at these speeds require the newer, buffered 16550 UART. This chip is found in some 486, and nearly all Pentium-based PCs.

Additionally, the native Windows 3.1 communications driver (COMM.DRV) supports data rates at, or below, 38.4 kbps. To overcome this limitation, some ISDN Terminal Adapter vendors offer enhanced drivers for their products. These drivers are specifically written to support faster Windows communications sessions.

Macintosh computers also have serial communications limitations. For example, Macintosh computers using the 68K architecture support 57.6 kbps as a maximum asynchronous serial port rate.

Will the serial port always be the slowest input/output port in the PC? Probably not. Work has begun on new technologies that will significantly improve the performance of the serial port. Already, the RISC-based Power Macintosh line supports faster serial rates through their Geoport serial port. Geoport-equipped Power Macs can handle throughputs of 230.4 kbps and, in some cases, up to 2.048 Mbps. Newer technologies, such as Intel Corporation's Universal Serial Bus or Apple's FireWire promise to enhance the serial port performance even further.

Still, the best throughput occurs with direct network connections, not with the serial port. Using Network Interface Cards (NICs), it is possible to provide connections close to network wire speeds of 10, 16 or even 100 Mbps. This is a vast improvement over the limited throughput rates that occur through the serial port. Decent WAN connectivity can be realized when connections are network passed over multi-channel ISDN connections, as we will see shortly.

PPP Over the D Channel

PPP or SLIP connections can be supported by analog modems and ISDN connections through Terminal Adapters. Common wisdom warns that no less than a 14.4-kbps modem should be used for PPP or SLIP connections. This is particularly true when graphical applications, such as web browsers, are used. Anything less than a 14.4-kbps modem will be much too slow to allow downloading of graphic images. If they can afford it, most people who access Internet services through PPP or SLIP connections are encouraged to use a 28.8-kbps modem connection.

These recommendations are relevant for both analog and digital services. The faster the connection, the better the performance. That is why ISDN PPP or SLIP connections to the communications hub are best supported over the B channel where the connection can be made at 64 kbps or above.

However, if speed is not a major issue, it is possible to operate PPP or SLIP connections over the ISDN D channel. This offers the advantage of allowing multiple users to access the network through a LCN over a single X.25 B channel.

Figure 10.6 shows how D channel users can take advantage of network connections through PPP or SLIP. As the figure illustrates, PPP over the D channel is done in much the same fashion as ordinary communications sessions are supported over the D and X.25 B channel. A PC running SLIP or PPP is connected to the D channel Terminal Adapter. A call is placed to a common number that connects to a communications server running SLIP or PPP. As we mentioned earlier in discussing ISDN X.25 service, multiple users can simultaneously connect to the communications server. They can do this over a single B channel at the network site with full network protocol support.

The biggest disadvantage of providing PPP or SLIP network access over the D channel is slow throughput. PPP and SLIP both have a degree of internal overhead that is added to the overhead of re-packetizing the PPP or SLIP packets before placing them on the D channel. The combination of the two throttles decreases

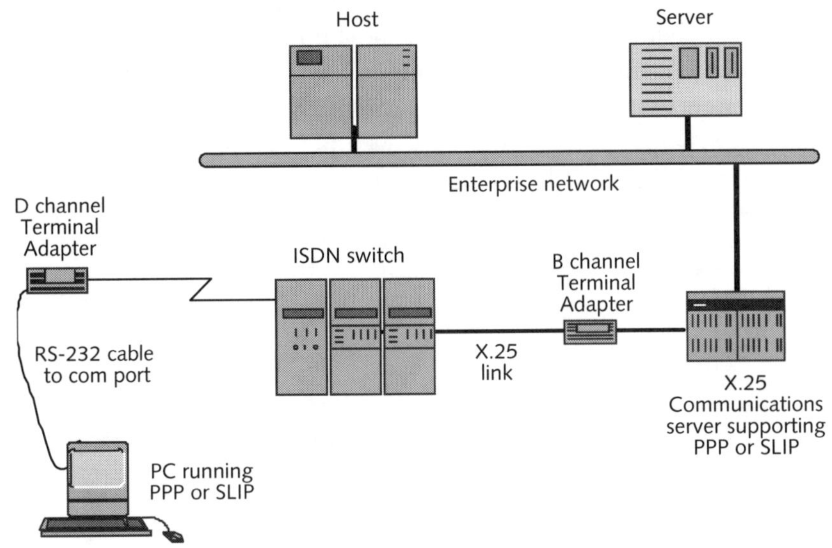

Figure 10.6   PPP or SLIP over the D channel

the effective speed of the 9600-bps D channel to around 5,000 bps. This makes the PPP or SLIP connection functionally equivalent to a 4800-baud modem, much lower than the minimum recommended 14.4-kbps rate for PPP or SLIP connections. While this is not exactly lightning speed, with some patience it is usable even with web browsers. This is particularly true if graphics are turned off in the web browser.

It may be unclear why anyone would want to run PPP over the D channel. After all, ISDN does well with 64- or 128-kbps B channel network access, but the D channel's 9.6-kbps throughput is definitely on the slow side. Perhaps an example would be useful to better understand why PPP over the D channel is of interest.

West Virginia University has many buildings in which there are no connections to the campus network backbone. Normally, that would isolate the users in these buildings from the network. However, a closer look at the department reveals that every user in the department has an ISDN telephone on their desk.

Almost every ISDN phone installed on campus has built-in D-channel capability. Using PPP over the D channel allows the department's workers to access the network and the Internet over their ISDN phones. They can do this simply by installing PPP software on their computers. This provides them with slow, but usable, network services. Importantly, it does not require the network to put up extra bridges for remote access, since the network access occurs over a common

X.25 communications server. This makes PPP over the D channel an inexpensive way to provide network connectivity for a large number of users.

Does this work? This answer is, "Certainly." For many users, this isn't even an issue. Slow connectivity is better than no connectivity. People can be very patient when necessary. West Virginia University even has people running Web browsers in graphical mode over the PPP D-channel connections.

11

Connecting to the Internet

It Takes Two to Tango

It is important to consider both sides of the WAN connection. It should be obvious that digital services are of little value if there is nothing to connect to on the other side.

Sometimes, in the fervor of a sales pitch, service providers overlook this important factor. Eager to close the sale, they tell potential users how wonderful the digital service will be for the customer's business. Somehow they fail to consider or even mention that it is one thing to install an ISDN, Switched 56 or Frame Relay service, and quite something else to provide real connectivity to a destination.

When it comes to finding a place to connect to, the Internet tops just about everyone's list. With its vast resources, worldwide reach, news groups and web sites, the Internet is as close as it comes to a limitless information source.

Accessing the Internet Through On-Line Services

There are several ways to access the Internet. One of the most common is through an on-line service, such as America Online, that offers an Internet gateway service. Users can send and receive Internet e-mail, FTP files, and use web browsers, right from the on-line service. Since many on-line services are accessed by modem connections, performance is sometimes slow. Adding to the slowdown is the internal performance of the on-line service itself. Particularly during peak hours (which are getting to be just about anytime), their internal systems can slow Internet access.

Of course, the advantage of accessing the Internet through an on-line service is that it is easy to do. Once you access the on-line service, you have Internet access. No additional equipment is required.

Accessing the Internet Through Enterprise Networks

Many enterprise networks are already connected to the Internet. This works out nicely for telecommuters, and for people who have SOHO remote connections to the enterprise network. Remote users who access these enterprise networks may automatically gain access to the Internet as well.

I said "may" because Internet access may or may not be provided to remote users, depending on the enterprise network's policy. Some corporations allow users on the enterprise, including remote users, free access to the Internet. Some do not.

Figure 11.1 shows how an ISDN or analog remote user can access the Internet.

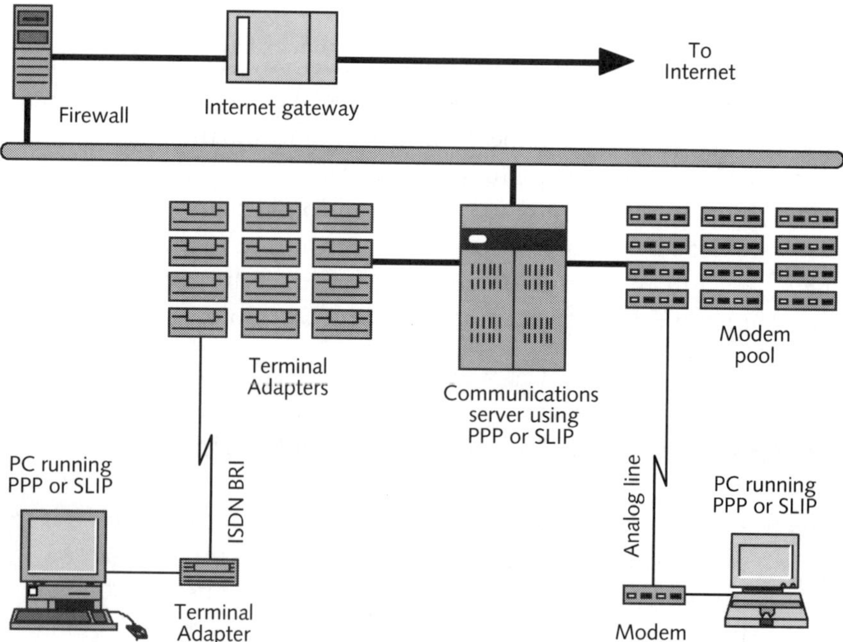

Figure 11.1   Enterprise internet connection

In order to protect their internal networks, many companies have installed firewalls. A firewall can be part of the Internet gateway device, or it can be a stand-alone computer. In either case, the firewall's job is to filter traffic going from the Internet to the enterprise network.

In a similar fashion, many Internet gateways are routers. Corporations install access lists in their routers. These access lists function somewhat like a firewall. They block certain traffic from going onto the Internet, or from transversing from the Internet to the enterprise network.

Whether a firewall, a router access list, or some other form of security is used, the result is the same. Certain Internet sites and Internet services are blocked. Typically, they are blocked for all users on the enterprise, including the remote user. However, some enterprise networks block Internet services to their remote users. These are services that are not necessarily blocked to users directly connected to the enterprise network.

The bottom line is that even if your corporation has its enterprise network connected to the Internet, you may or may not be able to fully utilize all the resources on the Internet.

Accessing the Internet Through Internet Service Providers

Internet connections from an Internet Service Provider (ISP) have become increasingly common. Connections to ISPs can be accomplished through analog or ISDN connections. Recently, however, ISDN access to ISPs has been on the rise. The reason for the growing popularity of ISDN access is the increased throughput, and faster connection time, offered by ISDN. It allows users virtually instantaneous access to the Internet at speeds that make the worldwide web browser performance very acceptable.

Analog ISP access is relatively simple. All that is needed is a modem, appropriately configured software and an account with an ISP. Unfortunately, ISDN ISP connections are anything but simple.

Ordering ISDN Internet Connections

There are several steps involved with ordering ISDN Internet connections. Remember that you are dealing with at least three independent agencies. You have to order the ISDN line from your local service provider. You need to order the appropriate and compatible ISDN equipment from a vendor. (We will discuss ISDN network equipment compatibility in detail in the next chapter.) Finally, as with analog access, you have to select your Internet Service Provider.

More than one individual has gotten a nasty surprise when attempting Internet connections over ISDN. After being lured by promises of great Internet connectivity through ISDN, they installed the service only to find that their local ISP did not offer ISDN connections.

Whether it's the corporate enterprise, the Internet or the National Information Infrastructure (NII), there must be a destination to connect to on the enterprise side. Therefore, it is wise to check with local Internet providers to see whether ISDN is being offered as an option prior to installing ISDN service.

Gathering and assimilating this information may seem to be an intimidating and time-consuming process. However, to save money and avoid wasted effort, it is necessary that you know this information beforehand. To help you in this process, here is a six-step guide you can use when ordering ISDN Internet connections.

Step One: Find out if you can get ISDN in your area

As we mentioned previously, ISDN deployment, while getting better almost by the day, is still far from ubiquitous. This is particularly true in North America. Step one is to find out whether ISDN is available in your location. Keep in mind that just having ISDN in your location is not enough. Your ISP must also have ISDN service installed.

Step Two: Decide how you want to use ISDN

Since ISDN is available as a voice, video and data service, you need to decide how you want to use it. When you order ISDN, you need to specify whether you want voice, data, or both bearer services on each channel.

Normally, if you expect to use ISDN for Internet access, you would simply choose ISDN data services on both channels. However, if there is a possibility you will want to connect a phone, fax or modem to the ISDN line, then you will need at least one voice channel designated on the ISDN BRI.

Step Three: Order the ISDN service

This is not as simple as it sounds. An entire chapter (Chapter 9, "Ordering Integrated Services Digital Network") is devoted to the process of ordering ISDN lines. If it has been a while since you read the chapter, a review might be in order.

Step Four: Order the ISDN equipment

If the ISP provides ISDN connections, you should find out what they require by way of equipment. Some Internet providers have selected specific network equipment they prefer you to use. If you purchase another ISDN device, it may not interoperate with ISP ISDN devices.

There are many variables involved in equipment selection. The devices have to use the same protocol to communicate. Whether it is PPP or V.120, it has to be the same on both sides.

Another variable to consider is the type of protocol the ISP is using to carry the network to your location. The ISP may only support PPP, or may have selected equipment that supports only SLIP. Some will support neither PPP nor SLIP, offering only basic terminal server access.

There are other equipment-related questions that need to be asked as well. Are connections being handled through a Terminal Adapter, or is connectivity offered via an ISDN bridge or router? Ask whether there is a recommended equipment list from which the ISP expects the user to purchase equipment for connecting to their network.

Step Five: Select a subscription class from the ISP

In many cases, Internet Service Providers offer different classes of service. They may offer dial-up, single-host service. The connection is made over a single PPP connection in a manner very similar to analog access to the service provider. The main advantage over analog in this class of ISDN service is better bandwidth and faster call set-up.

Another class of service frequently offered is called dedicated network access. This service is much like the nailed-up ISDN connections that we will describe in the next section. It yields a "permanent" connection to the ISP, because the call is made and never dropped.

The third class is on-demand network access. We will also discuss on-demand ISDN networking in this chapter. It is one of the neatest features in ISDN's bag of tricks. Basically, the connection is only in place when there is traffic passing to or from the ISP. While this can result in cost savings, there are many issues involved with on-demand network access. Later in the book, we will highlight and discuss each of these issues.

Step Six: Schedule an installation date for your ISDN services, the ISDN equipment and the ISP service

While not always possible, it is helpful if all the connections can be done at one time, especially if you can be present to see that everything is working as it should. Remember, you have to be concerned with three main variables. The ISDN line must be installed properly, the equipment must be configured properly, and your devices have to interoperate with the ISP's equipment. While this is not exactly rocket science, it can be complex. Congratulations! You have assumed the role of a systems integrator for yourself, your company or your client.

At this point, feel free to flip back to Chapter 8 and reread the section, "Testing ISDN Lines for Successful Installation." You will find some helpful hints that should help you get your ISDN service installed and working properly.

All the connectivity issues we have discussed in this section need to be carefully considered and fully understood before the first ISP connection is made. It makes no difference whether you are a consultant assisting in a remote access project, or someone directly involved in operating networks that remote users want to access. You will be called upon to decide what basis remote users can access network services and information resources.

ISDN Internet access is like going to a fancy restaurant. The menu may offer an intimidating array of selections, many of which may not be in English. It may take longer for the food to be prepared and served. However, when you begin to dine, the quality is so good that you find it was worth the wait and all the trouble.

Now that your appetite has been whetted, let us open the menu. It is time to look into some of the issues associated with ISDN Internet, enterprise network and LAN remote access.

12

Call Control

Once there is a destination and the access requirements are understood, the method that will be used for establishing calls needs to be considered.

Switched digital services, such as ISDN, offer several modes of call control. These include manual dialing, nailed connections and on-demand networking. Each mode has advantages and disadvantages, depending on how the connection is made.

Manual Dialing

Manual dialing is a relatively straightforward method of call control. It is very similar to the method used to dial a voice telephone. When it is time to begin a session, the user manually instructs the device to place a call to the destination telephone number. The user can enter the destination number through the keypad of the device or through a management console. Then, the device simply places the data call.

When the keypad is used, placing a call is exactly like dialing a telephone. There is usually a call button on the keypad that performs the on-hook/off-hook function. The number is then directly entered by the user.

Manual calls can also be made through a console if the device has a management port. The management interface allows call management to be controlled directly from the computer. This can be done through the PC com port using a standard or custom communications program. In many cases, call control can be managed through a network connection to the device using applications such as Telnet.

Some devices can store one or more manual destination numbers in a speed call list. In this case, the user simply selects the desired destination number from the call list.

Once a manual connection is made, it generally stays in place until a disconnect command is entered from the front panel or the management console. It is important to instruct users who use manual connections to manually disconnect the call once their session has been completed. Simply logging off the file server or host is usually not enough to disconnect a manual call. Otherwise, time and usage charges will continue to accrue even though the user is no longer using the network connection. Additionally, the call will tie up common network access devices.

Nailed-up Connections

Nailed-up connections are always in service. They are typically used for leased digital services like T1, Frame Relay and Digital 56-kbps service. As we mentioned earlier, leased lines expect to be connected all the time.

Although it is possible to nail up switched connections, switched digital services are not supposed to be continuously connected. When a switched service is nailed up (for example, the call is made but never dropped), it requires significant resources from the telephone network.

Switched data services use the same connection resources as a voice or fax call. The digital telephone switch allocates time slots, i.e., little sections of time, to each call. Although conventional design allows for a large number of simultaneous time slots within the switch fabric, each call owns its particular time slot. Once the time slot is assigned to a call, it is unavailable for other calls until the call is terminated.

Since telephone switches were engineered for relatively short connection times, nailed-up switched connections present a major resource problem to the telephone network.

The fact is, no telephone switch is engineered for 100 percent utilization. In sizing the appropriate number of time slots in a switch installation, design engineers assume three to four minutes as a common call-hold length. This allows more users to be served by the switch than would otherwise be possible. Switch engineers use contention, which allows a large number of users to be served by a single telephone switch.

Contention creates a ratio for the number of simultaneous calls supported by the switch, to a percentage of the total number of lines served by the switch. However, contention does nothing to increase the total number of time slots available in the switch.

While a switch might serve 10,000 customers, it may only have 4,096 total time slots. It is this total time slot figure that determines how many calls the switch fabric can support.

In most cases, the telephone switch is engineered for a finite number of short-duration calls. When that number is exceeded, the switch cannot process any additional calls. For example, when everyone tries to use the telephone switch at the same time to make calls, such as after an earthquake or flood, open switch time slots become rare. The result is that calls are blocked with fast busy (out-of-service) signals. When people attempt calls, they find they cannot get through.

Time slots dedicated to nailed connections can never be recovered. If enough slots are removed from service, this can lead to a situation that is analogous to the network overload that occurs during peak call periods.

A nailed-up connection or two is not likely to result in severe problems. However, if there are enough nailed connections and the local telephone switch is not adequately provisioned, it can quickly lead to trouble. There may be call connection problems for the telephone service provider and for the end users. Since central office-based ISDN switches typically serve thousands of analog and ISDN customers, over-utilization can cause problems for a significant number of callers. Therefore, it is incumbent on the switched services customers to use switch resources wisely and carefully.

Nevertheless, with care and consideration, ISDN can be connected in nailed-up configurations. It is easy to do, and reliability is typically quite good. ISDN connections can continuously operate for weeks or months and never unexpectedly drop. If your application warrants such connectivity, and leased digital services are impractical, nailed ISDN circuits may be appropriate. However, be sure to discuss this with your service provider first.

You should realize that some service providers attempt to protect their switch resources by charging data usage fees (also known as the "ISDN data penalty") of several cents per minute per channel. If, for example, the carrier charges two cents per channel per minute, this amounts to $2.40 per hour for a two B-channel connection. While this may not seem like much money, for nailed-up connections it amounts to $57.60 per day, or roughly $1,800 per month. For such 24 by 7 connections, leased services make far more sense and are generally less expensive.

On-the-Fly Connections

ISDN inherited a nice feature from the switched telephone network—it is capable of on-the-fly connections. Calls can be placed to a destination, information passed, and then the call disconnected. A second call can be immediately placed to another number. As before, information can be passed to the new destination and the call dropped again. This is true whether the call is voice, data or video.

With leased services, if the location of either the source or destination changes, the process of changing these connections takes weeks to accomplish. Service orders must be written, and telephone company technicians must be dispatched to the new site. There are order charges for changing leased line connections, sometimes running into the thousands of dollars.

This is not the case with switched digital services, such as ISDN. Unlike leased circuits, which are typically fixed between two destinations, ISDN can connect on an as-needed basis to multiple destinations. Just disconnect one call and place a new call to the next destination. This gives ISDN tremendous flexibility in call processing.

The flexibility of the switched digital network allows connections to be made automatically, based on traffic needs between two remote networks. If there is no traffic to be passed between the networks, the call is disconnected. Once traffic appears, the network device places the call to the appropriate destination.

Some network devices take advantage of this flexibility in a unique way. They keep a table of telephone numbers that have been associated with multiple remote network addresses. These devices, which function as matrix switches, have the ability to connect multiple networks on an on-the-fly basis. The network device automatically takes care of calling the proper WAN destination numbers when connectivity needs change based on individual packet destinations.

Call Set-up Time

ISDN distinguishes itself from analog, and even other digital technologies, in an important area—call set-up time. Anyone who has ever used an analog modem is all too familiar with the long series of tones and squeals that come from a modem as it is negotiating a connection.

ISDN functions in an entirely different manner. ISDN is extremely fast in connecting calls. As we mentioned earlier, local calls set up in about 600 milliseconds

(0.6 seconds). Long distance data calls set up in just a few seconds (typically, less than three). This is very important for remote network access.

On-Demand Networking

ISDN's fast call set-up and guaranteed bandwidth make it possible to provide on-demand networking. On-demand networking uses a call-management technique that is tied to network traffic utilization. When data is required across the WAN, the ISDN device simply places a call and connects to the remote network.

If, for example, a user wants to log into a remote file server, the packets generated for the file server's destination address cause the ISDN device to place the call to the remote network. When the user logs out or lets the connection go idle, WAN traffic no longer exists and the ISDN devices drop the call. This on-demand connectivity mirrors the bursty, stop-start nature of the computer network itself and can result in considerable cost savings. On-demand call management can save the user money. There are no usage charges unless the call is in place due to data passing over the link.

It is possible for a call to be originated based entirely on network traffic requirements from either side of the link. Since a host on the enterprise network may have traffic for the remote machine, there are some configurations that allow traffic from the enterprise side to bring up the connection to the remote user. In other configurations, calls are only allowed from the remote network.

When on-demand networking is in use, a packet destined to a remote network causes a call to be made to the network. If the connection takes too long to set up the call, the network protocol may assume that something has gone wrong. It will then take action based on how the protocol has been programmed to deal with link failures. Different protocols react differently to link-down situations, but all do react. Some of the consequences of excessively long call set-up times are hung sessions, packet retransmissions, and unacceptably long response delays.

Many switched data services, such as analog modems and Switched 56, take a long time, often ten or more seconds, to connect calls. This makes on-demand networking difficult or even impossible to achieve with these services. With services that have slow call set-up, calls must be left connected for longer periods. Obviously, this increases usage cost substantially.

Most network applications can tolerate some degree of call set-up delay. If it takes a few seconds or so to set up a call, the protocol will wait. After all, even directly connected networks are riddled with delays on a regular basis.

For those few applications and network protocols that cannot tolerate delays of any kind, the WANs can be permanently connected. As we have already seen, this can even be done with switched services. The call is simply made once, and is never disconnected.[1]

Dropping the On-Demand Call

While connecting calls using on-demand networking works well, dropping calls is somewhat more complex. There are considerations involving when to drop the call based on criteria like network parameters and billing issues.

It is important to realize that there are many instances where the telephone network is set up to bill based on sliding connection charges. In such cases, the most expensive connection time is the first minute of the call. A call, for example, that costs 18 cents per minute per channel once the connection has been up for a while, might cost 21 cents per minute for the first minute. If calls are frequently placed and immediately dropped, usage charges are always operating within "prime time" rates.

When a remote LAN connection occurs over a variable usage-charged connection, it makes sense to keep the call up for a few seconds even in no-traffic situations. This prevents calls from being prematurely dropped due to a momentary lull in traffic. Therefore, most ISDN devices provide a user-adjustable delay threshold to predetermine how many seconds a call is held up after traffic has ceased. A delay of twenty to thirty seconds after the last packet has been sent seems to be a good setting for the most economical call control.

Some RBOCs have become sensitive to call-management issues over switched digital WAN links. They have implemented six-second data calling rates to replace the older first-minute call rate. Where this has been done, connection costs drop after the first six seconds. This means that the threshold for dropping calls can be set to a shorter time.

---

1. Obviously, in the nailed-up configuration there is no call set-up time because the call is never torn down. This works wonderfully for local bridged connections, typically in ISDN Centrex service, where calls are not subject to usage charges. Outside the Centrex, data calls generally have usage-billed connections. Therefore, nailed connections are not a good idea unless there are no associated usage charges. Unless there is a critical need or a really fat budget, on-demand is a better method for WAN connections. If on-demand networking is not practical, leased service may be a better option than switched services. Consult your local telephone business office for more information.

When it comes to resources, users may wonder if continuously connecting and disconnecting calls places an extra burden on switch resources. There is little doubt that, in most cases, it does place some degree of additional strain on the switch. However, the digital switch fabric that handles call connections is usually well engineered. As a result, digital switches are not in the same resource-sensitive situation as time slots. So, continuously making and dropping calls places far less strain on switch resources than nailing up the calls.

Building Enterprise Networks From WANs

When people think of enterprise networks, they typically envision a large inter-connected campus high-speed backbone. This kind of topology is sometimes used by corporations and universities to build enterprise networks. However, more often than not, enterprise networks are simply made up of many separate, individual LAN segments interconnected by WANs.

Consider a publishing business such as the one shown in Figure 12.1. The publisher has headquarters in New England, and operates satellite sales offices in Atlanta, New York City, and San Mateo. The publisher wants the satellite office networks to be interconnected so workers in any office can access each other, common corporate resources and the Internet.

A number of Wide Area Network services can be utilized to construct the enterprise WAN. For example, leased services such as T1 or 56-kbps digital service can be used. With this configuration, a leased line interconnects each satellite office with the publisher's headquarters. As Figure 12.1 illustrates, the connection is made in a star configuration, with the headquarters at the center of the star.

While many companies use leased connections to form their enterprise network, cross-country leased lines are an extremely expensive proposition. Chances are, the satellite offices do not need to be connected all of the time. Therefore, a better solution would utilize a switched digital service such as ISDN. ISDN's networking-on-demand can create an ad hoc enterprise WAN. This offers several significant economic advantages.

With ISDN WAN internetworking, fewer lines are required at the headquarters. Using leased lines usually necessitates that a separate leased line be installed in the headquarters for each satellite office. Using ISDN with contention instead, a lower number of common lines can be shared by various satellite offices.

There are additional savings because ISDN monthly charges, in general, are much lower than leased line monthly charges. Therefore, this reduces the monthly

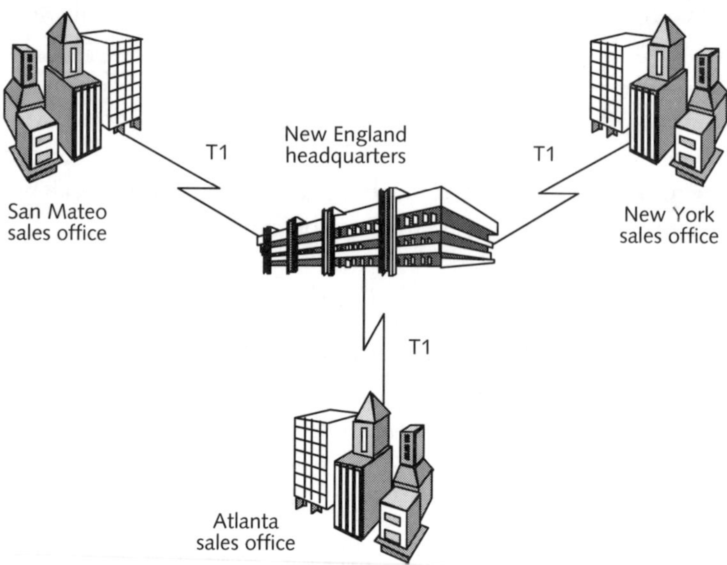

Figure 12.1   Enterprise WANs connected in a star configuration

charges associated with WAN connections by both reducing individual line costs, and by reducing the line count. There is also no mileage charge with switched services. Even though ISDN has usage charges, which are typically not incurred with leased lines, savings can also be realized because usage charges only occur when calls are in place. By using networking on demand, calls can be kept down unless there is traffic that needs to be passed over the WAN.

Figure 12.2 shows how an enterprise network can be built using standard WAN connections over ISDN.

One problem with leased lines, and even standard ISDN configurations, is that satellite offices are not directly interconnected. If the San Mateo office has a file that is needed in Atlanta, typically the connection must be made through the New England headquarters. This, of course, means that the traffic is passed twice. One call is set up from San Mateo to New England, and then a second call to Atlanta. Not only does this increase the cost of transferring information, it also creates unnecessary traffic on the intermediary network.

Some sophisticated ISDN network devices are able to take an enterprise WAN configuration to an even higher level. By creating routing-like tables, they can associate remote networks with their specific destination telephone numbers. This sets up the enterprise over something resembling a matrix-switched network. In a sense, this is an electronic version of the crossbar switches that were used for years in the telephone network. A crossbar switch connected any node directly with any other node. Today, we describe the crossbar configuration as a hub switch.

Hub switches have the ability to send packets directly to simultaneous, multiple, destinations without having to first transport them through an intermediary network. The value of this kind of connection-oriented internetworking is its efficiency. Since it functions in a manner similar to a switched telephone network, connection-oriented internetworking can make point-to-point connections to the final destination without having to go through an intermediate network.

Figure 12.3 shows how an enterprise network can be built using connection-oriented internetworking over ISDN.

Using multiple B channels, the devices can place simultaneous calls directly between a number of various nodes or networks. Now, the packets bound for Atlanta can travel directly over a call placed between San Mateo and Atlanta. After all, it does not make sense to travel from Nashville to Pittsburgh through Atlanta when you can get a direct flight.

What is most impressive about connection-oriented internetworking is that the call between San Mateo and Atlanta can occur even when another call is connecting the San Mateo office to the New England headquarters. This results in greatly enhanced flexibility in dynamically building or tearing down the ad hoc enterprise

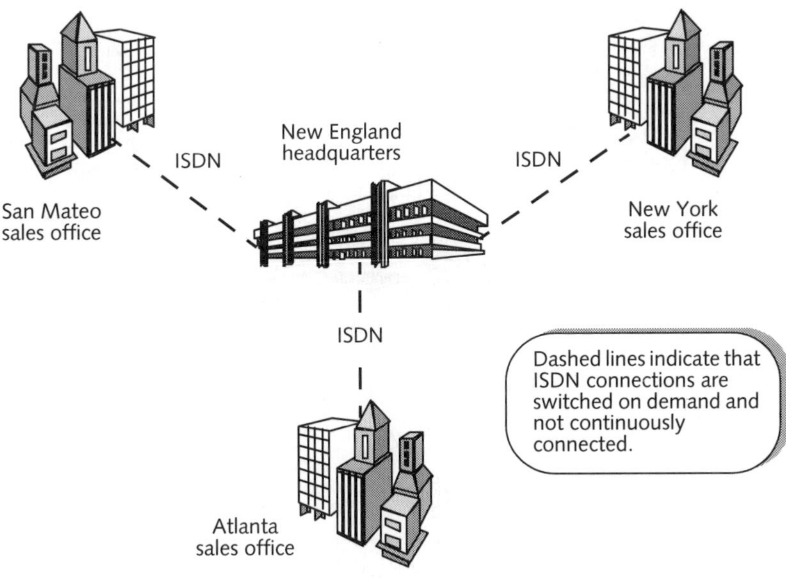

Figure 12.2 Enterprise sites connected over ISDN

WAN. Furthermore, this can be changed at will, based on moment-by-moment connectivity needs. This gives the enterprise the ability to establish a connection, on-the-fly and on-demand, from any site to any other site.

It is interesting to note that this kind of crossbar switching is a precursor to Asynchronous Transfer Mode. When it deals with LANs and networking, ATM uses a very similar connection-oriented technology.

There are some disadvantages involved in connection-oriented internetworking. Interoperability is not widespread. While there are devices on the market that utilize ISDN connection-oriented internetworking, solutions tend to be vendor-proprietary. Therefore, while connection-oriented internetworking is a good idea, it needs to be implemented in a standardized basis before it will see widespread acceptance.

Additionally, products that support connection-oriented internetworking tend to be expensive. Depending on the number of B channels they support, connection-oriented devices can cost three to seven times more than a standard ISDN bridge.

However, since these devices significantly reduce connection costs, there is a break-even point where the increased cost of the devices is offset by lower usage charges. The break-even point depends on a number of variables, such as the cost

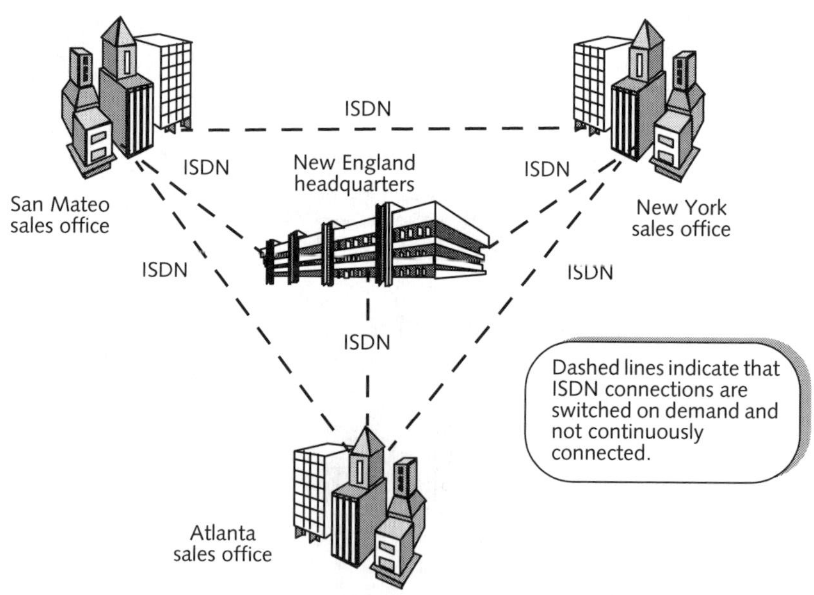

Figure 12.3   Enterprise WAN using matrix ISDN connections

of the ISDN service in the various locations, how many locations are to be inter-connected, and how often they connect.

Connection-oriented internetworking appears to be a viable alternative to multiple leased lines. It will have particular value for corporate networks supporting diverse branch offices. In this environment, the branch offices need to interconnect between themselves and the enterprise. It probably has somewhat less value for telecommuters, since people generally want to connect to the enterprise and not between themselves.

Virtual Network Connections

Networking on demand creates an interesting situation known as virtual network connections. During periods of user or network inactivity, the network WAN connections are down, even though the network itself may believe otherwise. In reality, the user is virtually, but not physically, connected to the network.

While these phantom or virtual connections can save usage charges, they can also lead to headaches. This is particularly true in situations where a Local Area Network assumes the user is physically connected, when in reality the call has been disconnected because no network traffic is passing over the WAN. This is an important consideration for companies planning to deploy remote LAN connections. We will discuss some of the ramifications and potential solutions when we cover LAN spoofing in Chapter 14, "Wide Area Network Considerations."

13

Making Remote LAN Access Connections

Early Remote LAN Access Development

The development of digital remote LAN access actually started as an attempt to evolve from Local Area Networks to Metropolitan Area Networks (MANs). The main difference between a LAN and a MAN is distance. While LANs provide local connections, typically within a building, MANs extended the connection to an entire campus or to an organization with multiple buildings.

The earliest MANs were connected with leased services, such as T1, and commercial-grade bridges. Sometimes a microwave radio link was used in place of T1 lines, but the theory was the same. The leased serial links were used to connect several independent LANs into a larger MAN that covered the organization's campus. Usually, that meant anyone on any LAN could exchange information and access services on any other LAN connected to the MAN.

In the late 1980s, several universities began to experiment with using MANs connected over Integrated Services Digital Network. Although the throughput would be lower, it was hoped that ISDN could deliver reasonable MAN capability at a lower cost than was required for leased lines.

West Virginia University tested ISDN MAN capability in July 1989.[1] Since the University needed to economically bridge LANs, ISDN was considered as a potential alternative to T1 bridge links.

---

1. Wolf, Dean. "West Virginia University Uses ISDN for T-1 Backup, *Telecommunications Magazine* **24** (February 1990): 47.

The objectives in testing ISDN for Ethernet bridging were fairly bold, particularly considering the early date that this testing occurred. The first goal was to learn how ISDN performed in heavy data applications.

Few applications are more data-intensive than LAN bridging. LAN bridging uses network devices and a communications link to connect one or more LANs into a MAN. Since LANs carry a wide variety of traffic at substantial throughput rates, they present a particularly interesting challenge for moderate-speed links like ISDN. Although ISDN is fast by conventional telephony standards, at 64 kilobits per second it is far slower than the megabits-per-second bandwidth typical on LANs.

When it comes to connecting networks, any technique that effectively increases bandwidth is very much of interest. Therefore, the second goal was to determine if data compression and parallel links could help offset ISDN's slower data rates.

To determine if ISDN, with its limited bandwidth, could be a candidate for LAN bridging, the test scenario shown in Figure 13.1 was devised.

Three campus Ethernet networks, normally interconnected by T1 circuits, were connected over ISDN. The LANs were at three locations. One location was the Engineering Sciences Complex. The second location was the Statistics and Computer Science department, located on a distant campus. The third location was off campus at the West Virginia Network for Educational Telecomputing (WVNET).

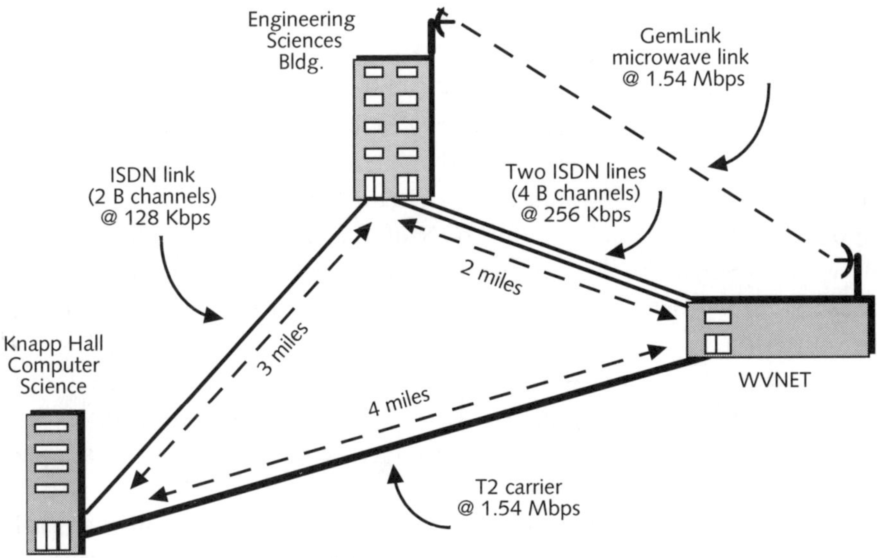

Figure 13.1   ISDN LAN bridging test configuration

WVNET is a state-wide computer facility co-located in Morgantown, West Virginia with the University.

The Engineering Sciences Ethernet served 300 users. Normally, this LAN connected to WVNET by a privately operated microwave link running at T1 speed. The LAN supported a DEC VAX minicomputer, a Sun Microsystems NFS server, a number of terminal servers and numerous PCs and workstations.

The WVNET Ethernet supported an IBM 3090 mainframe, a DEC VAX and an IBM RISC 6000, and connections to all 18 West Virginia state universities and colleges. The Statistics and Computer Science Departmental network supported several UNIX machines, a VAX cluster and numerous workstations. Prior to the test, the college was connected to WVNET by a leased T1 line.

Since an ISDN line offers two B channels, it made sense to take advantage of the parallel links and attempt to load balance the paths. By doing this, the effective link bandwidth could be doubled. The use of a Spanning Tree algorithm allowed redundant paths between bridges. This configuration provided more efficient data routing and the additional benefit of link redundancy.

Test Conclusions

After several months of testing, certain conclusions were reached by the evaluation team. They determined that ISDN's suitability for WAN links was primarily determined by the traffic demand level that existed over the WAN. In certain cases, the difference between T1 (1.544 Mbps) and BRI ISDN (0.128 Mbps) would be enough to remove ISDN BRI service from consideration as a WAN link. In other cases, the traffic across the WAN warranted consideration of ISDN as a backup service to the T1. Should the T1 circuit fail, essential WAN traffic could continue to operate over the backup ISDN link. In certain cases, the WAN traffic was low enough that the T1 bandwidth was really wasteful and unnecessary. In such cases, ISDN proved to be a less expensive and more efficient method of inter-LAN connection.

The tests were more successful than was first imagined. So much so, that West Virginia University began deploying ISDN as a routine method of interconnecting its campus networks. Eventually ISDN remote network access was expanded to the University's telecommuters and remote departments.

Today, West Virginia University has replaced its T1 connections with a Fiber Distributed Data Interface (FDDI) backbone. It also uses a mix of network connections to the backbone. Some forty departments and colleges that do not need high-speed access to the University's fiber-optic backbone are connected with ISDN remote connections. ISDN is also used for residential connections to the campus network.

Finally, with some restrictions, ISDN is used as an emergency backup should the FDDI network backbone collapse. This takes the form of ISDN connections to all router terminal ports and allows out-of-band management of these devices. The distant legs of the FDDI backbone are connected with ISDN LAN connections. In that way, should a major disaster occur on the network, limited recovery and emergency traffic can be moved across the WAN connections.

Can an ISDN BRI running at 128 kbps replace a 100-Mbps FDDI backbone? The answer is, "Certainly not." However, as we have seen, ISDN can provide reasonable, moderate traffic connectivity to the network backbone. It can also be called on to supply emergency backbone connections. Not bad for a technology that was sold primarily as a voice service!

Related Early Work

About the same time as West Virginia University was testing ISDN WAN connections, the University of Michigan was writing software to enable users to transport network protocols over switched digital links. As early as October 1989, a driver was written and distributed by the University of Michigan that supported TCP/IP over ISDN connections. This was ground-breaking work, although it went largely unnoticed by the media and users at the time.

The work of West Virginia University, the University of Michigan, and several other universities, made possible the eventual development of ISDN-based WAN devices. As we shall soon see, these devices extended network boundaries far beyond those envisioned by either LAN or even ISDN designers.

Communicating with Common Protocols

The good news for anyone desiring to move network protocols over ISDN is that it is protocol-transparent. ISDN operates at layer 3, and below, of the OSI model. The D channel uses protocols through layer 3 to establish network connections. The B channel, which is more frequently used for network data, provides layer 1 transmission; it is doing nothing more than handling a stream of bits. This makes the ISDN B channel essentially a bit pipe. Its mission in life is simple: To take a bit and move it to the other side.

For the most part, ISDN could not care less which protocols are in use. For either channel, a variety of protocols can be used. Protocols like PPP, when used on the B channels, are interpreted end-to-end, typically in network devices. None of this is seen by ISDN itself. The ISDN network is simply transporting the stream of bits over the B channel.

No matter what the network protocol, the only thing ISDN sees is data. Therefore, TCP/IP, PPP, IPX/SPX, AppleTalk, LAT, DECnet, SNA, and a myriad of other protocols can move seamlessly across an ISDN connection, given the right network devices.

What does make a difference, however, is the device's capabilities to handle the protocol. ISDN devices are generally designed for a specific protocol set. Therefore, they cannot support every possible protocol. So, while ISDN itself is protocol-independent, you will need to pay attention to supported protocols when you purchase ISDN network equipment.

It is important to know the equipment limitations when it comes to the protocols you wish to transport across the ISDN link. Terminal adapters, for example, do quite well with serialized protocols such as SNA, SLIP, and PPP, but not so well with network protocols like AppleTalk, TCP/IP, and IPX.

To support network connections, Terminal Adapters must have the ability to convert the asynchronous PPP data sent over the serial port to the synchronous PPP used by ISDN and network devices. Supporting network protocols over serial devices such as Terminal Adapters is the very reason the PPP and SLIP protocols were designed in the first place.

ISDN network devices can handle network protocols, but cannot handle serial or synchronous protocols like Kermit or SNA. For example, unless SNA is encapsulated in a network packet, ISDN bridges and routers do not have a clue what to do with it. Many ISDN bridges and routers can handle PPP, however, because it is designed into their internal code.

Similarly, some protocols have peculiarities that must be kept in mind. These idiosyncrasies extend beyond the actual hardware that is employed to carry them across the WAN. They are designed into the protocol. LAT and NetBEUI, for example, cannot be routed. They must be bridged. Other protocols, such as AppleTalk, do not handle multiple parallel paths very well. Put up a connection with two or more parallel paths and they fall apart. That makes it difficult to operate them over multiple B channels.

Designing Successful WAN Solutions

Using a little common sense and a decent measure of curiosity, you can handle most protocol peculiarities. The chances are that when you encounter protocols that offer WAN particularities, with a little research you will find workable solutions.

Knowing how various network devices handle the protocol idiosyncrasies will enable you to design successful WAN solutions. For example, using a bridge or a router that can also do bridging for selected protocols lets you handle LAT and NetBEUI across the WAN. Using a network device that presents multiple parallel paths as one large virtual path to AppleTalk will solve the protocol's finicky behavior with multiple B channels.

If you understand and follow the rules, it is not very difficult to make successful remote LAN access connections. It just takes a degree of planning, coordination and decent user support from the enterprise network staff.

For successful WAN implementations, the elements that must be in place are:

- A device on the enterprise to accept the remote connection. Typically, this device is called a Network Access Server (NAS). Very often, the NAS uses contention so several users can access it at the same time.
- A network device at the remote site. This can be a Terminal Adapter running SLIP or PPP, an internal PC card, or a standalone router or bridge.
- Digital connections at the enterprise and remote site to carry the WAN connection.
- Adequate support for remote user questions and technical problems.
- Consistent and meaningful network access policies.

Remote Installation Support Policies

Successful connections depend on selecting the proper equipment on the remote and enterprise side, providing adequate end-user support, and implementing consistent and meaningful polices.

Because there is so much that can go astray in any ISDN connection, particularly when it is first being brought up, having solid support behind your installation is important.

Installation Policies

One of the first support decisions that must be made is determining who will do the installation at the remote site. This is one instance where a clear policy must be worked out prior to the first installation. Will the network staff be expected to travel to the user's home and install the equipment? Will installations be left up to the user? Alternatively, is this something that will be covered by a third-party support organization?

Similarly, a decision has to be made as to who will load the appropriate software, and do the hardware and software configurations required by the remote access network device. Remember that besides the ISDN device configurations, installations will likely involve network protocol configurations, as well. Network configurations are required for the assignment of the proper network address, and for installation of the appropriate network drivers.

Will there be limits as to the supported network hardware software, or will the end user be allowed to use whatever they choose? Limited network support staff usually leads to a narrow selection for remote hardware and software installations. Allowing the user to choose their own equipment and network software provides greater flexibility. However, it taxes the support staff much more significantly since they need to deal with a variety of network software and drivers at the remote site.

Network Access Policies

Once the installation details have been resolved, policies have to be developed for managing dial-in access. Determine whether you want the network to call the user (in which case the network pays for the call, if there are usage charges) or whether the user is to call the network, or both.

If the network places the calls, a call-accounting mechanism may be required. When long distance or usage fees are accrued by the network, there may need to be a charge-back system in place. This allows the enterprise to bill the user for calls placed from the network.

Keep in mind there may be instances where two-way calling is desirable, such as when immediate recovery from an unexpected disconnect is desired. Placing calls from both sides can be necessary, but it can also be tricky. If the calling mechanisms in the remote and enterprise network devices are not timed properly, it is possible that both sides will try to call each other at the exact same moment. When both sides call simultaneously, this can cause call blockage and busy indications. This is similar to two people attempting to call each other at the exact same moment and both getting busy signals. Many devices allow different call time offsets to protect against call blockage. If an active connection is lost, for example, the network side may attempt calls every 10 seconds, while the remote tries to call every 15 seconds. That way, only one side will be calling at any given moment.

When it comes to network access policies, network security must also be seriously considered. If the remote user deliberately or unwillingly does things to compromise the network or the users, what will be the recourse? Will the user be reprimanded, disconnected from the network, or even fired? Because there are legal implications in each of these actions, security-related issues should not be handled casually.

User Support Policies

Finally, policies need to be put in place for user support. In the event of an outage or connection problem, should a remote user place a trouble call to the network control center, the service provider, or some third-party support organization? This is not just a matter of determining which support agencies may or may not be in place to assist the user with a trouble call. There is often a need for a single point of contact where users can enter trouble reports.

Regardless of who is chosen, the single point of contact must have the ability to sort out where the problem is likely to have occurred, and to relay the information to the appropriate repair personnel. Remember that remote access troubles can be very complex to sort out because a failure can occur almost anywhere. As an example, here are just a few of the possible points of failure:

- User cockpit problems
- Power outages
- Hardware or software failures in the remote PC
- Failures in the remote network device
- Cable problems at the remote location
- Failures in the ISDN line to the central office
- Failures in the telephone network
- Failures in the ISDN line to the network hub
- Failures in the network hub device
- Failures in the hub network segment
- Failures in any desired network host
- Failures in the network backbone

It is best to have a policy stating that there is one point of contact who will guide the trouble through the various agencies which are responsible for correcting the problem.

In addition, minimum response time should be stated depending on the nature of the problem. If the user reports a problem that turns out to be a partial or complete net down, it more than likely requires an immediate response on a 24 by 7 basis. On the other hand, if a single user's remote device has failed, a reasonable response might be the next business day.

ISDN Remote LAN Access Devices

Once support polices are in place, the specific devices used for remote access can be selected. Happily, there are a wide variety of remote LAN access vendors and solutions available today.

The remote side and the enterprise side will probably have different equipment requirements. Therefore, a single vendor solution may or may not be the most appropriate for widespread remote access. However, no matter what specific equipment is chosen for the enterprise or the field locations, the devices must have a high degree of interoperability. If they do not work together, your remote network access aspirations are doomed to failure.

Terminal Adapters as Network Devices

Terminal Adapters, once primarily used for serial communications capabilities such as PC-to-PC file transfers, are now finding their way into the arena of network devices. This is particularly true with Internet Service Providers, many of whom use Terminal Adapters to connect users to the Internet.

Some Terminal Adapters are well suited for remote LAN and Internet access. Terminal Adapters in this class incorporate the Point-to-Point Protocol (PPP) and the Multilink PPP protocol (MP) into their designs. PPP supports a single ISDN B channel, while MP aggregates up to six B channels for greater throughput.

The same method is used, regardless of whether Terminal Adapters are used to connect to the Internet or to enterprise networks. The SLIP or PPP package is installed in the PC. The Terminal Adapter is then connected to the PC serial port. Dialer software, generally included with SLIP or PPP packages, handles making the connection.

Before a connection can be made, a conversion process must take place in the Terminal Adapter. The serial port is asynchronous, but SLIP and PPP generally connect to synchronous devices like communications servers. Therefore, the Terminal Adapter must do an asynchronous-to-synchronous conversion for SLIP or PPP. Interestingly, not all TAs come with this capability.

Interoperability is often an issue, particularly when Terminal Adapters attempt to establish a SLIP or PPP session. Therefore, if your intent is to access an ISP or enterprise network, interoperability may be a problem. Be sure to check with your service provider and the TA vendor before purchasing any of these devices. You may also want to look at some of the ISDN bridge/router products. These devices seem to have a more robust and mature implementation of PPP and MP.

Bridges and Routers

ISDN network devices, whether they are external or internal devices, fall into two classes: bridges and routers. While there are clear differences between bridges and routers, their overall task is similar. They take LAN packet data from one network, and deliver it to the network on the other side. The method with which the device handles packet decisions determines whether it is considered to be a bridge or a router.

Sometimes the terms *bridge* and *router* are used interchangeably, but this is incorrect. As we will see shortly, from a cost, performance, security and operational viewpoint, there are very important differences between routers and bridges.

Bridges and routers are available from a variety of vendors over a wide price range. Depending on features, some cost only a few hundred dollars, while others can be as expensive as twenty or thirty thousand dollars. The price reflects the capabilities, intelligence and throughput rates of the devices.

Each device is implemented, or not implemented, for network interconnection based on its internal characteristics. Therefore, you must pay attention to each device's characteristics and how it impacts on remote LAN access for your enterprise network.

Bridges

A bridge has a relatively easy assignment. In its purest form, a bridge only has to decide if a packet is intended for the local LAN. It does this by looking at the address in the packet header. If the destination address is on the local network, the bridge simply leaves the packet alone. If the packet's destination address is not on the local network, the bridge throws the packet over to the other side of the WAN connection. It does not know exactly where the packet is bound, it only knows that it is not addressed to a device on its own network. Other bridges on the remote side of the connection will select or reject the packet based on whether or not it is destined for devices on their networks.

One of the biggest advantages of bridges is that they are protocol transparent. While some bridges do a limited examination of packet content, they generally make no attempt to distinguish different packet protocols. A pure bridge makes all its decisions at layer two of the seven-layer Open System Interface (OSI) model. It could not care less whether the packet is TCP/IP, IPX/SPX, or DECnet. The bridge sees them all as data, because protocol characteristics start at layer three of the OSI model. This means that any protocol existing on the LAN can be bridged over the WAN, which makes bridging relatively simple, inexpensive and efficient to implement.

Bridge Looping

Of course, bridges have their disadvantages. One of the most notable is a nasty ability to mindlessly handle packets. This can cause situations where packets endlessly loop around the WAN when the bridges are connected in a circular fashion.

Why would anyone want to use bridges connected in a loop? The answer is that no one in their right mind would want to do this. However, as the adage goes, "Stuff happens" (or words to that effect). Unfortunately, it is not particularly difficult to inadvertently create bridge loops. This is particularly a problem with remote access bridges that operate on switched services. Figure 13.2 illustrates how a bridge loop can be inadvertently created.

Suppose a bank branch office in Cambridge, Massachusetts installs a bridge to connect the branch LAN to the bank's corporate enterprise network in Boston. Three months later, a second bridge is added that connects the Cambridge office to a new branch bank in Framingham.

One day, unbeknownst to the Cambridge bank, the folks in the Framingham bank decide that their communications will be enhanced by a direct connection to the Boston headquarters. They install a bridge link between Framingham and Boston. Unfortunately, neither they nor the Boston office bothers to mention this to the Cambridge branch bank.

When the Framingham-to-Boston bridges are turned on, a triangle is created that runs from Boston to Cambridge to Framingham and then back to Boston. Packets travel merrily over the loop over and over again, never dying. This sets up the nasty condition that we know as bridge looping.

There is a tendency to assume that slower-speed bridged connections are harmless, so the issue of WAN bridging may not receive proper attention from the network administrator. An unknowing network administrator may think that a 64-kbps, or even 128-kbps, link can do little harm to the 10- or 100-Mbps corporate enterprise network. However, the network administrator should think again.

While bridges are an inexpensive and easy way to connect networks, to ignore the potential danger of bridge looping is a serious mistake. Bridge loops are wicked things. They can keep so many packets circulating in a neverending circle that the entire enterprise network can be brought to its knees.

Bridge loop concerns are valid for bridged connections, even over leased lines. However, there should be even more consideration of looping for switched digital connections. Since remote bridge calls can be connected and dropped at will, switched digital connections can create bridge loops that are very transitory in nature. This makes them especially hard to spot and potentially very troublesome.

Network managers have to exercise extreme care when overseeing their network topologies to avoid bridge loops. They should not underestimate the potential seriousness of this situation. Imagine the embarrassment when the network manager has to explain to management that a tiny pair of devices, no bigger than a modem and located fifty miles apart, crippled the entire corporate enterprise.

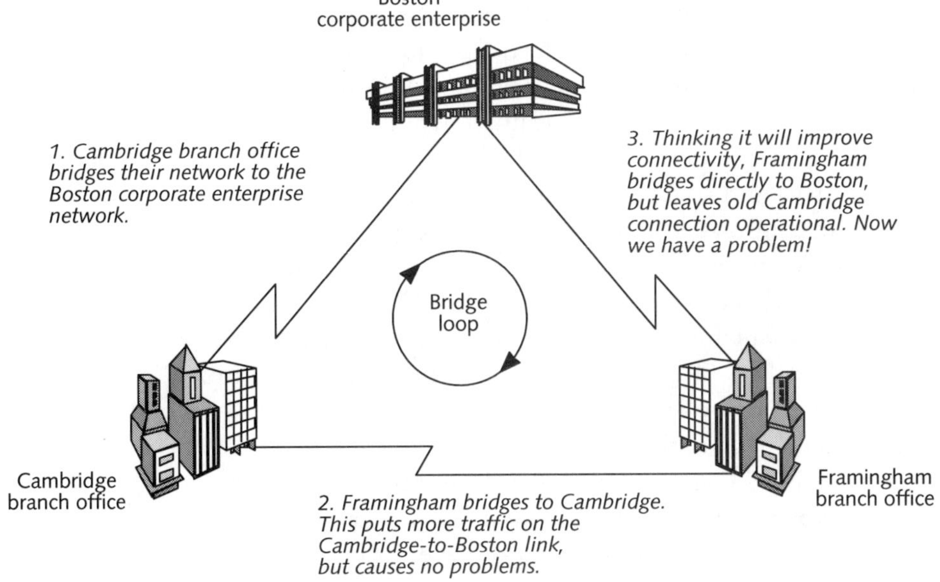

Figure 13.2   Bridge loops

Spanning Tree

A protocol called Spanning Tree has been designed to overcome bridge loops. Spanning Tree tracks the various bridge branches and prevents packets from circulating endlessly in a loop.

Spanning Tree is frequently used in leased line bridges. However, many switched services bridges do not support Spanning Tree because it adds to the cost and complexity of the bridge. The Spanning Tree protocol also adds extra traffic to the link. This can be tolerated in a T1 leased connection, but it is something we wish to avoid in lower-bandwidth WAN links such as are found in ISDN-based connections.

Routers

Routers tend to be slightly more expensive and somewhat more complex to maintain than bridges. However, they provide a degree of security and control that is not available in bridges.

Routers operate at layer 3 of the OSI model. Therefore, they are fully aware of network protocols. They know specific routes to various other networks, and they track hosts and workstation addresses, maintaining and exchanging tables telling each other where everything is located in the network.

A router processing engine has to be more powerful than a bridge, since it must examine every packet and match the destination address to a routing table kept in its memory. If the route to the destination is known, the router sends the packet out in that direction. If the route is unknown, the router either assumes a default route, or it queries other routers until it learns the route associated with the appropriate destination. It then adds that route to its routing table.

Routers are intimately concerned with the packet's contents. As a result, they are very network savvy. Their ability to inspect the packet's internals make them immune to the packet-looping problems encountered by bridges.

Routers prevent looping by assigning each packet a least-cost-routing figure, and a Time-to-Live (TTL). If there is more than one path for the packet to travel, the router will send out the packet in the direction that represents the least-cost route. Usually, this is the connection with the fewest hops. Packets that have exceeded their TTL are simply removed from the network.

It should be pointed out that almost all routers can function as a bridge for protocols that cannot be routed. In instances where it is preferred to bridge a protocol, the router can be told not to route it. Some protocols, such as NetBEUI and LAT, cannot be bridged. Therefore, routers deal with these protocols by bridging them.

Brouters

Some bridges go well beyond basic bridging functions. They allow the user to perform functions like address-, packet- and protocol-filtering. Some do a combination of bridging and routing. Other devices can be set up either as a bridge or router, depending on the customer's preference.

By definition, devices that support routing and bridging functions are not pure bridges, although they are sometimes mislabeled as bridges. Devices with this kind of capability are really bridge-routers, or brouters for short.

Deciding on Bridges or Routers

Every remote network connection needs to be supported by a bridge or router of some sort. It might be easy to assume that since routers are smarter than bridges, they should be the device of choice for switched digital connections. Actually, there are other factors to be considered.

Because they tend to do much less with individual packets, bridges are typically faster than routers. Since they require less processing power, bridges are cheaper and often physically smaller than routers. Finally, as we mentioned, bridges are usually much easier to set up and maintain than routers.

On the other hand, we have seen that bridges have weaknesses not found in routers. Therefore, all of the device's strengths and weaknesses should be considered when making a decision as to which kind of network device to deploy for remote LAN access connections.

Whether you use a bridge, a router, or a brouter for your remote network, connections are simply a matter of capability, cost and application. In many cases, you will not select a single type of device. Although bridges usually cannot connect to routers and vice versa, most networks feature a mix of routers and bridges staged in various parts of the network.

The reason bridges do not generally connect to routers is that there are significant differences in protocol stack architecture between bridging and routing. Figure 13.3 shows a comparison between a typical PPP bridging stack and a PPP IP routing stack.

Notice that the same interface appears at the top and bottom layers of both stacks. This is true whether bridging or routing is in use. The network protocol is on the top layer. The bottom layer is the PPP framing on the channels. Both stacks also employ compression (although not necessarily the same compression) and the Multilink protocol.

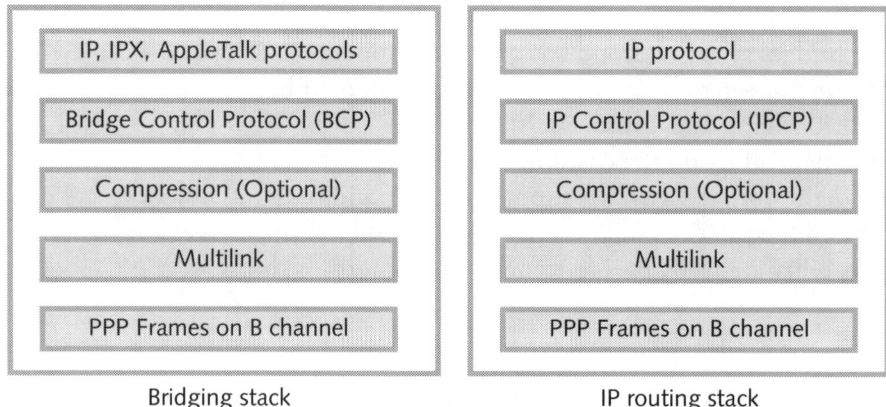

Figure 13.3　PPP bridging and routing stacks

The difference between bridging and routing stacks occurs with the protocol in use. The bridge stack uses the IETF-defined Bridge Control Protocol (BCP). BCP is responsible for examining the packets and determining their destination. The routing stack uses the IP Control Protocol (IPCP). Like BCP, this is an IETF-defined protocol. It performs the routing network functions. If IPX was implemented in a router, then IPX Control Protocol (IPXCP) would be used in place of IPCP. Control protocol have also been developed for other networking protocols.

ISDN PC Cards

Using a combination of special software and internal devices, it is possible to connect remote PCs to a remote LAN without requiring an external device. These internal devices take the form of ISDN PC cards, and can come in configurations either as routers or bridges.

Network applications, such as a World Wide Web browser, Telnet, or FTP, see some ISDN cards as an Ethernet NIC. This allows these cards to be installed without the need for special software to divert the packets to the ISDN port.

Usually, the installation is relatively straightforward. First, the user inserts the ISDN card in the PC. Next, they run an installer program to place the appropriate files on the hard drive. Then, they install the network drivers and application software. Finally, the user plugs an ISDN line into the back of their PC and reboots.

Like the external bridges and routers, ISDN network cards allow ISDN to be a carrier for a variety of LAN protocols like TCP/IP, AppleTalk, and IPX/SPX

(Novell). Like external bridges and routers, many ISDN PC cards can support PPP connections to standalone devices on the enterprise. However, unlike external bridges and routers that can support a number of devices, internal ISDN cards support only a single machine.

Network Drivers

Sometimes internal ISDN devices (bridges or routers) will come with firmware or software that emulates a network interface device. For example, an ISDN PC card may present an interface to the network driver that resembles a standard Ethernet card. This arrangement allows network drivers to work in their usual manner. Network applications are convinced they are talking to a real network card.

As Figure 13.4 illustrates, the ISDN card presents an interface to the network applications and drivers that is very similar to a NIC. In both cases, the network application speaks to the network driver. The NIC card processes the packets and sends them to the LAN. Similarly, the ISDN WAN card processes the network information and sends it to the ISDN WAN. Once it crosses the WAN, a network device on the far side simply puts the data on the remote network.

If the internal ISDN network device cannot emulate a NIC, it will require special drivers to replace the standard network driver. The special drivers need to be

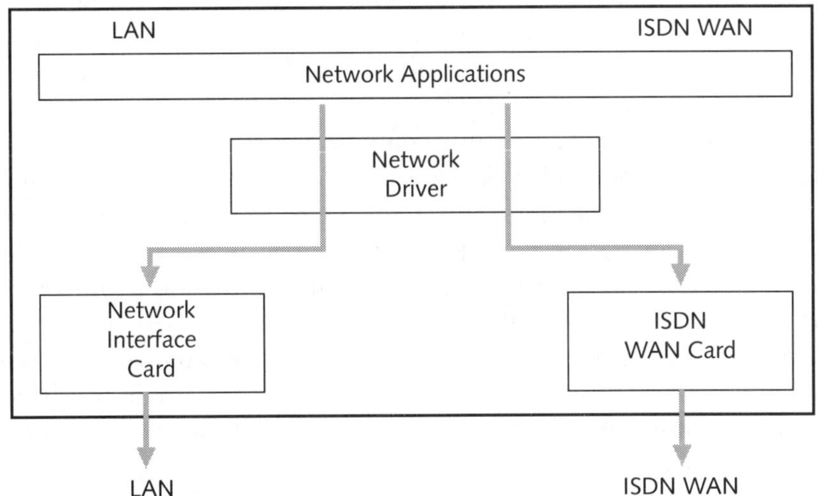

Figure 13.4 LAN and ISDN WAN network support

made compatible with the ISDN card. Therefore, they are typically included as part of the ISDN card's installation package.

These drivers present standard interfaces to the network software, but divert the data from the Ethernet card to the ISDN PC card or Terminal Adapter.

Another increasingly common approach is to build ISDN network drivers right into the operating system (OS) or network software. This has several important advantages. It makes ISDN appear as a standard part of the network options suite, leading to a high degree of integration with the OS. Plug-and-play becomes possible because ISDN remote access simply becomes another Application Program Interface (API).

The operating system can also be designed to anticipate and accommodate the unique characteristics of WAN connections. Several major vendors, including Microsoft and Novell, have been integrating ISDN into their network operating systems (NOS) and operating systems. We will discuss this in more detail when we cover network spoofing in Chapter 14, "Wide Area Network Considerations."

Personal LAN Devices

We started this book by pointing out that, not very long ago, network connections were extremely costly. Ethernet bridges were large, expensive devices costing tens of thousands of dollars. Homes were unlikely to have such high-priced gear in their dens, unless they were owned by the company president and had a Rolls Royce parked in the garage. Even if the company was willing to invest tens of thousands of dollars for devices operating in employees' homes, maintenance of the bridges was a difficult process.

Although some bridge maintenance could be done remotely, initial installation and many configurations had to be done on site. Therefore, it was often necessary to send a technician to the user's location. If there were enough devices and locations that were far apart, transportation costs could be quite significant. Therefore, it required an enormous investment of corporate finances and resources to install and maintain remote connections.

Things are very different today. Remote network devices have become less complex and much easier to install and maintain. They are downright small and lightweight. Many full-featured ISDN Ethernet bridges and routers are about the size of the average modem, and cost about twice as much as a high-speed modem. Clearly, the price for network devices has fallen to the point where a corporation can install a device that was totally unthinkable just a few years ago—a personal bridge. This truly is a product whose time has come.

Figures 13.5 and 13.6 illustrate how relatively easy it now is to provide remote LAN access for remote users. The top part of Figure 13.5 shows a number of remote computers that are connected to the enterprise. Each machine has decent access to the remote network through a shared ISDN WAN connection. Multiple machines connected in this fashion might be found in a branch office or in a telecommuting center.

The bottom part of the diagram in Figure 13.5 shows how it is possible for a home user to construct a very small, inexpensive home network consisting of nothing more than a single PC connected to the bridge. Using a 10Base-T reversing cable between the single PC and the network device eliminates the need to install a concentrator in the home.

Even though small, unmanaged concentrators are not very expensive, the ability to eliminate them can save the home user about two hundred dollars. It also substantially reduces the complexity of the home network connections. Thus, the

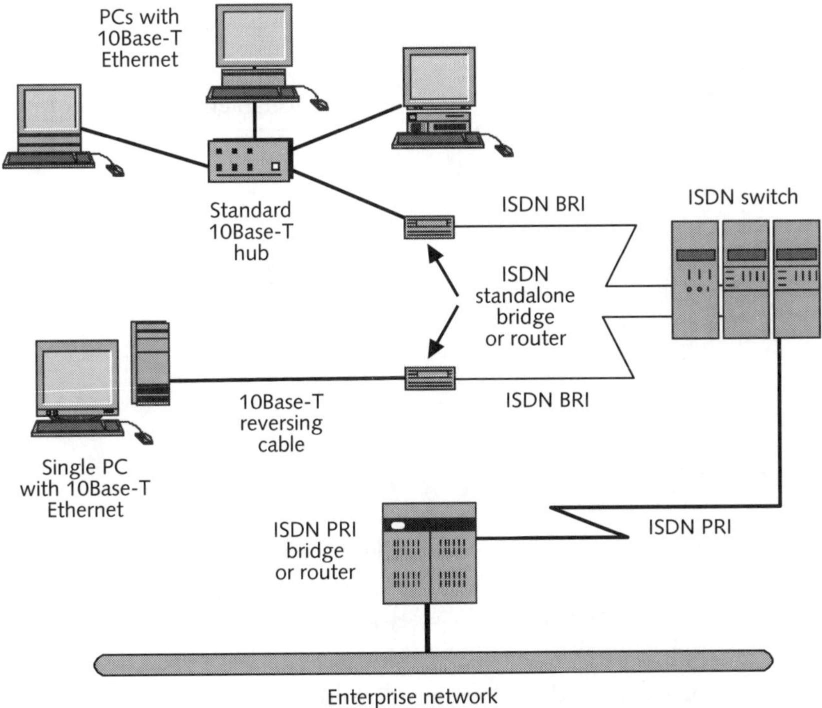

Figure 13.5 ISDN standalone WAN connections

work-at-home LAN consists of only two devices, the PC with a standard Ethernet card and the personal bridge. This dramatically reduces the hardware costs of the remote LAN connection.

By using network devices, it is also possible to cross media. This allows one side of the network connection to use 10Base-2 or thinnet cable, such as is typically found in a corporate computer center. Meanwhile, the other side can use 10Base-T network using twisted-pair cable suitable for installation in a home or office.

Figure 13.6 illustrates a remote network connection using an internal ISDN WAN card. While this configuration requires some additional installation and only supports a single machine, notice how much this simplifies the connection.

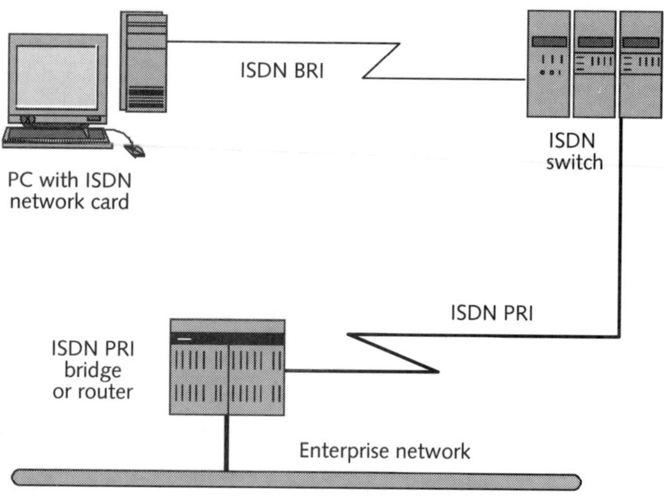

Figure 13.6   ISDN PC card WAN connections

The Enterprise Side

There can be cost savings on the enterprise side, as well. Significant cost reductions can be realized by sharing the network side resources. Often a PRI device can be used instead of multiple BRI devices. One PRI device can support 23 individual user sessions at 64 kbps each, or 11 user sessions at 128 kbps each. Using PRI also decreases the tangle of wires that is required to bring 11 or 23 individual ISDN and network connections to and from the network side device. It also reduces equipment costs.

Instead of installing a number of independent, standalone network devices, one for each remote connection, the network can use multi-user access devices. A large number of users can then simultaneously access the multi-user devices on the enterprise network. We will discuss how this is done in more detail when we cover contention in the next chapter.

Putting it All Together

Finally, let us put all the parts together. A complete remote access solution might look like the example shown in Figure 13.7.

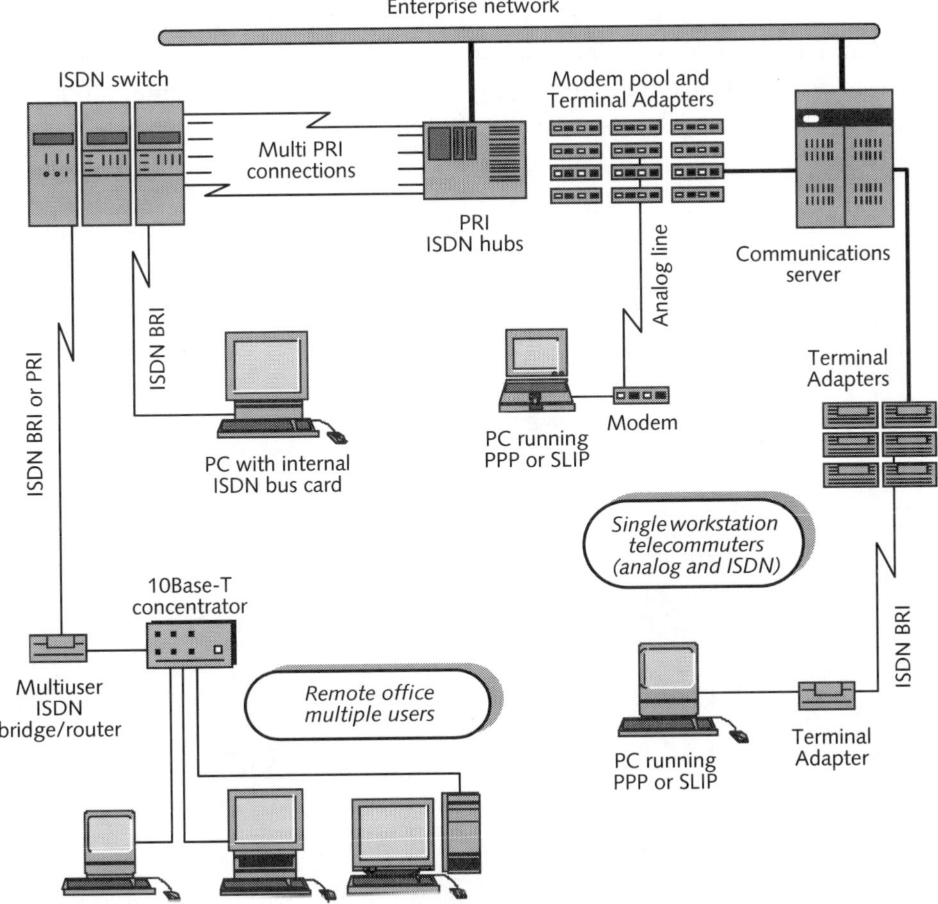

Figure 13.7 Remote LAN access examples

As can be seen, this example really covers a significant percentage of the remote LAN access methods.

A communications server allows serial connections using either analog modems or Terminal Adapters. The user only needs to have PPP- or SLIP-based applications running in the remote machine. If they are using an analog line, they dial in to the modem pool, which is connected to the communications server. ISDN users dial in to a bank of Terminal Adapters to start their PPP or SLIP sessions. Like the modem pool, the Terminal Adapters are connected to the communications server.

People with bridge or router capabilities dial in to a series of PRI lines to access the PRI bridge or router hubs. The hub supports N*23 connections if a single channel (64 kbps) is supported for user access. If two channels are supported (128 kbps), then the hub supports N*12 connections. For example, if there are two PRI lines going into the hub, there can be 46 simultaneous single-channel users. On the other hand, if 128-kbps connections are allowed, a PRI hub with two PRIs can support 23 simultaneous users. In any case, users connect to the same hub bank whether they use a standalone or internal ISDN network device.

14

Wide Area Networks

Many issues come into play with Wide Area Networks. Some of the most common considerations are conserving central site resources by using contention, proper network addressing, and spoofing.

Contention

There are two primary configurations that can be used for remote LAN access. The first configuration is a dedicated one-to-one configuration that provides unrestricted connections. A network device, a bridge or router, is provided on the network side for every remote user. In this kind of dedicated configuration, every user is guaranteed a connection whenever they want access to network services.

However, dedicated configurations are very resource-intensive. Therefore, management may decide it is too costly to provide network access with one-to-one network connections. Instead, they may prefer to have users share common network devices at the enterprise site.

Shared devices take advantage of the second method. Instead of providing dedicated connections, this method uses a shared connection with contention.

Switched digital services allow contention to service multiple users over common equipment. Contention cuts down on central site equipment expenses and line costs. For example a company may have 400 work-at-home users, but no more than 100 are expected to be on-line at any one time. This is based on an assumption, and it is usually correct, that not everyone will want to be connected at the exact same time. Instead of purchasing 800 network devices (two for each connection), the company can instead purchase 500 network devices. The company can install 400 remote network devices in homes. At the corporate site, 100 network devices can be connected in a "hunt group."[1]

Figure 14.1 illustrates how this configuration could be designed. In our example, four-to-one contention has been used (400:100 = 4:1). Each new user that accesses the network is given access to one of the common network devices on the enterprise network. Each time the user calls in, it is likely they will get a different network device.

If all network devices are configured in a similar manner (the same filtering is used in each device, for example), it makes no difference which device is accessed. The fact that the remote user gets a different network device from the last access is of no consequence. As each new user dials in, another enterprise network device is allocated. As users drop their sessions, the network side resources are made available for additional new callers.

This method requires a degree of "good citizenship" from users. Users need to be educated to drop connections when they are no longer needed. Alternatively, the network devices can automatically take care of dropping inactive calls.

When this configuration is used, some consideration must be given to on-demand networking. Suppose a user's connection has gone inactive, but the user is still logged into services with a specific network address. If the connection is re-initiated by user traffic, there is a likely possibility that the remote user will connect through a different device. The network will then need to know that the user is on a different network device. This is typically less of a problem with bridging than routing, but it is important to make sure that the network devices can handle this situation should it occur.

If all the devices have users connected and a new user calls in, the new user receives a busy indication and must try the call again at a later time.

In some cases, sophisticated call-handling applications are used for managing remote LAN connections. A bank of network devices can be used for call setup. The remote user's network device does not call the enterprise network device directly. Instead, it calls a special network device whose only purpose is to handle call management. Once connected to the management device, the remote device

---

1. This works the same as the hunt group that is sometimes used for voice service. Several incoming lines are placed in a circular loop. A call placed to a common number will find the first open number in the group. If the number is busy, the call will "roll down" or hunt each number until it finds an open line.

supplies authentication information (typically, an account and password) and requests a session. The management device authenticates the caller and drops the connection. It then instructs one of the network bridges or routers to call the remote user.

This process lightens the burden on the enterprise devices by accepting a pre-liminary set-up call, and by scheduling the first available network device to call the user back. It also automates the calling process for the remote user. If, for example, all network devices are busy, the management device will wait for an enterprise network device to become available. The management device then instructs the recently released device to call the remote user. This frees the user from having to attempt calls every few seconds if all the enterprise devices are busy.

In this case, the telephone bills are charged to the network side. The charges can be absorbed by central funding or, using call accounting, can be charged back to the original user—perhaps as part of a usage fee.

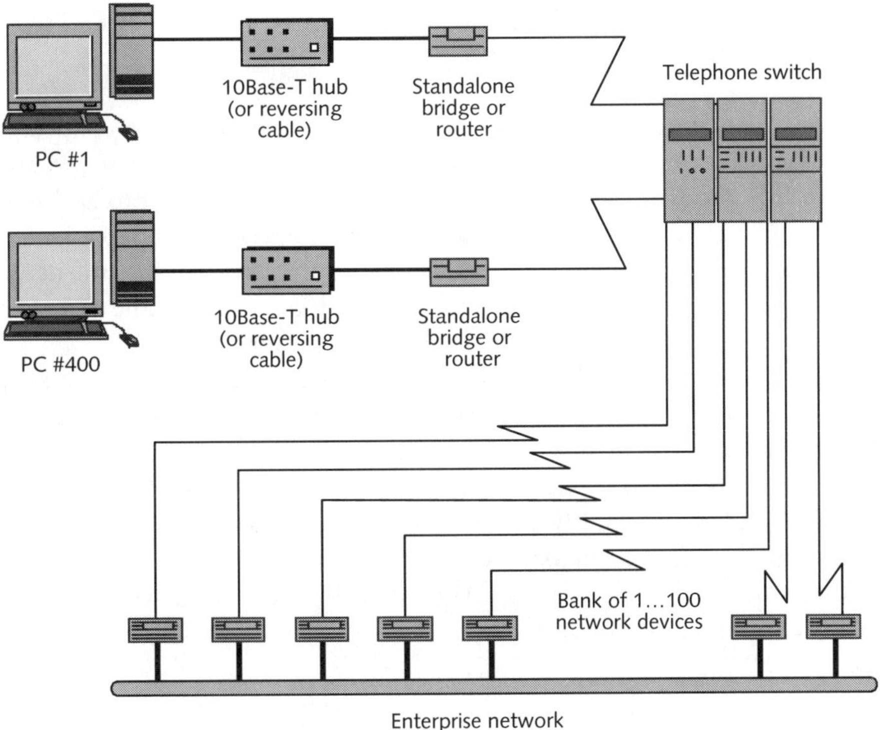

Figure 14.1 WAN contention

Whose Network am I Now, Anyway?

Network protocols use numbering schemes to determine where to send their traffic. All devices on the network must have a unique network address.

Network addresses are like subway tokens. Without them, you simply cannot ride on the train. This means that any network client, whether directly on the LAN or remotely connected, is required to have a network number.

In some cases, multiple numbers are required. For example, if a computer runs multiple protocol stacks such as TCP/IP, IPX/SPX, or AppleTalk, it will have multiple addresses, one for each protocol. Besides the protocol network numbers, each Ethernet NIC (Network Interface Card) has a unique Ethernet address hardcoded on the card.

Network addressing is an import issue for remote LAN access. To participate on the network, or to access the Internet, some manner of address assignment must be in place for the dial-in host or client.

Network Addressing Methods

With dial on demand, it is possible, even easy, for a remote user to connect to a number of different networks during any given work session. Users may want to connect to the corporate LAN to check their e-mail, then connect to an Internet Service Provider to access a World Wide Web site. Accessing these various networks through switched digital services can present problems, because the network address and subnet masks will change from network to network. The address and mask that were correct for the first network are wrong for the second.

This is a nasty situation. Without the proper address, the client will not be able to establish a network session. Worse, bad addresses can wreak havoc, especially on enterprise networks.

Unfortunately, network configurations are not always easy for the user to change—particularly for TCP/IP. Configurations are complex, being made up of multiple pieces of information like the network address, the subnet mask, the gateway address and the domain name server address. Figure 14.2 shows how a typical network configuration is assigned.

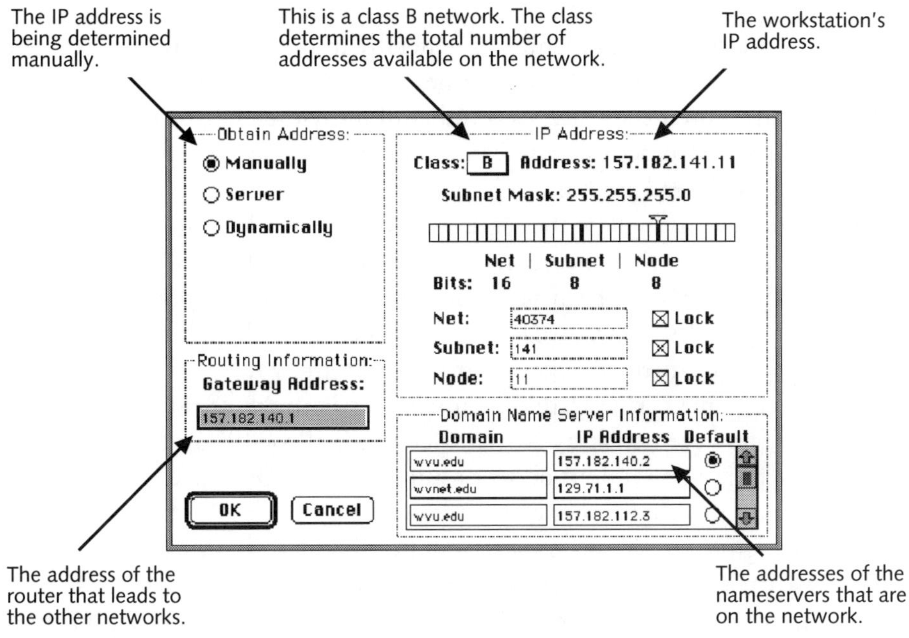

Figure 14.2   Network addressing example

Static Addressing

The network number assignments for a dial-in user can be handled in a number of ways. It is possible to use static addressing to pre-assign addresses to all remote network machines. If addressing is handled in a static manner, changing addresses usually means fiddling with a network configuration file, something that the casual user cannot and should not be expected to do.

Frankly, it requires some administrative overhead to manage the assignment of static network numbers to ensure no two users have the same network address. However, there is an important benefit to static addressing. The address is known in advance for each and every machine on the network and, importantly, the addresses rarely change. They usually stay the same for each individual computer on the network. This is a very big advantage when it comes to network security. Should inappropriate behavior be traced to a network address, it is easy to tell whose machine is the culprit.

Random Dynamic Addressing

If the addresses use static assignment, it is generally intended that the address will rarely, if ever, change. Of course, this assumes the user will always access a single network. If the user intends to access a number of individual networks, then static addressing will not be practical. For cases such as this, some type of dynamic addressing, such as server-based or random addressing, can be used.

Some network protocols allow the server to pick a network number for the user by using random addressing. Random addressing is handled in various ways. Sometimes the network server simply "guesses" an address for the workstation. This can be tricky and somewhat dangerous, especially if the addressed number has previously been assigned and the server does not know it.

Therefore, as a general rule, random number assignment is not a good idea. Some protocols, however, such as Novell NetWare's IPX/SPX and Apple Computer's AppleTalk, handle random network numbers well. Both take full responsibility for random network number assignments.

For example, AppleTalk nodes try a series of different addresses when they initially register with the network. Once they find a unique address, they save it. They do not need to reacquire a new address at each boot, unless another machine came up and took the previous address while they were off the network. In cases such as this, random addressing can work quite well.

Although the network number constantly changes every time the user turns on the workstation or connects to the network, this is seldom a problem for the user. The user does not know, or particularly care, what network number has been assigned to their machine. They are only interested in the network access that random addressing provides. Protocols that automatically manage the addressing function greatly simplify the task of the network staff in providing network connections.

Server-Based Dynamic Addressing

Server-based dynamic addressing is a form of addressing where addresses are assigned from a predetermined range of addresses. Server-based dynamic address allocation uses an addressing mechanism that easily allows automatic reuse of an address no longer needed by the machine to which it was previously assigned. Therefore, the addresses are only good for a single session.

If the user logs out, or turns off the workstation, the address is released for use by other workstations. Server-based dynamic allocation is particularly useful for assigning an address to machines that will be temporarily connected to the network, as in the case of remote LAN access. In short, dynamic address protocols allow for sharing a limited pool of IP addresses among a group of hosts that do not need permanent IP addresses.

BootP

In cases where static- or random-addressing assignment is impracticable or undesirable, it is possible to dynamically allocate network addresses from a specified range, on connection. IETF RFC 951, "Bootstrap Protocol," provides a mechanism for allocating dynamic addresses.[2] This RFC describes a bootstrap protocol called BootP.[3]

BootP was originally developed to allow a diskless client machine to obtain an IP address from the network. Once it had this address, it could connect to a server and boot from the network.

BootP servers allocate addresses that are only good for a single network session. When the user leaves the network, their address is no longer valid. When they reconnect to the network and start a new session, odds are pretty good they will get a different IP network number. BootP servers generally track the numbers they have previously assigned to other users. This ensures that the same number is not given out to multiple individuals at the same time.

Many BootP servers also log the assignment of network numbers. These logs can be a great value should any inappropriate actions on the network occur from remote users. They allow network administrators to identify the specific machine using a certain address at the time the inappropriate actions occurred.

RARP

An earlier protocol than BootP, Reverse Address Resolution Protocol (RARP) was created to allow a client to determine its own IP address. RARP created addresses

---

2. W. Croft, J. Gilmore, "Bootstrap Protocol," RFC 951, (updated by RFC 1395, RFC 1532, RFC 1497).

3. The term *bootstrap* is commonly believed to have come from the phrase, "lifting yourself up by your own bootstraps." People who went into business without previous experience or outside support were said to be bootstrapping themselves into businesses. This term applies very nicely to a condition where a PC is attempting, little by little, to lift itself into an operational mode. From this, of course, we get the phrase "booting a computer." Without this background information, users may be inclined to think that "booting a computer" is synonymous with throwing the bugger in the trash—something most of us have wanted to do from time to time!

based on the device's internal hardware address. However, RARP could only be implemented on hosts containing special driver modifications. It was largely replaced by BootP, since BootP provided improved IP addressing and did not require a special driver, as is the case with RARP.

DHCP

A newer protocol, Dynamic Host Configuration Protocol (DHCP), has been developed to handle dynamic addressing. DHCP is an extended version of BootP. It is described in RFC 1541, "Dynamic Host Configuration Protocol."[4]

Like BootP, DHCP is a de facto Internet standard that allows a server to assign IP addresses to remote clients. DHCP, however, is based on a client-server model. A designated DHCP server allocates network addresses and delivers configuration parameters to dynamically configured clients. Since DHCP is an extension of BootP, DHCP clients and servers can interoperate with BootP clients and servers.

Packet Resequencing

Remote connections can lead to all kinds of fascinating situations. We have already discussed issues involving bridge loops and network number assignments. Packet resequencing is another interesting problem that results from remote LAN access.

Suppose, as shown in Figure 14.3, a branch office network in Washington, DC is connected with a multiple ISDN B channel connection to an enterprise network in New York City. The connection on B2 (B channel two) happens to be routed by the telephone network over a fiber route directly from Washington to New York City. However, the B1 connection is routed through a satellite link that goes through Cincinnati, Ohio before it reaches New York.

This may sound strange, but the truth is that such routing happens all the time. While the Constitution states that, "all men are created equal," this adage does not hold for call-routing algorithms. Two calls placed immediately one right after the other between the same origination and destination will likely be given entirely different routing. The routes are not necessarily the shortest routes, either. The telephone network uses least-cost routing, not shortest-line routing, in establishing its call connections.

---

4. R. Droms, "Dynamic Host Configuration Protocol," RFC 1541.

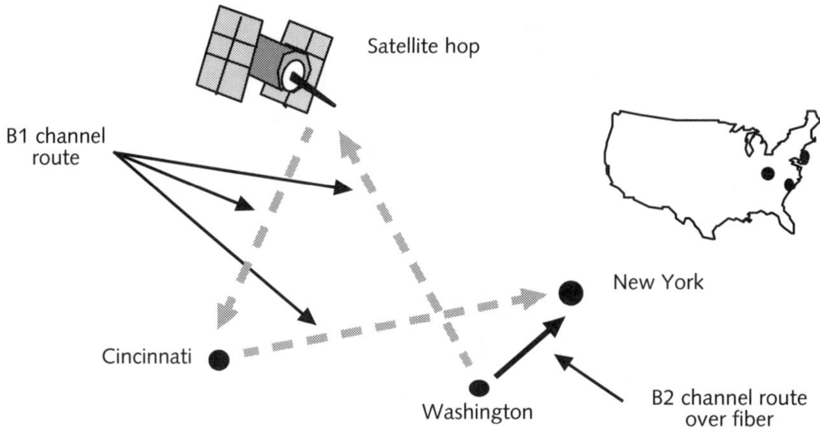

Figure 14.3   Typical telephone network routing

Once the connection has been established, the Washington branch office network will be ready to send its traffic to the New York enterprise network. Packets are to be placed on both B channels for transmission to New York.

Figure 14.4 shows the sequence that the packets are placed on the two B channels. It also shows the channel order when they arrive at the destination. As the figure shows, the Washington network device alternates channels, putting the first packet on channel one, and the second packet on channel two. Because the transmission delay is longer on channel one, packet number one will arrive well after packet number two has been received. Therefore, the network in New York City will see the packets arrive out of order. Because of the dissimilar delays, two packets will arrive from channel two for every one that arrives from channel one.

The delay causes the packets to arrive out of sequence. Instead of the packet arrival order being: 1, 2, 3, 4, 5, 6, 7, 8, 9, 10, the packets actually arrive: 2, 4, 1, 6, 8, 3, 10, 5, 7, 9. A very nasty situation, indeed!

Some network protocols, such as TCP/IP, are very robust. They are not bothered in the least by out-of-sequence packets. These protocols simply resequence the packets by themselves.

Unfortunately, other protocols are far less responsive to misordered packets. Their designers simply never considered the possibility that their protocols would ever have to deal with disparate delays over parallel links. Deliver out-of-sequence packets to these networks and the protocol comes completely unglued.

There are two ways to deal with this problem. One way is to ensure that the protocol is transmitted strictly on a single channel. Many routers, even when using

Input packet	Placed on channel	Arrival packet sequence	Output packet (Resequenced)	Comments
1	B1	2		Waiting on packet 1's arrival.
2	B2	4		
3	B1	1	1	
4	B2	6	2	
5	B1	8		Delay waiting for packet 3's arrival.
6	B2	3	3	
7	B1	10	4	
8	B2	5	5	Packet 5 delivered just in time.
9	B1	7	6	Now all packets have arrived.
10	B2	9	7	
			8	
			9	
			10	

B1 transmission delay = 2 * B2

Figure 14.4   Packet arrival table

multiple channels, can be configured in such a way as to allow distinct protocols to be assigned to a single channel. AppleTalk, for example, may be assigned to port 1, while IPX/SPX is assigned to port 2.

A better method, called packet resequencing, accommodates any protocol over parallel links. The protocol's packets are separated, sent over multiple links, and then reassembled on the far end. The key is that they are resequenced by the network device on the other side of the connection before being placed on the remote LAN. This creates a virtual channel that fools the network protocol into believing it has a higher-bandwidth connection existing over a one-channel link.

Packet resequencing is an elegant solution, because it allows multiple links to exist behind the scenes, increasing bandwidth for all protocols. That makes every protocol happy.

Packet resequencing does, however, create a bit of a problem. The remote device cannot resequence something it does not yet have. If a packet is delayed somewhere in the link, successive packets cannot be placed on the network, even if they have already arrived at the destination device.

The different channel latency forces delays, as all packets are held in buffers waiting for the errant packet to arrive. If you look closely at Figure 14.4, you will notice that packet resequencing introduces two delays in this example. In both cases, delays result because the network is being forced to wait for the slowest packet to arrive.

In the example given in Figure 14.4, the first delay occurs because the network device is waiting for the first packet to arrive. Once the packet arrives, the network device outputs packets 1 and 2. Then it has to wait for packet 3 to arrive before it can put the rest of the packets on the network. Fortunately, packet 5 arrives just in time, so there are no further delays in this example. In real life, it would be just a matter of time until another delay occurred. Worse, it is possible that a packet was dropped while transversing one of the WAN channels.

If the far side network device were to wait indefinitely for the dropped packet to arrive, the WAN connection would be effectively frozen. Therefore, most devices that support packet resequencing incorporate timers that limit the time that the device will wait for a wayward packet. If the packet does not arrive within a certain window, the device simply assumes the packet has been lost. It will then begin to introduce the remaining packets to the network. The network protocol will then be called upon to retransmit the packet that is missing.

Usually, packet delays due to resequencing are not that severe. Network protocols are usually designed to tolerate a fairly decent amount of delay. Many will wait several seconds before they begin requesting packet retransmissions. Usually, before the retransmission is required, the poky connection will have delivered its packets. However, if the network protocol is very impatient, it may retransmit delayed packets assuming that the packet was somehow lost in the network. In extreme cases where the retransmissions themselves are delayed, things can get very messy. As the retransmitted packets are delayed, even more retransmissions are generated. Things begin to degrade rather rapidly under these conditions.

Protocols Chatting Across the Backyard Fence

It is a known fact that network protocols love to talk. Nearly all network protocols spend some of their time sending and receiving packets for network or protocol management purposes. The nature of these packets varies from protocol to protocol. Many management packets take the form of routing updates and protocol keep-alives.

Network protocols send out keep-alives, or "are you still there?" messages, to ensure the network that all devices are indeed present and accounted for. Many protocols also use management packets to keep track of network topologies.

Information is maintained as to where devices are located, and how they can be reached. They share this information by exchanging routing tables across the network.

How often keep-alives and routing updates are sent across the network varies with different LAN protocols. Some LAN protocols send updates infrequently, maybe every few minutes or several times an hour. Other protocols are more assertive, sending updates every few seconds. For example, AppleTalk, one of the more chatty network protocols, sends out Routing Table Maintenance Protocol (RTMP) updates every ten to fifteen seconds. Adding to the mix are updates between the WAN devices themselves. These devices regularly exchange their own internal routing or bridging tables.

Users tend to see this management traffic as overhead. Network engineers see it as essential to maintaining the integrity of the network. No matter how they are seen, network management packets are busy overseeing the network, representing traffic the end user never sees but depends on for reliable connectivity.

When running on a LAN, protocol management packets simply place more traffic on the network. LAN bandwidths are wide enough that the extra management packets are seldom noticed. WANs, however, are an entirely different story. When protocol maintenance overhead is added to normal user traffic over WAN links, it can contribute to link saturation and can slow down response time.

Unlike LANs, which operate as a connectionless service, WAN links are usually connection-oriented services. Because a physical connection must be made, most WAN devices are configured to bring up the WAN link only when traffic is destined to or from the remote network. Similarly, WANs are configured to drop the link when there is no traffic to pass across the link. This process is called bandwidth management and its advantage is that usage charges are not accrued unless actual user traffic is present.

If users take a break from their workstation or PC, network dead time can last for minutes or hours. Perhaps the user went to the kitchen for a cup of coffee, or answered the telephone. Whatever the reason, there are significant potential savings for disconnecting a call when the user is not actively on-line. If there is no user traffic to pass, the connection can be kept down and the usage charges reduced to zero—at least in theory.

The problem is that whenever network routing updates or keep-alives need to be transmitted from either the enterprise or the remote side network, a connection must be in place. If the network device has timed out and disconnected the call, it will be necessary to reconnect the call. This happens even if there is no user data to pass across the WAN. Therefore, WAN connections are being made and charged just to pass internal device traffic and network maintenance packets. This is the case even when users are not at their computers.

If the network protocol sends out updates frequently, calls will be constantly made and usage charges will quickly accrue. As we have mentioned previously, the first minute of a call is typically the most expensive. This means network updates are being charged at the maximum rate, even though no user traffic is being passed. This is something users do not appreciate, and is something we clearly wish to avoid.

It's Not Nice to Fool Mother Nature

Clearly, the issue at hand is how to keep remote WAN connections for protocol management purposes to a minimum. Spoofing is one potential solution.

Webster defines spoof as, "to delude by underhand methods." That is actually a pretty good definition of network spoofing. Spoofing places the WAN in a stealth mode where the WAN network devices themselves, such as bridges or routers, answer up for the remote devices. When the enterprise network sends out a keep-alive or routing table update request, the device on the enterprise network answers up for the remote side. The same thing occurs for requests from the remote LAN, except they are handled by the remote site network devices. That deludes the network into thinking that everything is fine. The network goes merrily on about its business, none the wiser that the connection to the other side is not really in place at the time.

Figure 14.5 shows how this is accomplished. For example, a Novell file server on an enterprise network might send out a Service Advertisement Protocol (SAP) packet. If this occurs when the connection is down, the enterprise side WAN device will not place a call to the remote side to pass the SAP. Instead, it will acknowledge the SAP for the remote server to the Novell server on the enterprise LAN. This fools the server into believing the remote device is still connected and communicating. In reality, the connection is down and the device is temporarily off the network because user data is not being transmitted.

The same thing happens if the remote computer decides to sent a IPX Routing Information Protocol (RIP) update to the server. The remote network device acknowledges the RIP to the remote computer and, as was previously the case, does not bring up the WAN link just to pass the traffic.

LAN Spoofing

The spoofing process is not without its dangers. Protocols send out keep-alives and routing updates for a very good reason—they want to determine the status of the network. This little sleight of hand, called spoofing, can cause problems if something does indeed go wrong on the remote network, or if something in the network topology changes. Because spoofing fools the network into thinking that physically disconnected remote devices are really connected, spoofing defeats a network's native ability to assure itself that everything is as it should be.

When the remote side finally reconnects, the network may suddenly find that things are no longer as expected. While the connection was down, a remote machine may have crashed, been rebooted, powered off, or even hung. Whatever the case, the machine is likely to come up in a different state than it was the last

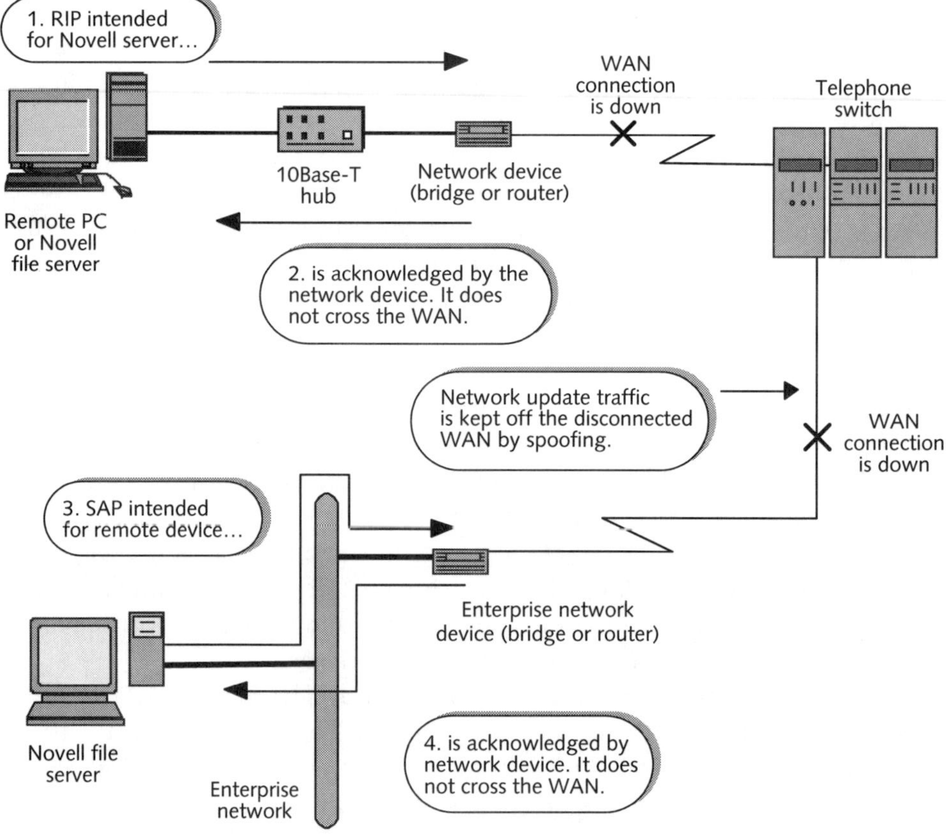

Figure 14.5   Network spoofing

time the network checked its status. However, the spoofed network does not realize that the remote host or workstation was out of commission. The fact that it has reconnected differently than the network expects leads to a myriad of potential problems. This is particularly true for file servers where reconnected users may wind up being logged in multiple times, using up precious license slots in the process.

Another frightening possibility can occur when the topology of one of the LANs is changed during the time user traffic is not present and the link is down. Perhaps a user turned off a workstation, or moved a device from one LAN segment to another. The LAN being spoofed is completely unaware of these changes. Its routing table still contains entries for old topology. After a period of time, user data causes the LANs to reconnect. During the next routing table update, the two networks suddenly realize their routing tables are different. Now both networks have a difficult decision to make: Which routing table reflects the real network topology, and which is out of date?

Clearly, implementing spoofing is not an easy matter. It takes careful thought and design. Spoofing needs to be implemented without causing serious grief for users or for the network.

Another issue that must be considered is the length of time spoofing can be in effect. The network can only be spoofed for so long before the connection must be brought up and actual management traffic is allowed to pass. Otherwise, routing tables will become hopelessly outdated. Whether the maximum spoofing interval is ten minutes, one hour, or longer, is something that network designers need to consider.

SNA Spoofing

While LAN spoofing is a relatively recent concept for WAN networking, it is not as new to other services. A form of spoofing has been in use for some time for IBM's Systems Network Architecture (SNA). SNA is a protocol used primarily for communications between IBM mainframes and remote synchronous terminals.

One of SNA's characteristics is a continuous handshaking between devices.[5] On dedicated or switched lines, there is a master/slave relationship between the communications controller and the remote unit. As a result, there is constant polling between devices.

---

5. It has been said that SNA has cornered the market on handshaking. Some SNA administrators claim the protocol does more handshaking than a politician running for election!

In the late 1980s, vendors took this into account in designing their Terminal Adapters. To spoof SNA, the controller side Terminal Adapter automatically answered status inquiries (polls) intended for the terminal. Similarly, the remote side Terminal Adapter answered up for the controller. This procedure worked well and both sides were happy, even though there was no actual response from the far side. Just as importantly, traffic over the serial connection was minimized, giving improved throughput to user data.

Interestingly, SNA uses a different tactic over LANs; it sends out a keep-alive every five or ten seconds. Therefore, it qualifies for the same treatment as LAN protocols.

WAN Integration into the OS and NOS

Network operating system (NOS) vendors have been re-evaluating how they handle network characteristics like protocol keep-alives and routing table updates.

Most LAN protocols were written at a time when interconnections of LANs were relatively rare. The designers knew they could count on the devices on the network being attached to the same physical wire. About the worst thing they had to worry about was repeater delays.

Having this degree of locality made it possible for network designers to assume certain things about the hosts and clients on the network. Unfortunately, these assumptions do not always hold true when the hosts or clients are on a metropolitan or Wide Area Network instead of a Local Area Network. As a result, some network protocols have not been able to keep pace with the changes produced by the Wide Area Network environment.

WANs have peculiarities not found in LANs. Many LAN protocols used by network designers failed to take into account characteristics that are natural to Wide Area Networks, such as packet fragmentation, parallel WAN links and on-demand networking. These issues do not exist on LANs, but become extremely important when Local Area Networks expand to metropolitan or Wide Area Networks.

The differences between LAN-, MAN- and WAN-connected clients are very significant. So much so that remote LAN access has been hindered because the operating systems (OS) and the network operating systems have not been fully aware of the Wide Area Network connection.

WAN equipment vendors have been attempting to deal with LAN protocol limitations. Unfortunately, they have met with only limited success. As we have already seen, spoofing has been tried, but it is far from the ultimate WAN solution.

The best place to deal with WAN-related issues is not in network devices, such as bridges or routers, but in the OS or NOS itself. If the NOS/OS is smart enough to realize it is dealing with WAN connections, it can control the calling patterns and adjust keep-alives and updates accordingly.

While major network vendors have come to realize they need to change the way their networks operate in order to support WANs as well as LANs, doing so is not a particularly simple or easy matter. For most LAN protocols, supporting WAN connections requires a major revision in the way the protocol operates. In some cases, it requires a complete rewrite of the NOS. In either case, it requires significant upgrades in network protocols to accommodate and better support WANs.

Desirous of supporting WANs in a better fashion, vendors such as Microsoft and Novell have begun to examine ways of incorporating WAN switched connections into their network protocol fabric. Microsoft believes that ISDN integration will make life easier for remote network users.

ISDN Integration into Windows 95

Microsoft developed an NDIS packet driver WAN Miniport ISDN architecture for Windows NT. They ported the driver to their popular Windows 95 operating system. Their goal in doing this was to ensure that computer operating systems offered users built-in ISDN WAN support fresh-out-of-the-box. No doubt, other NOS and OS vendors will follow suit.

ISDN connections can be handled in various ways under Windows 95:

- Terminal Adapters (TA) connected through the computer's com port will continue to work as before. For example, TA-based connections to Internet Service Providers (ISP) do not use the built-in ISDN support, but still work.
- ISDN bridges and routers can be connected, as before, with Network Interface Cards (NICs).
- ISDN PC cards continue to work with vendor-supplied driver software.
- Connections are possible with direct Windows 95 ISDN support.

This last category is where Windows 95's built-in ISDN comes into play. Windows 95 supports the Internet Engineering Task Force's (IETF) Point-to-Point Protocol (PPP). PPP allows network protocols, such as TCP/IP, IPX/SPX and NetBEUI, to operate over ISDN WAN links. Microsoft developed PPPMAC, an NDIS 3 PPP driver, that installs in the network control panel. To the network protocols, PPPMAC looks like a network (LAN) driver. However, behind the scenes it is responsible for getting bits to the other side of the ISDN remote connection.

Windows 95's ISDN support is relatively transparent. From an application or user point of view, nothing changes except the connection speed. Applications continue to create connections, using Windows Remote Access Services (RAS), Application Program Interface (API), or a Winsock.

Windows RAS is a software program that runs on a Windows NT server. It supports access to the server, or to the network the server resides on, depending on how it is configured. It also operates with Windows 95, making network connections an easier matter.

Third-party product integration is straightforward. Using the built-in ISDN protocol stack, the vendor's driver talks directly to WAN Miniport architecture. This eliminates the need to use third-party IP protocol stacks such as Chameleon or LAN Workplace for Windows. Native ISDN support also means that vendors are able to release products with shorter development cycles. This results in ISDN products being brought to the market faster, and at a lower cost than was possible when vendors had to write their own device drivers.

If you are interested in technical implementation details, Figure 14.6 illustrates how an independent hardware vendor (IHV) can create an ISDN WAN Miniport driver for their product. Briefly, the driver uses the Windows API to send information to the RAS. The RAS makes the TAPI calls to create the connection. A TAPI Service Provider, called the NDISWAN, then passes on the TAPI calls to an NDIS WAN Miniport via the NDIS Wrapper. Once the connection is made, PPPMAC sends and receives data to the NDIS WAN Miniport. Therefore, the RAS becomes the interface for all ISDN remote LAN access. Got that?

For developers, this capability really is a straightforward process—particularly compared to what they had to go through to create ISDN products in the past. However, it is an even bigger win for the user. When the user creates a new connection in the Windows 95 Dial-Up Networking folder, they simply choose the ISDN adapter instead of a modem in the dialog box. That is about as straightforward as it gets.

Early Windows 95 releases left out some features usually found in ISDN network devices. Multilink PPP (MP), for example, was not supported. This limited, at least initially, Windows 95's ISDN to 64-kbps bandwidth (the bandwidth supported by one ISDN B channel). Future versions will no doubt support Multilink PPP.

Additionally, Microsoft only supported their proprietary compression algorithm at first. Users were able to access devices that did not use Microsoft compression, but the connection defaulted to no compression. Also, spoofing was missing from the initial release. Microsoft plans to incorporate a similar feature they call suspend/resume in a future release.

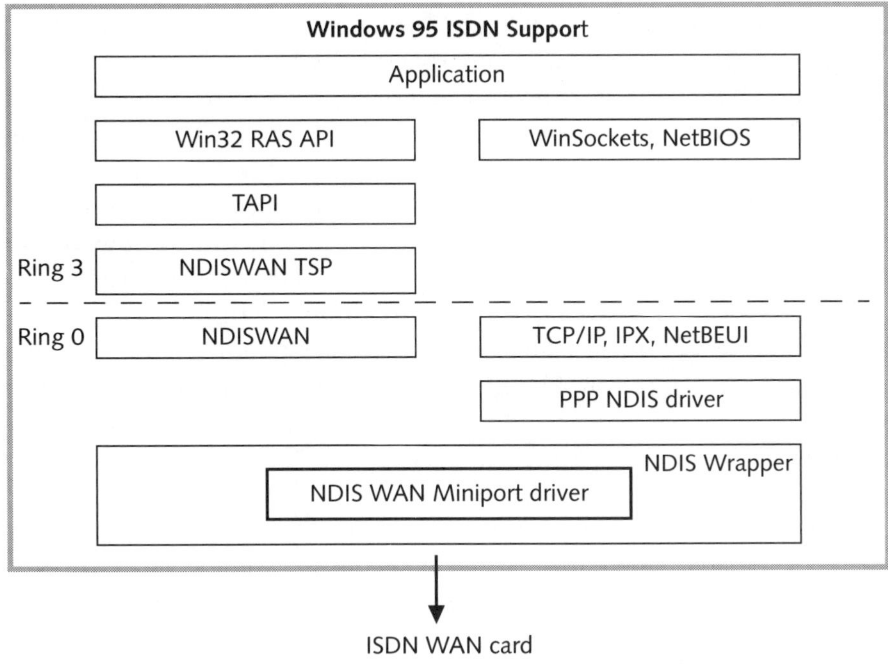

Figure 14.6   Windows 95 remote access support

Despite the limitations, the introduction of ISDN support into Windows 95 was an important first step in a process that will eventually lead to full WAN integration into the OS. Over time, this will reduce the complexity and cost of ISDN products. That is good news for users and vendors alike.

ISDN Integration into Novell NetWare

Although Microsoft integrated ISDN support into Windows 95, Novell has been relying on the NetWare Link Services Protocol (NLSP) and APIs to provide a tighter integration between their NetWare NOS and ISDN.

The NLSP protocol reduces the bandwidth consumed by IPX/SPX overhead. Prior to NLSP, IPX Routing Information Protocol (RIP) and Service Advertising Protocol (SAP) were used to broadcast updates over a network. NLSP is far less aggressive when it comes to exercising its update mechanism.

Instead of sending out updates every few seconds, which is common with RIP and SAP broadcasts, NLSP sends out a "hello" packet once every ten minutes. This significantly reduces the number of times the WAN connection is brought up just to pass network updates. When updates in the network do occur, routers running NLSP only pass along the changes instead of sending all of the information about the state of a network. This reduces the time it takes to perform the update.

The combination of fewer updates and more compact information in each update saves bandwidth, reduces WAN usage charges, and prevents the WAN link from being frequently connected for no other purpose than NOS updates. Clearly, NLSP is a significant improvement over the traditional RIP and SAP updates.

While NLSP reduces the need for mechanisms like spoofing, it does not entirely remove them. For that reason, Novell still relies on third-party vendors to support spoofing.

Novell also enhances WAN integration with their NOS through Novell's Open Data-Link Interface for Wide-Area Networks (ODI WAN) specification.

ODI WAN plays a role similar to that of a traditional network adapter card driver, except that it works for WAN connections. Basically, ODI WAN is an interface layer between a WAN adapter, the LAN communications protocols (IPX/SPX), and the WAN protocols. As is the case with Microsoft's Windows 95 ISDN implementation, this reduces the work required for ISDN WAN card vendors. To integrate with the NetWare environment using ODI WAN, a developer only needs to write a driver and a configuration database module for its WAN adapter. It is not necessary for the vendor to write the driver software from the ground up.

D Channel Solutions for Protocol Management

There may be another way of solving the protocol management problem. Some vendors are looking at the ISDN D channel, because it is a connectionless service that network devices can use for protocol control and management over WANs. Doing so means that ISDN connected networks could be managed by an out-of-band, packet based channel. Therefore, it would no longer be necessary to bring up a circuit-switched call just to transmit a keep-alive or to update a routing table.

It makes a great deal of sense for ISDN network devices to take advantage of the D channel for control and management of WAN devices. The D channel's primary function is the control and management of ISDN devices and connections. It was designed from the ground up for exactly this purpose. This makes D packet a natural for network protocol control and management. Users would be charged on a per-kilopacket basis, instead of a time-based usage basis for D channel management connections. Since management packets tend to be small compared to user data packets, these charges should be nominal.

Unfortunately, there are several problems with this otherwise ideal solution. Some vendors have expressed concern that a BRI D channel running at 9600 bps may be too slow to handle management traffic, particularly between larger networks.

Even if the D channel is deemed a good candidate for management traffic, there is a major deployment problem. North American telephone carriers have been very slow to implement national D packet access. Many central office switch D channel packet handlers have not yet been connected to the national Packet Data Networks (PDN). Therefore, D packet service is often restricted to connections within the local switch. The D channel can be used for local device management, but not for devices outside the local switch. That makes it difficult, if not impossible, for vendors to implement across-the-board D channel WAN management.

Despite these limitations, many vendors believe that D channel WAN management is viable, and plan to implement it once the telephone services providers support it. Stay tuned for further developments in out-of-band network management over WANs.

The ultimate solution for dealing with management protocol traffic is still somewhat elusive. As we have seen, there are many options to choose from, each with its own advantages and disadvantages. With the ever increasing number of telecommuters and the growth of SOHO WAN connections, one thing is sure. It is just a matter of time until users have a WAN protocol management solution that is both efficient and cost effective.

15

Optimizing WAN Connections

Ramming 10 Mbps Down a 128-kbps Pipe

Now that switched digital services are on the scene to facilitate remote network access, it is important to find ways of maximizing the efficiency of the slower speed WAN links. Let's face it, even 128 kbps is slow speed when compared to typical network bandwidths that are measured in the megabit-per-second range.

Mother Nature offers a good analogy for the kind of problems that can occur with narrow WAN pipes. We've all seen what happens during a heavy thunderstorm. If the rainfall is heavy enough, it quickly exceeds the capacity of the storm drains. When this happens, the streets get messy, flooded and dangerous.

The same analogy holds for connections between LANs. Ethernet LAN bandwidth is 10 or 100 Mbps. Token Ring has a bandwidth of either 4 or 16 Mbps. Compared to these bandwidths, ISDN's paltry 64-kbps bandwidth seems small indeed. An ISDN B channel is only a small fraction of Ethernet's 10-Mbps bandwidth (0.64% to be exact). The difference in bandwidth would cause us, at first glance, to think there simply is not enough bandwidth in ISDN to connect Local Area Networks.

Actually, this is not at all the case. Most network devices come equipped with a variety of tools they can use to help overcome the lower bandwidth capacity of ISDN lines. They can combine B channels for additional bandwidth. Network devices come equipped with compression, making them capable of effective throughputs much greater than 128 kbps. They can also filter unnecessary traffic from the WAN connection.

All these measures serve to make the WAN link perform more efficiently. We will look at each in detail shortly. Before we do, we need to consider the most important fact of all: WAN links are inherently different in nature from networks.

Contrasting LAN and WAN Bandwidth Requirements

Enterprise networks typically support a large number of hosts and clients. The range can literally be from hundreds to thousands. Remote LAN connections, on the other hand, usually support fewer clients than are found on a typical enterprise Ethernet LAN segment. Unlike an enterprise LAN, WAN connections typically support only a few users. Many support only a single user. This means that while there is less overall bandwidth, there is also less demand for bandwidth in WAN connections. However, there is an equally important point that must be made when contrasting LAN and WAN bandwidth.

In many ways, a 10-Mbps Ethernet LAN is not 10 Mbps. The real throughput in a 10-Mbps Ethernet rarely reaches anywhere near 100 percent utilization. A Digital Equipment Corporation study, reported in *Data Communications* magazine, stated that Ethernet utilization rarely exceeds 20 percent of peak capacity.[1]

Remember, this statistic represents the total traffic on the LAN itself. When comparing LAN and WAN bandwidth, it is important to recognize that not all network traffic crosses the WAN link. Local traffic on the LAN remains on the local network. Only traffic bound from one LAN to the other crosses the WAN link. This is typically a small percentage of the actual traffic on the LAN itself.

Keeping LAN traffic local is the reason networks are connected with bridges or routers in the first place. There is no need for local traffic to cross the WAN. Therefore, bridged traffic is considerably less than the twenty percent peak figure found on the LAN itself.

Clearly, it is possible to use switched digital services as a Wide Area Network link. The key is to determine whether the total interLAN traffic is appropriate for the WAN link.

There are various techniques that can be used on network protocols, such as Novell NetWare's IPX/SPX, to make them move more efficiently across the WAN. Window size can be adjusted, packets can be moved in a burst mode rather than serialized mode, and applications can be kept local to the remote machine. The

---

1. Callahan and Bradley, "New Token Ring versus Ethernet: Counterpoint," *Data Communications* **18** (January 1989): 127.

end result is that, while there is definitely a throughput contrast between WANs and LANs, the difference is not usually as dramatic as might be supposed.

Bandwidth-on-Demand

Not all Wide Area Network applications need the same bandwidth, and not all applications need the same bandwidth all of the time. A desktop videoconferencing session, for example, may be going along just fine with a particular bandwidth until the users start sharing a collaborative application or begin transferring files across the link. When additional demands occur, the current bandwidth is no longer satisfactory for the session and more bandwidth must be added.

Similarly, a remote LAN access connection may be running at a certain bandwidth until the user double-clicks on an application residing on the remote file server. All of a sudden, a remote application has been launched across the WAN and more bandwidth is required. Conversely, once the collaborative application work is done or the application is loaded into the local machine's memory, the extra bandwidth is no longer required. At this point, WAN bandwidth is wasted because much less is required than what is available.

Suppose that the requirements for the network connection change. More remote workstations are added, or a remote workstation is performing some data-intensive tasks. The single 64-kbps connection that was acceptable earlier in the session is no longer providing enough bandwidth. Perhaps two B channels (128 kbps), four B channels (256 kbps), or more, are better suited to support the user's needs. What is needed here is a variable, dynamic bandwidth system that can respond to network traffic at any given point in time.

Bandwidth Management

Bandwidth management is the key to providing this kind of dynamic throughput for WAN connections. Increases in bandwidth can be accommodated over ISDN by aggregating multiple B channels into one fast virtual B channel. For example, many ISDN Ethernet network devices can combine the two Basic Rate B channels to provide 128-kbps aggregate bandwidth. This magic occurs transparently behind the scenes using a technique known as inverse multiplexing. When implemented properly, inverse muxing is very effective. The user and the network application are none the wiser. They just see what looks like a wider data through-put path for the increased network demand.

The allocation or deallocation of extra B channels based on instantaneous and varying bandwidth conditions is called bandwidth-on-demand (BOD). If just one channel is sufficient, only one channel is used. When more traffic needs to be passed across the link, the network device places additional calls and adds B channels, according to the need.

Depending on the device, bandwidth can be scaled in 64-kbps increments, called N*64 or "N by 64," all the way from 64 kbps to T1 rates (1.544 Mbps). When traffic demands fall off, the additional channels can be dropped. If traffic picks up again, more channels can be allocated according to need. Therefore, only the required number of channels are in use based on network traffic bandwidth across the link at any given moment.

Bandwidth-on-demand minimizes connection costs. After all, it makes little sense to pay for peak bandwidth connectivity when the bandwidth is not needed. Bandwidth-on-demand WAN connections tend to be affordable, since the user only pays for the bandwidth required at a specific moment. No more, no less.

Dynamic Bandwidth Allocation

ISDN network devices that offer increased bandwidth by using inverse muxing generally do so with protocols such as BONDING and Multilink.

Bandwidth-on-demand interoperability (BONDING) is frequently used for aggregating B channels during videoconferencing sessions. Multilink Point-to-Point Protocol (MP), as defined in IETF RFC 1717, "The PPP Multilink Protocol (MP)," is more commonly used for network connectivity.[2] The main difference between the two protocols is in how additional bandwidth is handled.

BONDING does channel aggregation in hardware. All bandwidth negotiation is done when the call is set up. Once the call is in place, there is no mechanism within BONDING to allocate or deallocate additional channels. This is why BONDING is better suited for videoconferencing sessions. Typically, the band-widths required by the video and audio portions of the videoconferencing session are determined at the beginning, and remain constant throughout the session.

---

2. K. Sklower, B. Lloyd, G. McGregor, D. Carr, "The PPP Multilink Protocol (MP)," RFC 1717.

Multilink PPP channel aggregation, on the other hand, is generally done in software. This makes it less expensive to implement than BONDING. MP also has the ability to allocate and deallocate channels on the fly. Negotiation is rapid, making it ideal for bursty nature of network applications.

Inverse multiplexing, whether done by Multilink or BONDING, is typically a function of the individual device. Terminal Adapters, ISDN bridges and routers, usually come with one technique or the other incorporated into their designs. It is not at all unusual to see a device with both BONDING and Multilink PPP incorporated into its design.

Bandwidth Allocation Control Protocol (BACP)

Bandwidth Allocation Control Protocol (BACP) is an extension to the Multilink PPP bandwidth-on-demand capability. Basically, BACP describes a set of simple messages that are used to negotiate when it is appropriate to add or delete links from the Multilink bundle.

While Multilink provides a method to combine multiple B channels, it does not address the process of exactly how the devices should decide to bring up, or tear down, additional channels. When a MP session wants to add an additional channel, or shed one, the side that determines the need for more or less bandwidth simply connects or drops the call. The other side is totally unaware of this. It just sees the additional channel added or dropped, and reacts accordingly.

This kind of blind channel allocation can lead to problems. Since adding or deleting links is being done independently by each side, a condition called link thrashing can occur. For example, suppose that both sides react to the need for additional bandwidth by attempting to bring up a link at the exact same moment. Instead of an additional channel coming up, two channels are brought up, one from each side. Immediately, both devices realize that there is more bandwidth available than is actually needed. They then proceed to drop both links simultaneously. This, of course, reverts the channels back to the original condition. Now, there is not enough bandwidth. This symphony of channels being rapidly added and dropped is called link thrashing. Under extreme situations, it can go on for some time.

Link thrashing can also occur if both sides have different bandwidth-on-demand algorithms. This causes the links to behave in an unstable manner, with channels repeatedly coming up and going down due to differences in the two algorithms. There are other factors that can lead to link thrashing, as well. Therefore, there is a need to provide a coordinated method of allocating and deallocating links or channels.

With BACP, there is an early warning system. BACP allows both ends of a connection to inform the other when they are about to bring up an additional channel, or when they are preparing to tear down a channel. This allows for cleaner administration of bandwidth-on-demand changes, because the other side knows that a channel is about to be added or dropped before the change actually occurs. Thrashing is reduced because the well-behaved devices will not immediately add or drop links without first consulting the device on the other side of the connection. This makes the protocol proactive and allows for several interesting possibilities.

The device that wishes to add or drop an additional B channel has the opportunity to confirm the change before anything is done. If, for example, one side decides it wants to drop a link, it will signal this to the device on the other side. Perhaps the device on the other side of the link realizes that additional bandwidth will be needed shortly. It can signal the other device to hold off on dropping the channel. In another case, a network device might tell the other side that it is dropping a channel because someone has picked up a phone on the same ISDN multipoint line. Devices that support BACP can alert the other side not to bother with any additional call requests until the phone has been hung up.

Multirate ISDN

Besides Multilink PPP and BACP, an ISDN bandwidth-on-demand service is offered in certain areas. This service is called Multirate ISDN, although Bellcore often refers to it by the cryptic name Switched Fractional DS1 (SWF-DS1). It is also known by other names such as Wideband Switched Service, ISDN N by 64, and Switched Wideband Service.

Multilink PPP and BONDING depend on the device to do the inverse multiplexing. Multirate ISDN does the inverse channel aggregation in the central office telephone switch. This makes it somewhat hardware-independent.

The way Multirate ISDN handles channel aggregation makes it more appropriate for videoconferencing than for WANs. Bandwidth is determined on a call-by-call basis. Like BONDING, the desired number of channels is predetermined during call setup, and cannot be added or deallocated during the call. This is a problem for WAN connections that may want to add or shed B channels. However, in some cases a predetermined and constant bandwidth might make sense for network connections. In these instances, Multirate ISDN could be helpful.

Multirate has an important plus that should not be overlooked. Since channel aggregation is handled in the ISDN switch and not in the user's network equipment, this results in less expensive, less complex network equipment.

Compression

Compression effectively increases the apparent bandwidth of the WAN connection. It does this by taking a file of a given size and making it smaller. Therefore, it has real value for slower-speed WAN links.

Unfortunately, compression is one element of ISDN remote access that, as of this writing, has not been standardized. Although there are certain leaders in the field like STAC, Microsoft, Motorola and Symplex, no one method of compression has really dominated. After wrestling for some time with which compression standard to use, the IETF has had difficulty reaching consensus. There was even a strong sense at one time that the common point for agreement on compression should be simply no compression.

Even though compression is an unsettled issue, it is important when selecting ISDN equipment to pay particular attention to the compression algorithm that a particular piece of equipment supports. Unless both sides support the same compression suites, the connection will come up without compression. That can slow down the WAN link considerably. Therefore, it is important that you consult with all the sites to which you wish to connect, to determine what compression algorithms their equipment supports.

Your Mileage May Vary

Some really fantastic claims have been made for device compression recently. Vendors talk about 8:1 and higher compression figures. What is often left unsaid is the fact that compression figures are pretty much determined by file type. Ordinary text (ASCII) files compress well, binary files not so well, and pre-compressed files do quite poorly. Real networks have a combination of all three file types traveling across their wires.

Pre-compressed files are a problem for any compression algorithm. So much so that it can take longer to compress a pre-compressed file than to send the original uncompressed file. Some algorithms are smart enough to detect the pre-compressed file and let it be; others are not.

Vendor compression claims, like horsepower and gas mileage, are subject to much interpretation. If one vendor only measures compression with text files, they will get very high compression ratios. Another vendor, who uses a mix of text and binary files, will report a much lower and more realistic number. Both may be using exactly the same compression algorithm. As the fine print on the automobile sales sticker says, "Your mileage may vary."

Most ISDN network devices, working in the real world with a decent mix of text and binary files, are able to provide 3:1 compression. This means that a 128-kbps ISDN connection effectively offers approximately 300-kbps throughput.[3]

For users on a remote LAN, how does this equate to throughput for clients directly on the network? First of all, Ethernet, like almost every LAN, is a shared media. This means that everyone battles for their slice of bandwidth. Interestingly, with heavy client/server demands, the need for dedicated bandwidth became such an issue that vendors rushed in to release Ethernet and Token Ring switches. These switches are really intelligent bridges that provide dedicated network connections to workstations and servers.

While Ethernet switches can help by providing dedicated links between the switch to workstations, somewhere multiple-user packets will come together and compete for bandwidth. It might be in the switch's backplane or in the connection to a server. Whatever the case, the important point is that Ethernet and Token Ring networks operate over a shared media. No one gets all of the bandwidth all of the time. This fact must not be overlooked.

Additionally, network devices such as Network Interface Cards, routers, concentrators and repeaters, all conspire to lower throughput on the LAN. The end result is that a user directly attached to a 10-Mbps Ethernet LAN rarely sees throughput in excess of 2 Mbps. In many cases, the real throughput is considerably less—in the 600- to 700-kbps range.

This kind of throughput does not compare badly with an ISDN WAN connection. With two B channels and compression, ISDN can offer over 300-kbps throughput, or about half of the throughput found on a busy LAN.

Earlier, we discussed how an enterprise network can support hundreds or even thousands of users, while far fewer are generally served by WAN connections. To do a comparison, assume for a moment that we have a 10-Mbps Ethernet

---

3. All ISDN network devices have overhead. Therefore, no one really gets the entire 128 kbps for WAN traffic. Typically, the real bandwidth for a 2 B channel connection is 95 to 105 kbps. Therefore, with 3:1 compression, the measured throughput will generally be about 310 kbps.

supporting 300 users, and a 128-kbps ISDN WAN devoted to a single telecommuter. Doing a little arithmetic and a lot of cheating, we can see that if all 300 stations were to attempt to use the Ethernet at the same time, their effective shared bandwidth would be in the order of 33 kbps.[4] This is less than thirty percent of ISDN's 128-kbps bandwidth, all of which is dedicated to a single telecommuter.

Another fact usually forgotten in comparing ISDN with Ethernet bandwidth is that traditional Ethernet is usually a half-duplex media. Data flows in only one direction at a time. The transmitting station sends, and all the receiving stations remain quiet.[5]

ISDN, on the other hand, is a full-duplex media. It can receive data at the same time it transmits it. Therefore, ISDN is not just 64 kbps per B channel. It is 64 kbps bi-directional. It can simultaneously send and receive 64 kbps in both directions.

We might say that ISDN with 2 B channels and 3:1 compression is capable of handling 310 kbps in both directions simultaneously.[6] This implies, but does not necessarily mean, that two stations, one on each side of the WAN, can be transmitting at the same time. This is something that is not possible on standard Ethernet.

---

4. We get this figure by dividing 10,000,000 bits per second by 300 users. This gives us a per-user bandwidth of approximately 33 kbps. This math is for illustrative purposes only. These calculations are really a fabrication. Ethernet is a shared-bus media, where each station gets a short time slice to transmit their information. It is not likely that all 300 stations would want to transmit at the same exact moment. If all 300 stations did attempt to transmit simultaneously, there would be a considerable number of packet collisions, retransmission and a corresponding degradation in the network bandwidth.

5. At least we hope that the other stations will listen when a station is transmitting on an Ethernet segment. If this is not the case, the result is invariably a collision and retransmission.

6. From a marketing perspective, this makes things interesting. Several Ethernet switch vendors have been touting their Ethernet bandwidth as 20 Mbps, or 200 Mbps bandwidth for fast Ethernet. They claim this because many Ethernet switches support full duplex Ethernet. If ISDN network vendors were to follow this marketing perspective, they could state that ISDN devices offer in excess of 600-kbps throughput with full duplex and compression. Of course, this claim, like full duplex Ethernet, is somewhat deceiving. Most LAN workstations do not see large amounts of data traveling in both directions simultaneously. Most traffic, particularly on individual LAN segments, is primarily in one direction at any given moment in time. We can only hope that ISDN network vendors will continue to avoid this bit of marketing tomfoolery, and that Ethernet switch vendors will soon do the same!

16

Network devices intended to run on switched digital services can also make the best of a limited-bandwidth situation by supporting a process called filtering. Of all the steps that can be taken to equalize slower speed digital connections with higher-speed LANs, one of the most effective is filtering. Filtering improves bandwidth in the WAN connection by reducing unnecessary traffic. This allows more of the bandwidth to be dedicated to user data and less for other traffic.

Properly done, filtering results in the elimination of unwanted network traffic. Filtering can add up to 30 percent effective link bandwidth for remote LANs connected to an enterprise network, operating with a wide variety of protocols and devices.

Network devices usually have the option of assigning filters on protocol, address or on a custom packet basis.

Protocol Filtering

Protocol filtering is important for remote LAN connections to enterprise networks. Enterprises tend to support many protocols, not all which are of interest to the remote users.

The remote LAN may support only one or two of the many protocol suites found on the enterprise network. There is absolutely no sense to moving these protocols across precious WAN bandwidth if they are not needed on the other side. Protocol filtering allows these non-essential protocols to be blocked from traveling over the digital connection to the remote LAN.

Protocols can be filtered to the appropriate remote locations by various methods. Depending on how the network device is configured, it can block or permit certain protocols across the WAN. In some cases, all remote users will need the same protocols filtered or passed. More typically, some remote users need some subset of enterprise protocols, while others are interested in a different subset. Figure 16.1 illustrates how filtering can be used to provide the correct protocol suites to the appropriate users.

A network device determines which packets are to be passed or dropped based on their protocol number. People generally talk in terms of specific protocol names, such as AppleTalk, TCP/IP, etc. Rarely do users refer to the code numbers used by WAN devices for filtering by protocol.[1] Someone who was configuring an ISDN router, for example, and wished to filter AppleTalk, would need to know that Ethernet type 809b was AppleTalk over Ethernet.[2]

So how do we figure out what these magic numbers are for the various protocols? Usually the device documentation provides the hexadecimal Ethernet-type codes for common protocols in their technical documentation appendices. If not, a call to the vendor's technical support department might be helpful. If you have access to the operational documentation that comes with high-end routers, there is generally a large section devoted to protocol-type codes.

Filtering can be either inclusive or exclusive. Inclusive protocol filtering allows the network device to pass only selected protocols to the remote side. All other protocols are blocked by default. Exclusive protocol filtering, on the other hand, blocks selected protocols from moving to the remote side. All other protocols are passed by default.

It is not hard to determine when to use inclusive or exclusive filtering. Inclusive would be used when the remote network clients or hosts are using a single protocol, or only a limited number of protocols like TCP/IP and IPX. In this case, the number of protocols you want to pass to the remote side are few. Therefore, inclusive filtering is easiest to use. You can simply enter the protocols you want to pass. All other protocols are blocked by default.

---

1. Protocols may have more than one number assigned to them. Sometimes this is because protocols have different sockets to cover different applications running under the protocol. Many networkers are convinced that multiple protocol socket numbers are there just to confuse the issue as much as possible. This is networking, after all. There is no need to make things too easy or straightforward!

2. Those in the know are aware that AppleTalk over Ethernet is best known by the Apple-derived name EtherTalk.

If, on the other hand, you wish to pass most of the protocols and block only a few protocols, then exclusive filtering is easier to implement. You enter the protocols to be blocked into the network device. All other protocols are passed.

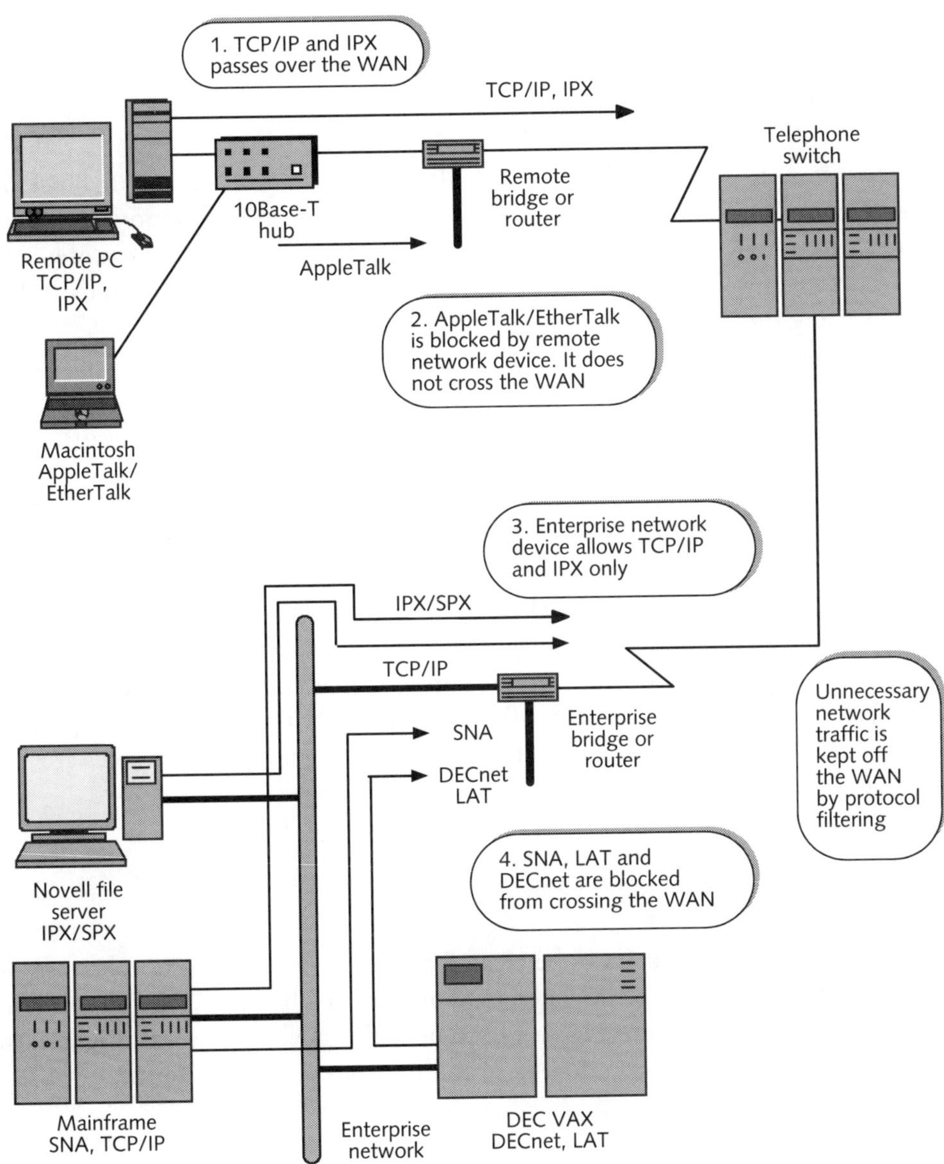

Figure 16.1   Network protocol filtering

For example, suppose you want to allow any protocol except Digital Equipment Corporation's LAT across the WAN. You would give the network device a command like "SET PROTOCOL 6004 BLOCK." The network bridge or router would be set up to block DEC LAT packets.[3]

Address Filtering

Address filtering is a little like protocol filtering. Instead of passing or blocking packets according to protocol type, it filters based on a workstation's Ethernet address. It can block packets intended for any host that is not on the remote LAN from crossing the WAN. Like protocol filtering, this limits superfluous traffic from crossing the WAN.

Address filtering can also be useful for security purposes because it can be used to prevent access over the WAN to sensitive hosts. Since every device has a unique Ethernet address, filtering on device address allows packets to be passed or trapped based on the destination device's specific Ethernet address.

Most bridges are able to learn the various addresses of network devices. This means they can keep track of the Ethernet addresses of stations on either side of the link. In a single-user environment, all the enterprise LAN bridge needs to learn is the address of its remote side client. Since the remote workstation's Ethernet address is known and does not change, the corporate side bridge can be set to forward only traffic bound for the remote address. Other traffic is filtered out at the corporate LAN side. This keeps traffic over the WAN link dedicated to packets destined for the remote computer. This is the reason that learning bridges are frequently used for telecommuters.

Custom Filtering

Custom filtering allows filters to be created for very specific purposes. For example, a custom filter might be designed to allow e-mail while denying FTP or Web access. However, custom filtering should come with a government warning sticker. Like hard whiskey, it is an acquired taste and not for the novice drinker.

---

3. This isn't a real command for a network device—it's just to give you an idea of a typical filter command format. Nor is it intended to imply DEC or their LAT protocol should not be allowed over a WAN connection. It's just an example, for heaven's sake!

Custom filtering is extremely complex because it works inside the packet and filters based on specific byte patterns. Most users will find filtering based on an Ethernet device address or protocol to be of much greater value. Unless you really know what you are doing, custom filtering is best left to advanced users.

Unicast, Multicast, and Broadcast Filtering

Networks are notorious for sending out unicast, multicast, and broadcast packets. These packets occur when there is something every station needs to know, or when the network is looking for an unknown address.

Unicast means that the packet is addressed to a specific device, which may or may not be the device across the WAN. Multicast packets are destined for a defined group of addresses. Again, computers in this group may or may not be located across the WAN. Broadcast packets are simply sent to everyone.

Unicast, multicast, and broadcast packets do have their purposes. However, these "tell all" packets are also the enemy of any WAN network connection. They consume considerable bandwidth and, in many cases, represent superfluous traffic.

There have been cases documented where large enterprise networks have carried well over 128 kbps in multicast traffic alone—more than enough to gum up an entire ISDN WAN connection.

Unicast, broadcast, and multicast traffic that is intended strictly for devices on the enterprise network have absolutely no business transversing the WAN to the remote side. Therefore, most bridges and routers can filter unicast, multicast and broadcast packets.

With on-demand calling, unicast, multicast, and broadcast packets can be especially troublesome. Any traffic sent across the WAN will result in a call being placed—even if there is no directed traffic for the remote computer. Therefore, network administrators must be especially careful to add appropriate filtering when bridges or routers are configured for on-demand calling. It is best to filter unicast, broadcast and multicast when possible to avoid extra usage charges.

While filtering can significantly reduce multicast and broadcast traffic, filtering broadcast and multicast packets should not be done indiscriminately. It is important not to eliminate them without first analyzing whether network services will be adversely affected. Some network protocols require broadcast or multicast traffic for proper operation.

For example, a device on the network may be looking for a remote workstation. It seeks the workstation by sending out a broadcast packet. If broadcast is filtered across the WAN, there will be no response. Then the network host or router will then consult its Address Resolution Protocol (ARP) entries, only to find that the workstation's entry has aged out of the routing table. In this case, the network will not find the remote workstation even though it is really on line.

Additionally, some protocols such as IPX/SPX rely on multicast and broadcast traffic for tasks such as assigning network addresses. Novell's Service Advertisement Protocol, for example, is often used by network applications to update information between servers. It depends on multicast to transmit the update information. Without multicast, servers connected across WAN links may not be able to exchange necessary information. Even worse, without this exchange of information it is possible that two network devices on the same LAN will come up with the exact same network address. Not a very pleasant situation!

Filtering on the EDN Side

Most network devices can impose filtering on either the enterprise side, the remote side of the WAN link, or both. If multiple protocols do not need to be transported across the link, it is better to filter them out on the enterprise network side rather than on the remote side.

Filtering at the enterprise side prevents unwanted traffic from transversing the link. Almost without exception, the enterprise has a number of protocols on its various segments. If unnecessary protocols are filtered on the remote side, they will have already traversed the WAN link, taking up valuable bandwidth in the process.

Filtering on the remote side keeps extraneous protocols from the enterprise off the remote LAN, but does nothing to keep them off the ISDN WAN connection. However, it may prevent unnecessary remote LAN traffic from traversing the WAN to the enterprise network.

Protocol Efficiency

There is no escaping the fact that some protocols behave poorly over WANs. Their designers optimized them for Local Area Networks, not for wide area connections. Whether the protocol is IPX/SPX, DECnet, AppleTalk or TCP/IP, there are things that need to be considered when using these protocols over WANs.

For example, Novell users should use the newer VLMs. This prevents IPX/SPX from becoming cautious and sending out small packets, and then waiting for an acknowledgment before proceeding. On LANs, this kind of pessimistic approach works. However, on serialized WAN connections the latency introduced by the WAN causes delays that slow down the protocol considerably.

Servers and clients should also be configured to use PBURST and long packets to optimize Novell NetWare's operation over WANs. Other things that can help reduce delays include keeping applications locally (including logon and logoff applications), setting buffers carefully, and adjusting the protocol's window size.[4]

---

4. Of course, there's always the "cup of coffee" approach. Launching a large application like Microsoft Excel is much the same as downloading a 5-MB file across the WAN. It can take several minutes. Common wisdom says that such applications should be kept on the local hard drive of machines connected by WANs. Some network administrators, however, prefer to keep applications on the server, even when remote LAN users are involved. In this case, remote users should be told to launch the application and then go get a cup of coffee. Once the file is launched, for the most part it remains in memory as long as the machine is not rebooted or the application closed. From then on, the WAN is typically out of the picture as far as loading the application is concerned.

17

Interoperability

Interoperability is like the weather. It affects everyone and everyone talks about it, but until recently no one really did anything about it.

Imagine the following scenario. I want to call you to discuss a business proposal. Before I can call, I have to first send you a letter asking what brand of telephone you have. This is necessary because I do not know which vendor made your telephone. I need to know the vendor because my telephone set will only work with the same manufacturer's telephone equipment. If your equipment is different from mine, we will be unable to talk.

Perhaps this sounds totally ridiculous to you. Unfortunately, in the early days of remote LAN access this was a very common situation. People wanting to connect various networks faced it time and time again. WAN equipment, particularly ISDN WAN equipment, was proprietary. Vendor A's WAN equipment simply would not talk to vendor B's device. This made it next to impossible to connect LANs on the fly.

Things are much better today, as the result of hard work on the part of several ISDN user groups, and the cooperation of many network vendors. These vendors realized that it is just plain good business to allow devices from different vendors to interoperate with their products. However, not all is rosy—at least not yet.

The ISDN Tower of Babel

Even today, non-interoperability rears its ugly head from time to time in remote LAN access. Before users can connect networks, they must know the answer to a number of important interoperability questions. Here is just a sample for your viewing pleasure:

- What equipment is on the other side? Is it a bridge? Is it a router? Is it a Terminal Adapter?
- Which vendor made the equipment?
- What network protocol, or protocols, is supported?
- Is PPP, BONDING, or some other form of channel aggregation in use?
- What is the protocol used by the ISDN link? Is it PPP, HDLC, V.120, or some other protocol?
- Is the communications protocol proprietary?
- Is the telephone network able to provide end-to-end digital connections between the networks?

Gathering all this information for each and every network users might want to interconnect with is an absolute nightmare. It is enough to drive an otherwise sober network administrator completely insane!

Interoperability, or the lack of it, is a particularly nasty problem with ISDN. Interoperability can flounder at any point—and there are so very many points for it to fail.

Provisioning

For starters, ISDN provisioning can be extremely complex. There are many different flavors of ISDN, and they do not all interoperate. Compounding the confusion even more, there are a myriad of configuration parameters. All of these must be set properly to ensure a successful end-to-end connection. Interoperability must exist between switches, between switches and CPE, between CPE and network devices, and between ISDN networks. Even if everything in ISDN interoperates, vendor equipment may or may not interoperate.

In a sense, this Tower of Babel situation is understandable. Interoperability is not particularly easy to achieve. It goes against the natural flow of things, including marketing pressures and governmental actions. Since common laws drive interstate commerce, you would think that, as a rule, the governments would be instrumental in promoting interoperability. Unfortunately, this is not always the case. Ironically, one of the biggest obstacles to interoperability over the years has turned out to be the United States Government.

The Big D: "Divestiture"

In 1984, the Justice Department, ever vigilant to investigate and break up anything it considered to be monopolistic, went after large companies like AT&T and IBM. In an event called "divestiture," the government investigated and successfully broke up the AT&T Bell System.[1] At the time, the Bell System was a model of interoperability.

With very few exceptions, the Bell System was one unified telephone network. Its cohesive structure meant that a person could pick up a telephone and call anyone else, no matter where they lived. The process was simple and intuitive. Telephones operated in the same manner and—except for minor cosmetic touches, some innovations like touch tone, and a few model variations—they even looked alike.

The hallmark of the telephone network was consistency. Things were done uniformly within the telephone network. This was true in each and every state and region. It was even somewhat true when using the telephone system in different countries. As a rule, overseas travelers did not find foreign telephones dramatically different from what they knew and loved at home.

As near as is humanly possible, everything in the telephone network worked together in harmony and unison. Sadly, for the United States, divestiture changed all that.

Literally overnight, one large cohesive Bell System was broken into seven smaller companies called Regional Bell Operating Companies or Baby Bells. Each RBOC formed its own corporate leadership, and soon each developed its own agenda for telecommunications deployment.

Telecommunications service offerings became unique to each RBOC. Tariffs were filed for the same services with widely differing rate structures. The wide variety of services caused confusion, user frustration and, most importantly, cost the network its simplicity. While many worthwhile benefits, such as competitive products and reduced equipment costs, came from divestiture, things have not been quite the same since.

---

1. Once again, our old friend Webster offers a definition that helps us understand what has really occurred. *Divestiture* is defined as the "act of divesting," or "the sale, liquidation, or spinoff of a corporate division or subsidiary." Mr. Webster informs us that the word *divestiture* is from the Medieval Latin word *dhvesthtus*. The word literally means, "to undress." Undressing is an extremely appropriate definition of the 1984 AT&T divestiture. It is exactly what the government did to the old Bell System!

While voice services still remain relatively consistent, the breakup of the Bell System caused widespread diversity and a lack of standardization for digital data services.

Interoperability, particularly for data services, immediately went by the wayside. The seven RBOCs, and thousands of independent telephone companies, began operating diverse networks that offered radically different data services at widely varying prices, with limited interconnection. Some carriers can offer a variety of digital services to their customers. Others offer only a limited number of digital services. Still others do not have a clue when they will be able to provide their customers with digital services.

Digital Nightmares

Pity the poor administrator of an enterprise network who is charged with the task of interconnecting the various corporate branches and hundreds of telecommuters scattered throughout the country. It has become virtually impossible to do this in a unified manner using digital telephone services. The administrator must deal with a plethora of state tariffs and widely varying carrier capabilities.

Out of one company came a myriad of different regional and local telephone companies. There are Regional Bell Operating Companies like Nynex, Bell Atlantic and Ameritech. There are interexchange carriers like AT&T, MCI and Sprint. Both can provide local service. Providing ubiquitous, interoperable communications in such an environment is a complete nightmare.

The confusing array of choices came at the very moment that many telephone carriers began to aggressively deploy switched digital services such as ISDN. Given that renowned national and international standards bodies spent years developing ISDN, it is reasonable for users to expect consistent and interoperable deployment of the service. However, reason and telecommunications services do not always go hand-in-hand. Largely due to divestiture, the worldwide telecommunications standard called ISDN has been deployed in so many flavors that it has become anything but standardized.

Compounding the confusion, users seeking information on switched digital services are likely to receive misleading advice from inadequately trained telephone sales representatives.

Horror stories about ISDN service ordering faux pas are legendary. Some network administrators, attempting to order ISDN for their corporate networks, have been told to send in photographs of their computers. The order takers insisted this was necessary before an order could be approved for processing. Others have been asked a series of completely irrelevant questions by telephone order takers. There was even a recent instance where a telephone account executive told their client to avoid ISDN "because it did not work." This was not a representative of some backwoods Mom and Pop telephone company. This account executive worked for one of the most aggressive RBOCs in ISDN deployment.

While telephone service providers attempt to get their act together in this area, ordering ISDN service remains the most difficult part of almost every ISDN installation. Users face interoperability issues between carriers, central office switches, long distance data calls, and even in selecting equipment like ISDN bridges, routers, and Terminal Adapters.

Users ordering ISDN face an intimidating array of options. Cumbersome deployments, confusing switch specifications, and service ordering, are disconcerting even to veteran ISDN users. The day when a user can take their ISDN network device on a business trip, connect it to the local hotel phone system and access their corporate network, is a long, long way off.

Ironically, business travelers would find high-speed digital connections from their hotel room to a desktop video or the corporate LAN extremely valuable. Yet, for the most part, telephone carriers are not even thinking about how digital services can be deployed in the hotel industry. Many hotel chains, even larger ones that cater almost exclusively to business travelers, have failed to grasp the potential of offering ISDN connections in their rooms.

It may be years before this kind of digital in-room capability is made available to the business community, even though technically the capability exists today.

No one thinks of calling a hotel in advance and asking for an ISDN connection when they make their room reservations. It is a shame, too, because hotels providing ISDN could offer in-room videoconferencing, and remote LAN access to the corporate enterprise network, right from a hotel room. While this is an unfortunate situation, no one can really blame the hotel industry, or even the business traveler, for the lack of digital in-room services. ISDN never has been a simple, portable, plug-and-play affair.

The situation is terribly complex. If a user decides to add a new line, or to move their ISDN equipment to a new location, the ISDN service has to be installed and configured. The installation requires that users understand highly technical issues that even many telephone company technicians do not fully comprehend.

To set up a line for an ISDN network device, users need to know and understand telco-speak words such as terminal type, Service Profile Identifier, and bearer service. It is a very intimidating process for users who wish for nothing more than WAN connectivity.

Ordering ISDN lines involves the telephone company service ordering system, the very same slow and awkward system that makes leased connection changes so difficult and time consuming. It typically takes a week or more for an order to be processed after it is issued to the telephone carrier. Do not assume you will get overnight service installation or changes with ISDN. It rarely, if ever, happens.

Equipment Interoperability

When remote ISDN LAN devices first made their appearance, most used proprietary communication protocols. There were a variety of reasons for this. Proprietary protocols tend to be easier and faster for vendors to implement since they have full control over the protocol. Unlike standards-based protocols, there is no committee to deal with, and there are no competitive interests at stake. This means that proprietary protocols can, in many cases, be made more feature-rich.

A proprietary protocol also helps the vendor gain market share because all the devices that wish to interconnect must be purchased from the same vendor. Thus, network users are forced to stay within one vendor's product line, making WAN interconnection between different networks very problematic. It also forces users into buying decisions that they might not wish to make.

The problem is that proprietary protocols do not interoperate. Unless there are tight corporate purchasing requirements, there is no guarantee the remote user's network device will be made by the same vendor as the enterprise network device. When the remote user attempts to connect, the different proprietary protocols will block any attempt to make the connection. That makes it impossible for vendor A's network device to connect to vendor B's device. In the past, this has left users and network administrators in a quandary as to how to deploy remote connections to the enterprise.

As we mentioned previously, a white knight has appeared in the form of Point-to-Point Protocol. The specifications for PPP are found in several RFCs.[2] Two of the most relevant are RFC 1661 and RFC 1717.[3]

---

2. The RFCs concerning Multilink PPP can be found at a number of Internet FTP and WWW sites. As of this writing, RFCs and Internet drafts are available by anonymous FTP from ds.internic.net. Look for RFCs in the directories /rfc and /internet-drafts, respectively. From time to time, the IETF updates RFCs. Usually this results in a number of changes for revised RFCs. A list of relevant PPP RFCs can be found in the Appendix.

3. W. Simpson, "The Point-to-Point Protocol (PPP)," RFC 1661. K. Sklower, B. Lloyd, G. McGregor, D. Carr, "The PPP Multilink Protocol (MP)," RFC 1717.

Since the Point-to-Point Protocol provides a standard method for transporting multiple protocols over point-to-point links, virtually any device running PPP or MP can talk with any other device, no matter which vendors are involved. PPP was initially designed as a single-channel specification for analog and digital connections. Multilink PPP allows the same interoperability between multiple B channels.

Many ISDN network equipment vendors have realized that interoperability is critical to sales. Several ISDN user groups, realizing the importance of interoperability to users, have worked with vendors in developing interoperability Implementation Agreements (IA). An IA complements an RFC. It describes how the vendors will implement the RFC or other standard into their ISDN equipment.

Referring to the PPP RFCs, the North American ISDN Users' Forum's Enterprise Network Data Interconnectivity Family has developed an implementation agreement for PPP over ISDN.[4] The Interoperability Agreement has provided networking vendors with the opportunity to work together to produce agreements for core ISDN WAN technology.

The California ISDN User's Group (CIUG) has taken this process one step further by creating interoperability bake-off sessions. These are common meetings where vendors can test between each other's WAN products in a neutral environment. In a past bake-off, network equipment vendors demonstrated interoperability between ISDN devices using MAC layer bridging and IP routing. Each vendor uses the bake-off to demonstrate the ability to connect and pass data to other vendors' equipment. Where interoperability problems exist, the vendors' engineers can go back to their offices and rework their code.

The work of the IETF, ENDIF and the CIUG has produced big benefits for the end user. It is now possible to connect remote branches and telecommuters to multiple remote networks with different vendors' equipment, and to have reasonable assurance the connection will work. This is an very encouraging development.

The emergence of full device interoperability—coupled with national and international standards and the simplification of digital line ordering—is exciting. It is entirely conceivable that from these efforts, plug-and-play ISDN networking may yet be possible. The indications are that many of today's interoperability issues will eventually vanish. As vendors approach full interoperability, installing and making ISDN WAN connections will become as easy as plugging in a telephone and picking it up to place a call. Network users and managers require and expect no less.

---

4. The implementation agreement is found in the North American ISDN User's Forum document NIUF 436-95, "5.1.11 Remote LAN Access (Additional section to the NIUF Applications Catalog as approved in the NIU-F Plenary June 9, 1995)."

National ISDN

Interoperability problems extend beyond ISDN device considerations. They extend right to the digital telephone network itself. When ISDN first appeared, the big three switch vendors (AT&T, Northern Telecom and Siemens) were not able to agree on how ISDN should be handled between their various switches.

There were many subtle, and not so subtle, differences in how each switch vendor had chosen to forge their own ISDN implementation. This prevented ISDN equipment from being moved from one switch to another and, more importantly, made ISDN data calls possible only within the local switch. Data calls could not be placed between different vendors' switches, nor even between similar switches in different locations.

This intolerable situation created islands of data connectivity, and presented a terrible problem for corporations trying to use ISDN for enterprise WAN connectivity. Ironically, interoperability was never a problem with ISDN voice service. From the beginning, an ISDN voice call could be placed from an ISDN phone to any telephone anywhere in the world. It did not matter whether the phone was digital or analog. Complete interoperability of voice service over ISDN existed from day one. One has to wonder why the designers, switch vendors and carriers were so slow to recognize how important fully interoperable ISDN data was to their new technology.

Bellcore, the research arm of the regional Bell operating companies, was one of the first to realize that deploying ISDN islands was not a good idea. They developed a standard called National ISDN (NI). National ISDN provides progressive standards for interconnection for ISDN voice and data services.

There were initially three versions of National ISDN, labeled NI-1, NI-2 and NI-3. Each version added features and built on previous generations. The National ISDN standards have been widely accepted by switch vendors and service providers. The NI-1 and NI-2 versions were the earliest deployed. An even more robust version, NI-3, was the next iteration of National ISDN.[5]

Interoperability, however nice, comes at a price. In ISDN's case, it comes at a great price. Individual switch manufacturers, such as AT&T, created their own flavors of ISDN, usually called Custom ISDN. To create a garden-variety interoperable ISDN, Bellcore and the various ISDN vendors determined that National

---

5. According to Patrick Donovan, Chairperson of the National ISDN Council (NIC), National ISDN is now denoted by using the term National ISDN-95 (NI-95), National ISDN-96 (NI-96), etc. The details of NI-95 and NI-96 are contained in Bellcore SR-3476 (Issue 1, June 1995).

ISDN would incorporate only the most basic of the custom ISDN services. This means that virtually every form of Custom ISDN is more feature-rich than National ISDN. Therefore, almost every vendor's Custom version has features and capabilities that vary widely depending on the specific switch manufacturer, but far exceed those found in generic NI.

Does the feature disparity make a difference? It may or may not, depending on the application. Many of the Custom ISDN features are pointed towards voice services, and have limited impact on the switch data capability. For data purposes, more often than not, Custom ISDN does not offer significant advantages over National ISDN. Therefore, for interoperability and flexibility in the data world, it is preferable to order National ISDN lines and vendor equipment that supports N-ISDN.

Despite its lowest-common-dominator approach, National ISDN addressed the interswitch compatibility issues rather well. It is now possible to place data calls between a number of different vendors' switches. Thanks to National ISDN, many ISDN devices can easily be moved from one switch to another with minimal reconfiguration. Now, it is up to telephone carriers to deploy signaling standards necessary to knit the various ISDN switches together.

18

Extending ISDN to Your Doorstep

Network Signaling

Network signaling is essential for connecting calls. Without it, telephone calls would never make it to your doorstep. It is the telephone signaling network that determines call routing, from the source to the destination. It is also the signaling network that alerts the far end that a call is incoming. Finally, the signaling network disconnects the call when the user indicates the connection is no longer needed.

There are two kinds of signaling systems used in the telephone network—in band and out of band. Earlier, we mentioned that SS7 handles call control in an entirely separate network from the one that provides user connections. This is called out-of-band signaling. Older networks, including POTS and Switched 56, handle call control in-band.

In-band signaling steals some of the user bandwidth to handle call management functions like call set-up and tear-down. In the process, in-band signaling reduces the bandwidth of the connection. Digital 56-kbps service, for example, actually uses 64-kbps links with 8 kbps reserved for call control. Besides reducing the throughput, in-band signaling also increases the call connection time.

Because in-band signaling is carried over the same facilities as the call itself, it must use a serialized call set-up protocol. Therefore, each switch node along the network has to be set up in sequence. A switch node cannot be set up for call routing until the preceding switch node has been set up. If there are a large number of nodes between the source and destination, the setup time can be considerable. Transcontinental Switched 56 calls, for example, take 13 to 15 seconds to set up end-to-end calls. By comparison, out-of-band signaling networks, such as ISDN, are lightning fast at connecting calls. A transcontinental ISDN call is set up in about 3 seconds.

Figure 18.1 shows a greatly (perhaps overly) simplified view of how out-of-band signaling compares with in-band. However, it should give you some idea why out-of-band signaling is so much faster than in-band.

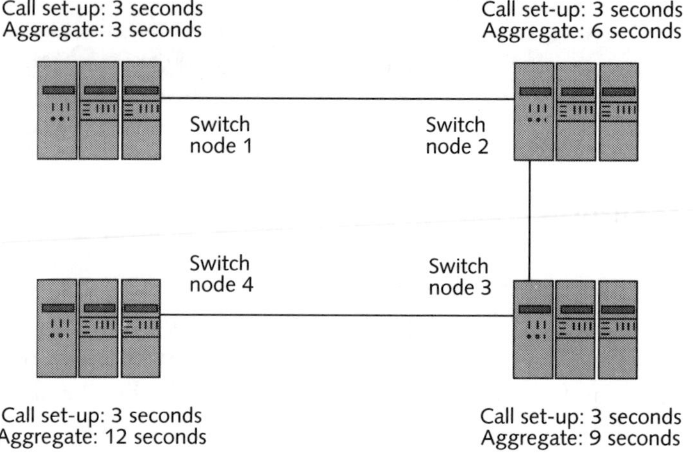

Switched 56 node call set-up

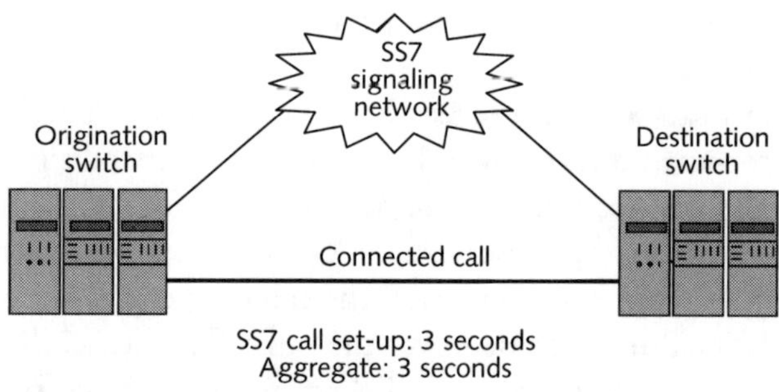

SS7 call set-up

Figure 18.1 In- and out-of-band call set-up times

Signaling System 7

You might think that something sounding as arcane as Signaling System 7 (SS7) would be something you do not need worry about, but think again. The SS7 deployment directly affects the way you make your ISDN calls.

It is possible to deploy ISDN without SS7 connections in the local telephone switch. Since SS7 forms the basis for out-of-band signaling, without it, ISDN works locally but cannot go outside the switch. While this will rarely cause problems for voice services, it will limit your ability to place data and video calls outside your local switch. Therefore, it is important you find out how much SS7 connectivity is available.

Table 18.1 illustrates how SS7 deployment affects ISDN data calls.[1]

Possible Data Calls	Not deployed	Within LATA	To IXCs
Local Calling Area	✓	✓	✓
In LATA Calls		✓	✓
National Calls			✓
International Calls			✓

Table 18.1   SS7 deployment table

- Does your Local Exchange Carrier (LEC) have SS7? If not, you will only be able to place data calls within your local calling area or LATA.
- Does your RBOC have SS7? If not, you will be confined to placing data and video calls within the regional company's area.
- Does your Interexchange Carrier (IXC) have SS7? If not, your data calls will be confined to the LATA.

---

1. A little trick can sometimes determine how much SS7 connectivity is available at your site. Monitor incoming calls on your ISDN phone, or on your analog phone if it has Caller ID. If a number is displayed for calls from other exchanges, chances are you have SS7 connections between your location and the originating exchange. For long distance calls, SS7 is entirely carrier-dependent. Therefore, depending on your long distance carrier, you may or may not have the same outgoing SS7 connections as you have incoming. For example, suppose someone whose carrier is Sprint calls you. For discussion, we'll assume that Sprint has SS7 connections to your LATA. The incoming call number would display on your phone. Now, let's assume that your carrier is AT&T and they do not have SS7 connections to your LATA. In this case, you won't be able to make an ISDN data call to the same exchange using the National ISDN networks. This is confusing and more than a little frustrating to people who need SS7 capabilities.

It takes SS7 connections between the LEC, or RBOC and IXC to place data calls anywhere you wish, and SS7 must be available on both ends. Keep this important fact in mind when ordering ISDN for your various branches and tele-commuters.

Eventually, this will be a nonissue as SS7 become ubiquitously deployed and cross-connected throughout the telephone networks. For now, remember that it pays to check with all your telephone service providers to find out just how extensive SS7 support is in each area you desire ISDN connections.[2]

Clear Channel Capability

It is important to realize that not all ISDN connections operate at the full 64-kbps rate, even with SS7 deployed. Signaling System 7 determines how calls are set up. It does not determine at what transmission speed the connections occur. In order to operate at 64 kbps from end-to-end, an ISDN connection must have 64 kbps Clear Channel Capability (64 CCC). Unless all the elements in the connection support 64 CCC, the call will go through at 56 kbps.

PRI connections need another element before they can support 64-kbps clear channel calls. They must be configured to use a line coding called Bipolar 8 Zero Substitution (B8ZS), instead of the Alternate Mark Inversion (AMI) code.

Do not let these cryptic terms throw you. Simply make sure your carrier configures your PRI circuits with B8ZS, and you should be able to connect at a full 64 kbps over the PRI.

The Last Mile

The infamous "last-mile syndrome" occurs when everything seems to be favorable for an ISDN installation. The service provider has an ISDN tariff in place, the local central office is ISDN-equipped, and the installers are well trained in ISDN

---

2. The FCC issued an order requiring all carriers to implement SS7 by December 1, 1995. That date came and went without much change in SS7 deployment. Perhaps by the time you read this, SS7 will be ubiquitously deployed and you will not have to be as concerned about the issues in this section. On the other hand, given the FCC's slow enforcement and the carrier's even slower deployment, SS7 deployment may be an issue no matter when you read this book.

installations. However, when you apply for ISDN service, you are told the service is mysteriously unavailable to you. This leaves customers scratching their heads in wonderment as to what could have possibly gone wrong.

More than likely, what has happened is that your location has exceeded the ISDN distance limitation from the central office. You are simply too far to get connections from that "last mile" to the central office. This may sound like a rare occurrence, but it happens more often than you might expect.

The specified distance for a 2B1Q ISDN connection is 18 kilofeet (approximately 3 miles) from the telephone company's local central office. This is not 18,000 feet as the crow flies, or even as the car drives. It is 18,000 feet in total wire length from the switching office to your location. Since telephone cables rarely take the shortest route, a user can be relatively close to the central office and still not be within ISDN range.

Before the service provider will honor your request for ISDN service, they will have their customer engineering division check out the wire length from the central office to the destination. If it exceeds 18 kilofeet (or a certain dB loss), the provider will not accept the ISDN order.

The last mile can be very frustrating, especially when ISDN would otherwise be advantageous for remote LAN connections. However, try not to get too discouraged if the service provider initially says no to your ISDN request. Using a little creativity and some tactful negotiations, you may well find there are ways to get around the 18-kilofoot limitation.

Overlay Technology

One method used to overcome the last-mile syndrome is overlay technology. Overlay is most often used when the local serving office is not ISDN-equipped, but another office some distance away is ISDN-ready. As Figure 18.2 illustrates, a digital link is established between the serving CO and a distant CO that does have ISDN capability. This link is part of what is known as an Interoffice Carrier System (ICS).

In the ICS, each ISDN B channel takes up a DS-0 64-kbps channel in the carrier. Interestingly, a Basic Rate Interface D channel also takes up an entire 64-kbps DS-0, something that seems like a terrible waste of bandwidth.

BRITE (BRI Terminal Extender) cards are used at both central offices to extend ISDN over the ICS. Once the carrier arrives in the non-ISDN office's channel bank, it is carried to the destination over a regular ISDN BRI.

Using overlay technology, RBOCs can extend ISDN for very long distances, anywhere from several miles to as much as 200 miles.

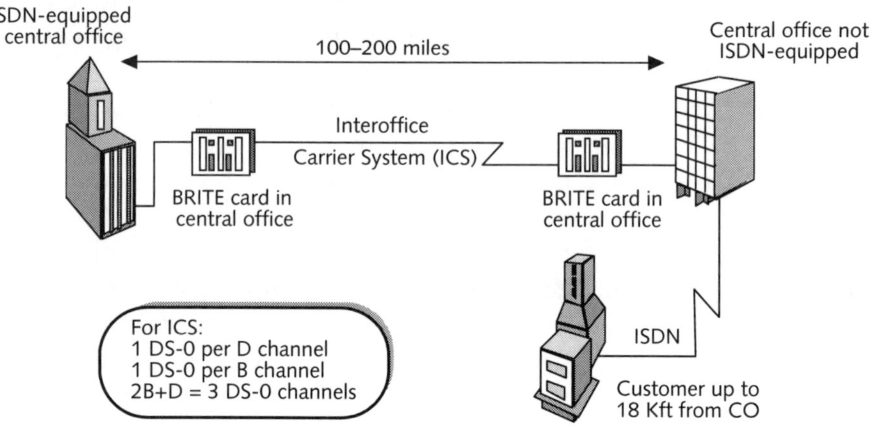

Figure 18.2   ISDN extension using ICS and BRITE cards

Midspan Repeaters

Midspan repeaters are another technology commonly used to extend ISDN from
an ISDN-equipped office. These devices, which are illustrated in Figure 18.3, are
actually digital repeaters. Midspan repeaters can be placed in locations where the
digital signal has begun to degrade. They then take the degraded digital signal and
reconstruct it. The newly replicated signal regains the full ISDN distance. This
buys the customer an additional 18 kilofeet distance.

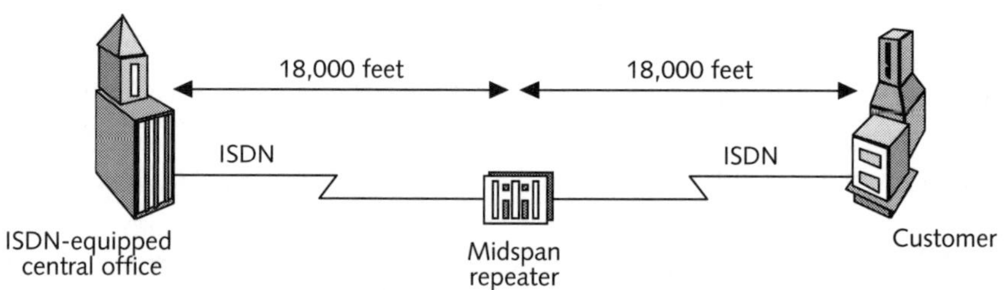

Figure 18.3   ISDN extension using midspan repeaters

Subscriber Line Carrier

Sometimes carriers use Subscriber Line Carrier (SLC) to extend ISDN. (SLC, by
the way, is pronounced *slick.*) SLC services are usually fiber-based connections

with many independent channels multiplexed onto the fiber. The SLC originates in the hosting central office, and terminates either in a local central office or close to customer locations. SLC systems have a fairly long range and are relatively inexpensive to operate, and so they are often used to extend analog services. However, many SLC units have the ability to carry ISDN over their carrier systems.[3]

As you can see, telephone carriers have many tricks up their sleeve when they are really interested in extending ISDN service. That, more than anything else, is allowing some RBOCs to ease up, or drop completely, the distance limitation for ISDN. When a customer wants service, some carriers will use whatever technology they can cost-justify to deliver ISDN to the customer's doorstep.

The down side is that each of these technologies involves extra expense in equipment procurement and installation costs. Therefore, each service provider has to decide how much of this expense they are willing or able to absorb, and how much they are willing or able to pass along to the customer. Similarly, each customer needs to decide how much extra expense they are willing to justify to enjoy ISDN connections to their various last-mile destinations.

ISDN Anywhere Programs

As we mentioned earlier, several telephone service providers offer "ISDN Anywhere" programs. The goal of these wonderful-sounding programs is to provide ISDN service anywhere it is wanted. Therefore, they all aim at ubiquity. Some ISDN Anywhere programs come close, some do not; some have so many conditions that they completely miss the mark.

People sometimes confuse "ISDN Anywhere" with "ISDN Everywhere." They are not the same thing. There is usually some fine print about exactly where "anywhere" is. It pays to read that fine print. Some carriers are very generous in what they will do to get ISDN to your location; others are not.

The point is that ISDN Anywhere programs are a good start, but they are not always what they seem to be. "ISDN Anywhere" programs are definitely worth looking into, but do some research before you get too excited by them.

---

3. Some SLC systems don't support ISDN, and are limited to analog services only. Other SLC systems are digital but functional only up to 56 kbps. Incidentally, telephone companies have a neat name for 56-kbps SLC service: "Slick Fifty Six." No, that's not a motor oil brand name!

Using Switched 56 to Extend ISDN

The good news for network administrators seeking digital connections into areas where ISDN service is not available is that ISDN interoperates well with Switched 56 services. Calls can originate from ISDN to Switched 56, or from Switched 56 to ISDN. It is even possible to connect two ISDN switches over Switched 56.

The high degree of interoperability between ISDN and Switched 56 is particularly valuable if ISDN is available in switches on both sides, but there are no SS7 connections between the switches. The local carriers can program the central office switch to pass an ISDN data call over a Switched 56 service. Digital switches can be quite smart about doing this. They can recognize an ISDN voice-bearer call and pass it along a standard network connection routing. When a data or video call comes along, they can point it to the Switched 56 network.

The Copper Umbilical Cord

Dick Tracy's famous wrist radio was transportable. It allowed Tracy to be anywhere in the city and still stay in contact with the people and resources he needed to do his job. By contrast, switched digital services are anything but portable. Most switched digital connections are firmly lashed by twisted-pair copper cable to wall-mounted faceplates.

As with most digital services, ISDN has been a tethered service requiring physical connections to the fiber- and copper-based telephone network. Considering the wide range of voice, video, and data applications supported by ISDN, its lack of mobility has been extremely constraining. This lack of portability reduces flexibility and restricts user access. It also creates dependency on outside agencies, like the telephone carriers, to provide service to the faceplate.

Fortunately, there is an alternative form of Integrated Services Digital Network, called Wireless ISDN or ISDN radio, that is breaking the copper umbilical cord and offering users communications freedom.

Wireless ISDN comes in two flavors, satellite and radio. One flavor is based on Very Small Aperture Terminal (VSAT) satellite technology. VSAT uses transportable satellite link equipment and relatively small uplink/downlink dishes. Connections are made using leased- or call-based satellite channels. The other flavor, ISDN radio, uses specialized modems called spread-spectrum modems. These modems distribute the signal over a wide bandwidth, thereby reducing interference and improving security.

By using radio or satellite connections, ISDN can be made available to any location, whether it has wired ISDN service or not. Not only does this overcome the last-mile problem, it also gives ISDN links immediacy and flexibility.

Satellite ISDN is the super version of wireless ISDN. Like Superman, it can leap tall buildings in a single bound, is faster than a speeding bullet, and can literally span continents. ISDN radio is intended for local, more restricted communications. Its range is much more limited, since it operates primarily with unlicensed transmitters operating with one watt or less output power. This low power restricts the range, depending on antenna height and terrain, to a maximum 30-mile radius. This is usually enough range to overcome the last-mile problem, but is not enough to span continents the way ISDN satellite can.

The bandwidth a wireless ISDN connection can provide depends on the amount of spectrum bandwidth available to the connection. A BRI, for example, requires 160-kbps full-duplex radio bandwidth. Two ISDN BRIs require 312 kbps; three, 464 kbps; four, 616 kbps; and so on. Obviously, transmission equipment and satellite channels must have wide enough spectrum to support the desired ISDN bandwidth

As we have seen, wired ISDN's biggest drawbacks are lengthy, complex installations, distance limitations, and a lack of ubiquity. ISDN radio can help resolve each of these shortcomings by providing transportability to ISDN services.

Wireless ISDN can help speed up the installation process. While terrestrial ISDN orders take days, or even weeks to process, ISDN radio equipment can set up nearly on-the-fly connections. Even with satellite connections, it is not unusual to have service in place within 24 hours.

Wireless makes ISDN available wherever it is needed. Transportability makes ISDN radio especially valuable when unexpected events take place. It can handle with equal aplomb a network outage, an urgent last minute site coming on-line, or a network demonstration that was scheduled without advance notice.

Wireless ISDN offers a degree of independence from the service providers. Do not dismiss this point too casually. Independence from the telephone service providers carries with it tremendous options. For example, where terrestrial ISDN is not available, ISDN radio can step in as an extension service. ISDN radio's transportability can bring ISDN to any non-ISDN location. Even if there is no ISDN-equipped CO for miles, wireless ISDN can provide service. Satellites can extend ISDN from any ISDN public network to remote locations that do not have access to terrestrial ISDN.

ISDN Radio Connections

As Figure 18.4 illustrates, wireless ISDN can connect an assortment of ISDN equipment over a variety of digital links. Devices like radio, satellite, cable, microwave, laser, infrared, and multiplexed networks can all be used to transport ISDN. This adds mobility, flexibility, and ubiquity to ISDN—especially where the last-mile syndrome would otherwise prevent ISDN's use.

Wireless ISDN connections make use of the usual ISDN Terminal Adapter or bridge/router. Instead of plugging the device into the wallplate, the network bridge/router or Terminal Adapter is connected to a satellite or radio converter. Adding a spread-spectrum modem or a connection to a digital uplink completes the installation.

Wireless ISDN uses radio modems that operate in the 900-MHz band (902 to 928 MHz) or the 2.4-GHz band (2.400 to 2.485 GHz). The radio antenna is

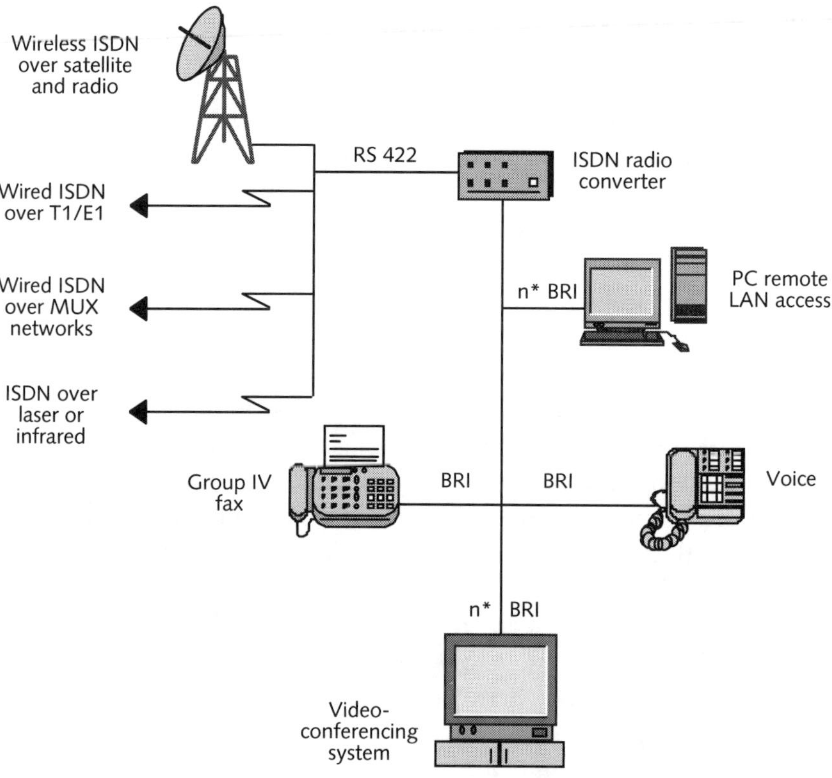

Figure 18.4   Mobile ISDN versatility

usually a Yagi or a 0.75-meter dish. Satellite dishes are somewhat larger than those used for radio. Their size depends on the particular satellite being used, the location in the satellite's footprint area, and the frequencies in use.

Satellite ISDN connections use a technology based on a signaling protocol called Demand Assigned Multiple Access (DAMA). Like ISDN, DAMA uses out-of-band signaling. This happy coincidence makes DAMA compatible with ISDN signaling.

Satellite channels can be obtained directly from a satellite owner or through a satellite distributor. Distributors often take care of all the access details, which includes providing a private earth station and VSAT equipment.

Satellite service is available in a number of configurations:

- Point-to-point service that connects two sites.
- Point-to-multipoint service that connects a central hub to a number of different locations.
- Mesh service that acts like a matrix switch connecting any point to any other point.

Each of these services can be ordered as a full-time service, equivalent to a leased or dedicated line, or as a usage-based plus monthly fee satellite service, similar to terrestrial ISDN.

Redundancy

Wireless ISDN has an important advantage when used in conjunction with wired ISDN. It provides redundancy.

Redundant circuits are often used for critical data connections. Most customers do not know this, but truly redundant telephone circuits are not very common. Even when the corporate networking department orders separate primary and secondary leased circuits, they may not be redundant. The circuits often run in the same cable sheath or over the same carrier. If a cable is cut or a tandem telephone switch inexplicably goes down, redundancy goes right out the window along with essential connectivity. The unexpected outage leaves the beleaguered network manager wondering what happened to the company's carefully developed redundancy plan.

By nature, ISDN radio is redundant. Connections are not made over the terrestrial telephone network, but through radio or satellite channels. The local telephone company is either out of the loop entirely, or is ancillary to the connection. This makes terrestrial outages of far less consequence.

Figure 18.5 shows how a redundant WAN satellite connection can provide backup service for terrestrial connections. ISDN connections over radio or satellite, if not already in place, can often be made available within 24 hours. Therefore, for critical business applications that must stay connected no matter what, wireless ISDN is very attractive.

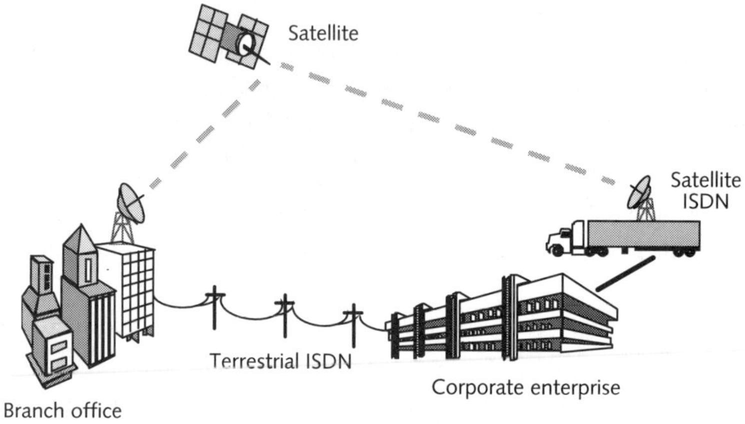

Figure 18.5   Redundant WAN satellite connections

Network administrators who are challenged to keep their networks alive regardless of the situation will find ISDN radio particularly attractive. Should a natural disaster, such as an earthquake, fire, flood or tornado, disrupt terrestrial-based WAN connections, the network manager can call on ISDN radio to restore services in short order. ISDN radio can also be kept in hot standby, or can even function in active service. When the terrestrial connections go down, the ISDN radio links can be quickly pressed into service.

ISDN Radio Disadvantages

ISDN radio is not without its disadvantages. The most obvious, and potentially most costly, is that it requires extra equipment, some of which is fairly high-priced and difficult to transport.

Besides the usual networking experience, ISDN radio requires personnel who know how to set up, maintain and operate radio equipment. Technicians have to understand how to aim satellite dishes and adjust microwave antennas. They also need to deal with radio transmission equipment and interference.

As most radio technicians know, radio transmission equipment is part science, part art, and part black magic. People versed in both networking and radio are very hard to find. All of this extra baggage can add to the expense and complexity of network operations.

Quality of Service

ISDN radio is subject to the same limitations as any radio service. Interference and poor signal quality can quickly cause problems. Changing weather conditions can interfere with microwave transmission frequencies. Fog can play havoc with radio transmissions. Snow and ice are deadly to satellite dishes. Even tree growth can drastically alter the transmission characteristics.

Most importantly, satellite delays can adversely affect ISDN radio's Quality of Service (QOS). Satellite links introduce a fair amount of transmission delay. If severe enough, delays can drastically reduce ISDN's QOS. This results in garbled voice transmissions, scrambled video and collapsed WAN connections.

Table 18.2 shows comparative delays between various leased and switched services. As can be seen, a terrestrial ISDN connection delays the signal about 10 milliseconds (ms). An international terrestrial circuit experiences end-to-end delays on the order of 140 ms. A single satellite hop has a marginal range one-way delay of 260 ms. Bi-directionally, satellite delays can be well over 500 ms. This puts satellite delays in an unacceptable range for some applications.

Service	Delay (ms)	QOS
National T-1 service	1	Acceptable (< 150 ms)
Terrestrial ISDN Basic Rate Interface (BRI)	10	Acceptable (< 150 ms)
National analog service	25	Acceptable (< 150 ms)
International terrestrial circuit	140	Acceptable (< 150 ms)
Single-hop satellite	260	Marginal (= 150–400 m)
Bi-directional satellite	520	Unacceptable (> 400 ms)

Table 18.2   Quality of Service due to path delays

Delays can cause problems for isochronous applications that require audio and video synchronization, or that are intolerant of disruptions in information flow. Delays can also cause big problems for network applications. If the delay is long enough, the network protocol may assume that the communications link has been lost and time-out the session.

Network response to delays can cause unnecessary retransmissions, collisions and, in severe cases, broadcast storms. Users considering ISDN radio for network or time-sensitive applications should take steps to assure themselves the technology is workable for them.

Any solution to extend ISDN requires additional equipment and knowledge, and often adds to the cost of the installation, the monthly charge, and the operational expenses for the service. Even so, where the option is no connectivity or even more expensive digital service alternatives, wireless ISDN appears worthy of consideration. ISDN radio's ability to supply services to any location anywhere in the world, regardless of whether or not ISDN is available from the telephone carrier, gives users better options for remote LAN access. If your local service provider gives you a blank stare when you ask for ISDN connections, ISDN radio could be your answer.

19

The Compleat Telecommuter

Telecommuting involves much more than remote LAN access. The aim of telecommuting is to set up an environment in the home that duplicates, as much as possible, the environment the worker finds in the office. Therefore, when designing a telecommuting solution, some consideration must be given to things other than network connections to the corporate enterprise.

Consider, for a moment, the set-up most workers have in their offices. Offices typically have at least one computer connected to the corporate enterprise network, a telephone and some form of access to fax services. This being the case, network devices that provide access to remote LANs are only part of telecommuting. Setting up a remote LAN connection without including voice and fax services provides only a partial solution and may not fully empower the telecommuter.

If you do not think this is an important issue, consider a survey recently conducted by *U.S. News & World Report*. In an interview of 820 adults concerning telecommuting, an overwhelming majority of almost 70 percent said they preferred to work in the office because at home they did not have access to a copier or fax machine. Clearly, there is much more to telecommuting than simply dropping a data line in the home.

A Few Words on Voice Capabilities

The telecommuter usually needs voice services to keep in touch with clients, with co-workers in the office, and to check voice mail. The telecommuter may also need fax or modem capability from the corporate LAN, through fax modems, or with standalone fax machines.

Just as remote LAN access requires some understanding of networking requirements, voice and fax requirements must also be taken into account. Therefore, the same technicians who install data services also need to understand something about fax and voice services. They may also need to install equipment that supports these services.

Before the crew arrives, an analysis of voice and fax services for the telecommuter should be conducted. The analysis should answer several key questions:

- What do corporate users do with their telephones? The answer to this question may not be as obvious as you think.
- Do they use voice mail?
- Should their phones be part of the corporate Digital Centrex or Private Branch Exchange (PBX)? Or should they be on standalone lines?
- What voice features should the users be given? For example, do they need to forward their phone to another extension, send calls to voice mail, or be able to program speed dial buttons from their home office telephone?
- Should users have access to their office line at home?

Working through these issues requires close coordination with the company's telecommunications specialists. Unfortunately, coordination between networking and telecommunications staff is not necessarily a foregone conclusion in most corporate environments. The fact is, there is often a wide chasm between telecommunications and network services staff.

Generally, the folks on the telecommunications side, such as voice technicians and telephone service providers, may use the network but not understand networking very well. They usually have their hands full with new installations, trouble calls and call maintenance issues.

While network managers and network operational staff usually understand how to use telephones, they do not necessarily know how to deploy voice telephone systems, nor understand the issues involved in voice service. Like the voice specialists, network folks are generally kept busy with network requests, updates, data problems, etc. They do not have time to study or understand the voice system.

Typically, both staffs are so overwhelmed by their own daily work they often do not have much time to spend interfacing with each other. They may even reside in different departments and have different management channels. As a result, one side may have absolutely no idea what the other is doing, and often know even less about how each other's equipment works. This often leaves the home worker out in the cold in terms of achieving a complete telecommunications solution.

Before a telecommunications initiative occurs, it is important for the voice and data managers to get together and map out a course that intertwines the two groups. Installations, end user support and upgrades need to be done in a coordinated, careful manner. Cross-training between voice and data staff on the other unit's equipment does not hurt either.

Supplying Voice Services

There are several different configurations that can be used to supply a complete telecommunications solution. Figure 19.1 illustrates the first of three of the most common ISDN related methods.

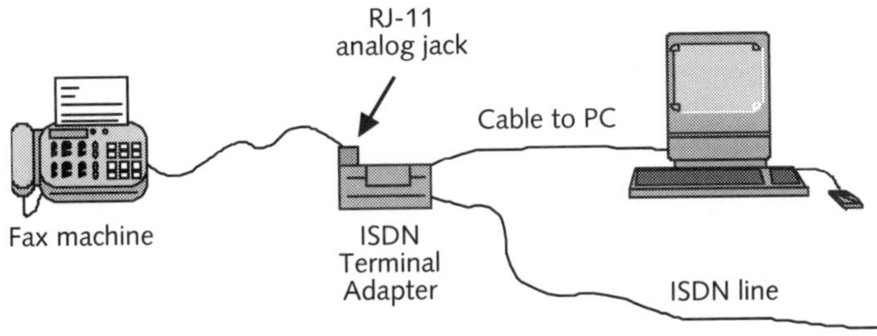

Figure 19.1   Telecommuting method 1

Method 1: RJ-11 Connectors on ISDN Devices

Method 1 takes advantage of a number of ISDN data products on the market that allow one of the B channels to function as an analog telephone line. These products include an RJ-11 telephone jack, allowing the user to plug in a POTS telephone, modem, or fax machine into the unit. Since the B channel can be set up for voice-bearer services, POTS devices that connect to the RJ-11 jack think they are connected to an analog telephone line. This allows the POTS devices to make, and sometimes receive, calls from analog telephones, modems, or fax machines.

In method 1, one device is responsible for all the telecommuting support. This makes the installation and support of this method relatively straightforward. However, it also limits throughput by temporarily or permanently removing one of the B channels from the network connection.

One feature often found in devices that support this method is multi-service bandwidth allocation. Suppose an analog phone is plugged into the RJ-11 jack on the device. When the user lifts the telephone handset to make a voice call, the device is intelligent enough to recognize this and respond. It automatically removes one of the B channel network connections and uses it for a voice call. Once the voice call has been terminated, the ISDN device automatically re-establishes the network call on that channel.

Method 2: ISDN Multipoint Lines

Figure 19.2 illustrates the second common method of providing comprehensive telecommuting access.

Method 2 uses an ISDN multipoint line to support both voice and data devices. An ISDN BRI is available as a single-point or multipoint line. A single-point line supports only one device on the line. A multipoint supports up to eight individual devices all on the same line. Each device has its own telephone number, courtesy of our old friend the SPID. Multipoint ISDN makes it possible to simultaneously connect a network device and telephone to the same line.

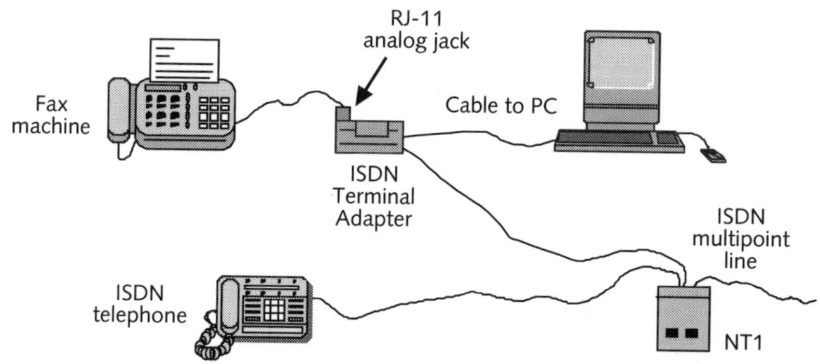

Figure 19.2   Telecommuting method 2

Each device can have access to the B and D channels. Since the D channel uses a packetized X.25 protocol, all devices can simultaneously access the D channel. This makes it appear as if each device has a dedicated D channel connection that operates independently of all the other devices on the same multipoint. By the way, all National ISDN lines are configured as multipoint lines. Therefore, they can be used to support this telecommuting method.

The B channel works a little differently. All devices have to contend for the two B channels on the multipoint line. Once both B channels are occupied with any combination of voice or data calls, no other device can make calls. Both channels can be occupied either by one device that takes both channels, or by two devices occupying a single channel each.

POTS devices cannot directly operate on multipoint ISDN lines. Therefore, unless the ISDN device has an RJ-11 analog jack, only ISDN devices are supported in this method. However, not all ISDN devices support multipoint lines. If you plan to use this method, be sure your devices support multipoint services from your local switch.

Method 3: Multiple ISDN and POTS Lines

Figure 19.3 illustrates the third method of providing telecommuting access. It is more comprehensive than either method 1 or 2.

Method 3 employs two or more ISDN lines to support voice and data services. This method works well with a mix of analog lines. Doing so combines fax, voice data and possibly video to provide comprehensive telecommuting services. This method allows the connection of any device, voice or data. Therefore, it is the most straightforward and also the most robust.

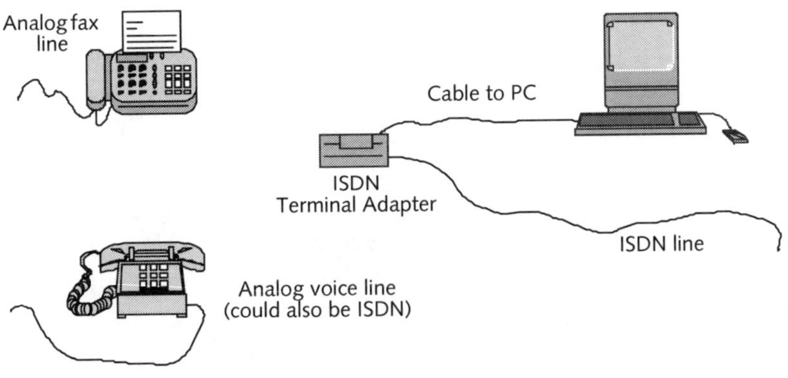

Figure 19.3   Telecommuting method 3

Since method 3 requires the installation of multiple telephone lines, this method carries the disadvantage of being the most expensive method of providing full telecommuting services. As can be seen from Figure 19.3, each device is connected to a single line dedicated to that device. The voice service can be supplied through an analog or an ISDN line, depending on the desired features.

Intelligent B Channel Connections for Analog Services

With the right equipment, methods 1 and 2 can be installed with intelligent channel contention. The intelligent network device connects to the remote LAN using as many B channels as are needed, based on the number of available channels on the single or multipoint line. If both B channels are free, the device has the option of taking both. If only one channel is available, the device will connect at 64 kbps over a single channel. In either case, the intelligent network device continuously monitors the D channel. By watching the D channel, it can tell if any other device on the ISDN connection has requested or wants to release a B channel.

If, for example, the intelligent network device has both B channels in service and notices a call set-up message coming from another device, it simply releases one of the channels. That makes the channel available for the other device. If the other device happens to be an ISDN telephone, the B channel will be freed up for a voice call. During the call, network throughput will slow down to the single B channel rate, but the connection will still be in place.

After the voice call has been completed and the user hangs up the phone, the B channel used for the voice call will be released. Once the intelligent network device notices that the channel has been released, it can grab it if additional bandwidth is required by the network connection. If the additional bandwidth is not necessary at the moment, the intelligent network device may decide to simply leave the channel alone so it is kept open for other devices. Keeping the channel open when it is not needed also saves usage charges.

The intelligent ISDN equipment takes care of automatic call control and on-demand bandwidth management. The user knows nothing of the magic occurring behind the scenes that makes this all possible. Having been given simultaneous, non-blocking access to data, voice and fax services, the worker has the ability to work at home much as they would in the office. Implemented properly, this capability can be very slick indeed.

It takes network equipment specifically designed for this function to take advantage of this intelligent bandwidth management and automatic call control. Obviously, not every ISDN network device supports this functionality.

Earlier, we mentioned Bandwidth Allocation Control Protocol (BACP). By using BACP, devices inherit the intelligence to manage B channel resources effectively.[1] Multiple voice and data devices can occupy the same multipoint BRI line and make very effective use of the bandwidth provided by the two B channels.

---

1. See Chapter 15, "Optimizing WAN Connections," for more information on Bandwidth Allocation Control Protocol.

Home Equipment Issues

Providing a full complement of telecommunications services involves sorting through a number of complex issues.

Earlier, we said the telecommuter should have the same facilities available at home as in the office. However, in deployment, telecommuting is different from office setups in many ways. Usually, there are issues related to telecommuting that are not the same as those faced in the office. Some of the issues are technical. Many of the issues are procedural and legal.

Ringing Voltage

Placing calls in an analog environment is easy. When the caller takes the receiver off the handset or starts a fax or modem connection, a switch is thrown in the device that closes the circuit to the central office switch. The telephone switch, seeing the circuit closed, then issues a dial tone to the analog device. This signals to the user or the device to start dialing. The switch collects the series of touch tones or pulses that allow dialing, and then connects the call to its requested destination.

Answering calls is nearly as straightforward. When an incoming call is intended for an analog device, the telephone switch places a ringing voltage on the line.[2] The voltage causes the bell or ringer in the telephone to operate, alerting the user or the device to the incoming call. When the handset is picked up, or the modem or fax machine goes off-hook, the switch turns off the ringing voltage and the connection begins.

Ringing voltage is almost taken for granted these days. However, when it comes to digital devices, it creates a problem. Ringing voltage can be quite substantial, in the order of 100 volts AC.[3] This is brute force compared with digital services, such as ISDN, which signals connections entirely through the D channel.

---

2. Telephone installers often refer to ringing voltage as *ringing current*. Either is appropriate for, as Ohm's Law points out, a device with impedance and an applied voltage has current.

3. Analog ringing voltage creates an interesting situation when ISDN and analog devices are accidentally interchanged. Both analog and U-interface devices (ISDN devices with built in NT-1s) use RJ-11 jacks. That makes it all too easy to plug the wrong device into the wrong jack. Plugging an analog device into an ISDN line does no harm. The analog device simply does not work. Plugging an ISDN device into an analog line is another story altogether. ISDN devices work at considerably lower voltages and currents than what is sent down the line when the central office switch wants to ring an analog device. Should a call be placed to that line, the ringing voltage is enough to completely destroy an ISDN device.

D channel signaling uses digital packet data that operates in a significantly lower voltage range. Under ISDN there is no ringing voltage, so the power to ring the connected analog devices cannot come from the central office. Therefore, ISDN devices that support RJ-11 jacks must generate ringing voltage for any attached analog devices.

Incorporating ringing voltage in ISDN devices requires much larger power supplies than are normally necessary for the ISDN device itself. To reduce cost and size, ISDN devices that support RJ-11 analog jacks may not support the ringing voltage. This allows connected analog devices to make, but not to receive, calls. Those ISDN devices that do supply ringing voltage to their RJ-11 jack, more often than not, use external power supplies.

Radio Frequency Interference

In the United States, the Federal Communications Commission (FCC) certifies devices in terms of their radio frequency (RF) emissions. At first, it might seem strange that the FCC should be concerned with devices that have no antennas—especially since digital devices are not designed to broadcast radio signals in the first place. However, there is a very good reason for the FCC's involvement.

Computers, routers, bridges, and even digital telephones emit some level of RF energy. Inside each of these devices are oscillators that are used to generate a clocking frequency. The computer clock frequency determines, in part, how fast the microprocessor operates. The faster the clock, the faster, in general, the PC. That is why users often hear of new CPUs that run 100, 150 and 200 megahertz (MHz).

The internal oscillators in digital devices such as computers typically operate in the broadcast frequencies from 1 MHz to 200 MHz. Therefore, they can and often do act like tiny radio transmitters. The wiring inside the computer, the cables connecting it to peripherals, and even the power cord, can act as radio antennas. Radio Frequency Interference (RFI) from computer devices operating in this range can easily cause interference to devices operating in the broadcast spectrum.[4]

---

4.   In North America, AM stations transmit from 550 KHz to 1.6 MHz and FM from 88 MHz to 108 MHz. In between the two broadcast bands are various shortwave services such as radio amateurs, military communications, and shortwave broadcasting services. A computer emitting excessive RFI can interfere with a broadcast frequency near its clock frequency or in multiples of that frequency, known as harmonics. For example, a computer bus running at 50 MHz has the potential to interfere with stations near that frequency, and with FM stations at 100 MHz.

If you are curious, turn on your computer and hold a portable shortwave radio close to the computer's CPU or monitor. Tune the radio bands and listen to the various noises and spurious signals. Now, turn off your computer or move the portable radio a good distance from the PC. Listen again. Chances are that many of the spurious signals and noises you heard when the radio was near the computer are now gone.

FCC Device Certification

In an attempt to reduce interference caused by digital devices, the FCC has created certification requirements for devices sold in the Unites States.[5] Manufacturers are required to submit their devices to laboratories operated by the FCC. The FCC lab evaluates the device and assigns a "type acceptance" to the device, depending on how much RF leakage occurs. Devices that are accepted by the FCC are assigned to one of two classes, Class A or Class B.

According to the FCC, Class B certification applies to equipment, "designed to provide reasonable protection against harmful interference in a residential installation." Therefore, all equipment intended for use in a home must carry a Class B certification. However, there is no guarantee offered by Class B certification "that interference will not occur in a particular installation." In other words, the FCC expects that the Class B device will not cause problems in home use. Still, they are warning that we are using the device at our own risk. Even Class B devices may cause interference.

The second certification class, Class A, is intended for use in an office but not in homes. Class A is less restrictive in emission control than Class B. This is because the FCC believes that offices seldom have radios or televisions.[6]

What happens if a device with Class A certification is assigned to a home user? Several things. First, it must be said that if the device does not meet Class B certification, it is technically illegal to install it in a residence. From a practical point of view, there is some risk of interference with home communications devices. However, despite the legality and the risk, Class A network devices do manage to get installed in homes all the time.

---

5. The United States government is not unique in setting RFI certification standards. Many other countries have done the same through their regulatory agencies.

6. Given the number of television and radios that have been showing up in corporate offices lately, one has to wonder if the FCC can make this statement with a straight face!

Sometimes Class A units find their way into home installations due to a lack of education. Some network installers simply fail to pay attention to the FCC's type certification. Even if they do check, they are still likely to install Class A equipment in the home. There is a very practical reason for this.

Many remote network device vendors are concerned with type B certification. However, a few are not. The vendors who are not expect their bridges, routers, Terminal Adapters and telephones to be used only in the office. Understandably, to save money and (sometimes) time, they sought and received only type A certification.[7]

Should you install type A devices in a worker's home? Probably not. To keep things legal and to avoid possible interference, devices intended only for office use should not be placed in workers' homes.

Four ISDN Home Weaknesses

When it comes to home use, ISDN has four weaknesses: availability, expense, a lack of powering from the central office, and the inability to provide extension telephone service. All of these issues work against using ISDN as a total home solution. Depending on the installation, they may have somewhat less impact on using ISDN for telecommuting. However, each must be taken into consideration when considering ISDN as a telecommuting solution.

Expense and Availability

As we mentioned earlier, depending on the local telephone tariffs, ISDN can be moderately expensive. Incredibly, some RBOCs are increasing their ISDN rates instead of lowering them. This cannot help deployment of the service.

---

7. As might be expected, devices meeting Class B certification for home use must have additional shielding. Several computer vendors who have submitted their machines to the FCC have been told that they must add extensive shielding to gain type B acceptance. Adding extra shielding increases the costs and weight of the product. If you are curious about your device's certification, look on the back or bottom. There should be a label dealing with Part 15 of the FCC Rules and Regulations. The device's label should state whether it achieved type A or B certification. If the device is not labeled, look in the operations manual. The FCC type certification should be found either in the front of the manual, or in the appendix in the back. If you find no mention of type acceptance either in the manual or on the device, you should worry.

The equipment price situation is a little more tenable. ISDN equipment is dropping in price. While some ISDN devices remain on the expensive side, others are becoming quite a bargain. ISDN network devices often fall into the same price range as high-end modems.

Availability can be an issue, even if price is not. We have already discussed problems in ISDN deployment. ISDN service is simply not available everywhere.[8] The same holds true for ISDN devices.

You may find ISDN devices hard to locate. They are not readily available everywhere. For example, you cannot go to Radio Shack or CompUSA and buy an ISDN bridge—at least not yet. Your telecommuters may need assistance in locating the appropriate ISDN devices. The good news is that many computer mailorder houses routinely offer selected ISDN equipment. The situation is indeed improving, but it still has a long way to go.

Because of availability issues, your company may decide to sell, lease, or outright provide ISDN equipment for telecommuters. If so, this will save telecommuters the trouble of searching for devices. It will also help prevent telecommuters from purchasing devices that are not compatible with your corporate network.

External Powering

ISDN devices cannot be powered from the telephone network itself, as is the case with many POTS devices. Analog devices plugged into a POTS telephone line are operational even during power outages, because analog power comes from the telephone network. Not so with ISDN. Every ISDN device requires its own powering. The power supply might be built into the unit, or it might be an external plug-in brick. In some devices, such as ISDN telephones, powering comes from the NT1. No matter what the source, ISDN devices must be locally powered.

For home use, lack of powering from the central office can be a real disadvantage, particularly in an emergency. Unless the ISDN device and the NT1 are connected to a back-up battery or Uninterruptable Power Supply (UPS), they will go dark whenever the power fails. Therefore, it is unwise to use ISDN as the only telephone service in homes.

---

8. I am sure you are as tired of reading this as I am of writing it. Maybe someday, we will be able to eliminate the ISDN deployment subject altogether. Until that day arrives, I want to be sure you know that it is not available everywhere. That is why I have stressed deployment so heavily throughout this book.

Extension Phones

There is another disadvantage to ISDN when it comes to home installations. Just about every home installation has multiple phones connected in parallel to the same telephone line. These extra phones are called extensions.

Extension phones all work the same way. Usually, every extension phone will ring whenever the number is dialed. This allows the user to answer the call from a number of locations in the home. Similarly, outgoing calls can be made on the same line from any extension phone. It is easy for several people to simultaneously pick up extension phones and participate in the conversation.

ISDN is another matter entirely. Since ISDN does not have an extension phone equivalent, it is not well-suited to home use. It is difficult to duplicate extensions with ISDN phones. About the only way to emulate extension phones is to assign the same call appearance to multiple ISDN phones on the same multipoint.[9]

Therefore it is difficult to replace POTS home voice service with ISDN unless the home only has, and only plans to have, a single telephone. This being the case, telecommuters should be dissuaded from replacing their POTS service with ISDN. Given the expense, powering, and extension phone issues, ISDN works out best as an ancillary service. Encourage the telecommuter to keep their analog line or lines, and to use the ISDN line for additional functionality. Fortunately, most telecommuters want business connections that supplement, but do not replace, their home POTS service. In this kind of home arrangement, ISDN works out quite well.

---

9. Multipoint is a type of multiple telephone service configuration for ISDN. It is usually expensive to install and requires the assignment of multiple phone numbers. Multipoint allows multiple ISDN devices, typically up to eight, to share a single line. Each device, if it is a telephone, can have a call appearance of each of the other devices. This gives it extension phone functionality, but each device is independent of the others and has it own assigned telephone number.

20

The View From the Deck of the Enterprise

When selecting equipment for the central site, a number of factors must be considered. Firstly, there has to be some assurance that the equipment in the remote locations is functionally compatible with the network central site equipment. This involves several levels of interoperability, including authentication, compression and inverse multiplexing. Compatibility with the enterprise network's operating systems and protocols must also be assured.

With all these factors to consider, there is no doubt that remote access to the enterprise changes things for the network itself, for the network staff and for the users. From the enterprise point of view, changes need to be made in network management, in billing procedures, in support issues and in security policies.

Network Management

ISDN's interaction with most networks is nearly seamless. An ISDN bridge or router should appear as just that to the network. Where network management is being used to administer the enterprise, ISDN represents just another link on the Simple Network Management Protocol (SNMP) topology map.

ISDN network devices that support Management Information Bases (MIBs) can be managed from SNMP management consoles. Network staff will be able to get parameters, monitor performance and, if allowed, set parameters like passwords and configurations, even in remote devices.

From a network management point of view, ISDN can be considered transparent. It functions the same as any serial link. However, the network administrator must decide whether the remote network device will be managed in telecommuter homes, or in corporate remote offices.

The enterprise network bridge or router should always be managed by SNMP. This allows the network staff to monitor the status of the network site's remote access devices. However, it may or may not be a good idea to manage the remote side of the connection.

There is a case to be made for managing or not managing devices on the remote side of the WAN connection. If large numbers of telecommuters or branch offices are connected to the enterprise network, the considerations for managing remote-side devices become more complex.

If the remote device supports SNMP, it is a candidate for management. The same thing holds for the remote user's PC. However, unless extensive trap-filtering is done, every glitch that occurs in the remote location will be reported to the management station. If, for example, there is a local power failure or telephone outage that affects the worker's home, the network staff will receive an alert. If the telecommuter turns off their PC or, heaven forbid, turns off the remote LAN device, an alert will also be sent to the network management console.

This can be a mixed blessing. On the one hand, it is good to know if the telecommuter has done something that affects their network connections. This allows the staff to be proactive instead of reactive in supporting telecommuters when they call in for assistance.

On the one hand, if an outage occurs at the corporate president's house, the staff may appreciate being alerted immediately. On the other hand, if there are hundreds or thousands of telecommuters, the network staff may not be as excited about receiving events of this magnitude from every single telecommuter.

SNMP monitoring becomes an even larger issue when on-demand networking is in use. Connections coming up or dropping due to dial-on-demand or bandwidth-on-demand changes, will cause triggers on the SNMP management console. When the network devices drop the call due to a lack of user activity, it will look to the SNMP console as if there has been a line failure. A device that was previously reachable is no longer on the network. Typically, this is will set off a trap alarm.

Unless some form of spoofing is used, the network staff will need to adjust the SNMP traps for the remote devices according to how often they are actually connected to your network. It may be a good idea not to allow the SNMP software to ping the remote device on a regular interval. This will eliminate many of the false trap alarms. It will also reduce network traffic on the WAN, and will prevent a call from being made to the remote side.

If a decision is made not to manage the remote side of the WAN connections, it will make things considerably easier to handle. However, from a support point of view, there is also something to be said for managing the remote side of the connection. Obviously, each network's administrators will have to decide which method best suits their needs.

Billing Issues

An entire book could probably be written on billing policy issues for telecommuters. Virtually no policy has the potential to be more controversial or contentious than billing.

A thumbnail of some of the more common billing issues includes: Whether to order the line as flat rate or measured service; whether to bill the line to the telecommuter or the corporation; and whether or not to charge the telecommuter for network access. Each has its own relative advantages and disadvantages; and each is best determined by establishing solid, well-thought-out corporate telecommuting policies.

A decision needs to be made whether to send telephone bills directly to the telecommuter for reimbursement, to the department, or whether to cover them in the central corporate telephone bill. The decision will probably be based on corporate billing policies and procedures, and on the carrier's billing capability. If charges will be received centrally and billed to telecommuters or departments, appropriate consideration must be given to charge-back structures built into the corporate accounting system. On the other hand, if calls will be absorbed centrally, then other considerations come into play.

There are cost advantages to consolidated billing, but there is also an associated loss of detail and accountability. Auditing telecommuting bills for legitimate toll and usage charges can be an important issue to the corporation or department. The relative advantages and disadvantages must be weighed and a decision made based on what best serves the telecommuter and the corporation. Unfortunately, the goals of these two groups are not always the same.

Network access charges can be a tricky issue. There is much controversy when it comes to remote network charges, particularly if the company is already billing users for telephone charges.

Some managers argue that the telecommuter is remotely accessing the corporate enterprise at the pleasure of the company and, therefore, all related costs should be absorbed by the corporation. Other managers argue that telecommuting reduces expenses for the telecommuter since their travel, lunch and clothing costs are nil. This being the case, the telecommuters should pay for the privilege of accessing the corporate enterprise.

The issue is clouded by the fact that, along with gaining access to the corporate enterprise, telecommuters frequently gain Internet access. Many corporate enterprise networks are connected to the Internet. Therefore, unless Internet access is filtered by a router, or blocked by a firewall on the enterprise, anyone who has access to the enterprise network can also access the Internet.

There are conflicting camps with regard to providing Internet access to telecommuters. One camp believes that Internet access should be considered a perk. After all, telecommuters are being given remote access to the corporate enterprise because it is in the best interest of the company to do so. If Internet access comes along with the package, so be it.

The other camp is not willing to provide services for free that others have to pay for out of their own pockets. They reason that all services from the enterprise network, including Internet access, should be charged back to the telecommuter. Still others argue that, while services on the corporate network should be made freely available to the telecommuter, Internet access should not be part of the package.

In the final analysis, it is up to each company's management to make a policy judgment. The company must decide what connection and service charges, if any, the company will absorb for their telecommuters. In some cases, it makes sense for the corporation to absorb all expenses. In other cases, having telecommuters pay for their own telephone charges, their own network access, their own Internet access, or any combination of these, makes more sense.

No matter what the case, the important point is to create a policy and consistently stick to it. Nothing is more deadly than providing remote LAN access to telecommuters, without a policy. Dealing with remote network access on a case-by-case basis is generally not a good idea.

Providing Telecommuter Support

An illustration of how complex it can be to provide full telecommuting services can be seen from the experience of Don Radick, Senior Network Analyst for

Holiday Inn Worldwide. As someone who is responsible for network support involving hundreds of telecommuters for Holiday Inn, he understands the complexities of supporting telecommuters.

Don points out that, "Each corporate department has a slightly different set of telecommuting requirements. Each telephone service provider has different capabilities to offer for telecommuting."

This creates a confusing array of requirements that must be sorted out for each new telecommuter. Don believes potential telecommuters should be repeatedly surveyed during the design and planning stages of the telecommuting project. This must be done frequently to determine and confirm their requirements.

According to Don, "Every application, file and print service, and communication need should be assessed, analyzed and documented."

There is a problem that often occurs when companies decide to extend their network resources to telecommuters. Management fails to realize that supporting remote users requires an investment of additional corporate resources, especially when compared to supporting an equivalent number of office-bound users.

Ironically, in many cases company management expects to support hundreds or thousands of telecommuters with the very same networking and telecommunications staff that already handles their corporate network and telecommunications services. Pushing the staff to this very widespread support limit is extremely tricky business. If the company is not willing to add additional resources to support telecommuting, it is important to carefully set users' expectations for support response time and speed of problem resolution.

While network backbone failures may fall in the emergency response category and require immediate attention at any hour of the night or day, telecommuters are typically supported on a much less aggressive basis. Trouble calls may be assigned next working day preference, and may take a back seat to more mission-critical outages and projects.

In some cases, telecommuters are left entirely on their own. When a telecommuter calls in a trouble, all the network staff will do is verify the network is alive. If it is, they will simply tell the telecommuter to call the telephone company.

Users need to understand and accept the level of support offered to them. If support plans are not agreed upon in advance by all parties, misunderstandings and frustration will result. Telecommuters, managers, and the support staff themselves, can become very dissatisfied with the level of service and support that is provided. This is not an acceptable situation from any point of view.

Network Security

There is endless debate on a number of issues surrounding remote LAN access. However, there is one area concerning remote network access where there is virtually no debate at all.

When it comes to security, every experienced networker knows that allowing dial access of any kind to their networks without appropriate network security is just plain stupid. It is amazing to what extent some network managers will go when providing for network security. They spend thousands of dollars on firewall systems and expensive security devices to prevent unwanted access to their networks, only to overlook the security risks of dial-in access to their network.

It is a simple fact of life that remote office connections increase the risk of security compromises and break-in attempts from outside the corporate net. There is just no way around this. It does not matter whether the remote access is provided through ISDN, Switched 56 or analog modem pools. In every case, security must be one of the major concerns network administrators consider when extending their enterprise networks to telecommuters, remote branches or other remote locations. It just makes sense to protect valuable network resources and information by having reasonable security in place for any form of dial-in access.

Without appropriate precautions, anyone can dial in to the network and do whatever they wish. That situation frequently spells disaster for the network. It can also spell trouble for other networks, particularly if the enterprise is connected to the Internet. Hackers frequently gain access to networks through remote access security holes on other networks. They use these as pass-through networks.

When it comes to protecting network resources, there are several things that can be done to reduce the risk. Most remote network devices provide some form of network security. The most common methods are user passwords and call back.

Passwords

Clearly, allowing remote access to the enterprise network creates additional security hazards, such as unauthorized individuals gaining access to network resources. Therefore, remote access to the network should be controlled, at the very least, by passwords. No one should be allowed access to the enterprise without first having to enter an account and password.

Passwords can protect against unauthorized persons accessing network services from work-at-home workstations. Suppose that Johnny, the hacking nephew, is visiting his Uncle Phil, the telecommuter. While Uncle Phil mixes drinks for his parents, Johnny wanders into the den. Noticing that Uncle Phil's PC is turned on, Johnny connects to the network and decides to have some fun. Unfortunately, since there is no password blocking access to the network, the fun is at Uncle Phil's and the network's expense.

Requiring user account authentication and frequently changing passwords is necessary for adequate security. It is also the first line of defense in protecting the network. Passwords should not be obvious and should be changed often.

Telecommuters should be encouraged, or even required, to use passwords that cannot be easily guessed. They should not be allowed to use obvious passwords such as *ISDN* or *remote access,* or their own names.

The network staff needs to consider how often passwords should be aged out. Increasing password life periods weakens security somewhat. Decreasing it makes access more difficult for telecommuters to remember their passwords. Whatever frequency is used for changing passwords, remote users should be cautioned that writing their passwords on Post-It notes attached to their computer monitors is not a wise idea.

Other Precautions

Other precautions can be taken to prevent unauthorized access to the enterprise from telecommuting workstations. Many of these are much the same as the precautions observed by those directly connected to the corporate network.

Restricting physical access to the workstation is one method that is frequently useful. Doing this in homes is somewhat more difficult than in the office, but it can be done. The workstation itself can be password-protected. Additionally, the room where the workstation is located can be kept locked when not in use. Again, this is one area where clearly defined policies are important. Telecommuters and home workers must understand the rules that the company has set for remote network access.

In the case of passwords and information that must be kept extremely confidential, data encryption can also be used. There are several security protocols, such as PGP or the DES encryption algorithm, used by the United States government. Security protocols and applications are available to protect passwords, as well as the data itself. A number of remote LAN access devices provide one or more encryption protocols in their products.

Call Back

If passwords are considered the first line of defense, call back is usually said to be the second line of defense.

Call back works in a fairly straightforward manner. The user calls in to establish a network session. A host or device on the network validates the fact that the user has supplied a legitimate account and password. At that point, the network-side device drops the connection and calls the user back. This allows the network to ensure that a device connected to a legitimate telephone number has been given access.

Call back is very flexible. It can be used with any switched service, digital or analog. However, it is not foolproof. Therefore, call back should never be used as the only form of authentication.

Call back does not validate the user, or the computer; only the telephone number. Unless other security measures are in place, anyone calling from that number is allowed access to the network. It is also possible to trick call back by using something as simple as call forwarding.

Another problem with call back is that the enterprise network winds up being charged for the call. Therefore, unless some charge-back mechanism is put in place, it increases the cost of operating the central site connections.

Incoming Calling Line Identification (ICLID)

One advantage offered by some digital services is that the incoming telephone number can be checked before the connection is allowed. ISDN, for example, passes the calling number as an Incoming Calling Line Identification (ICLID).

ICLID, also known as Calling Line ID (CLID) or Automatic Number Identification (ANI), is like dial-back security, but without the need to drop the connection and call back the remote user. On call set-up, ICLID passes the number of the calling party to the called party. Therefore, the network device can determine if the call is coming from a legitimate number. The network device can be configured to only accept recognized numbers, and to reject connection attempts from unauthorized telephone numbers.

This works well as an early line of defense, but it is a very basic method of handling security and far from foolproof. Like call back, LAN administrators must realize that the ICLID only validates that the correct telephone number is being used; it does not validate the user. Also, ICLID is not universal. Checking the ICLID will not work if the call is coming from a switch or location that does not issue the calling telephone number, or from one that blocks Caller ID.

Because it is provided by the ISDN service provider and not the ISDN user, the ICLID tends to be fairly reliable. However, like call back, ICLID can be fooled by using call forwarding through a second number.

While not particularly easy to do, it is possible to create a false ICLID. The ICLID can be hacked to substitute a fake Calling Party Number (CPN) in place of the real CPN. Doing this requires access to the telephone switch database, and hours of intensive work. It is unlikely that such internal shenanigans would go unnoticed by telephone company officials for very long. Still, be aware that it can be done if the hacker is enterprising enough.

If used with care and intelligence, ICLID can be a valuable network security tool. ICLID, along with password protection, can provide a reasonable basic level of security control.

Authentication

A better method of implementing security is through a process called authentication. As the connection is made, the remote device sends a password, or a random number called a *challenge,* to the network device. The network device compares the password with a stored string or performs a computation on the challenge sent from the remote device. If they match, voilà, the user is authenticated and given access to the network. If not, the call is refused.

Authentication can be handled in the network devices themselves, or a separate authentication host can be used. Authentication can be done by a remote host or a network device that serves other functions, or it can be done by a host or network device that has only one purpose in life: to validate the user.

Figure 20.1 shows how an authentication host can be set up. As can be seen from the figure, the authentication device accepts calls from the remote users. It then uses a procedure similar to what we have just described to validate the user. Once it verifies that the call originated from a legitimate user, the authentication device drops the call from the user. It then finds an open device in the remote network bridge or router bank, and instructs the open network device to call the remote user back. These validation schemes combine call back with user authentication.

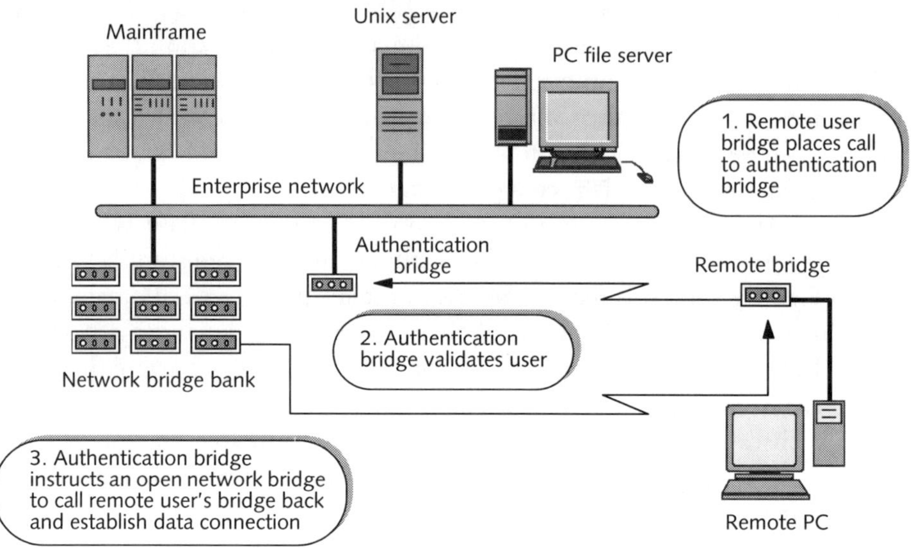

Figure 20.1 Dial-In access with authentication

Not only does this arrangement provide security, it can also support detailed logging and accounting mechanisms. This makes it possible to bill calls from a central location, and charge them back to the users. The log can be used for security monitoring purposes.

PAP and CHAP Authentication

The IETF has defined two protocols for security over PPP connections: Password Authentication Protocol (PAP) and Challenge-Handshake Authentication Protocol (CHAP). Both are specified in RFC 1334, "PPP Authentication Protocols."[1] These authentication protocols are intended for use by hosts and routers that connect to a PPP network via switched circuits or dial-up lines, but they can be applied to leased links as well.

Both protocols allow authentication of the remote device by creating a series of encrypted numbers. However, PAP provides only basic authentication. An identification password pair is repeatedly sent by the remote device to the authentication device until authentication is acknowledged or the connection is terminated. Since PAP sends passwords "in the clear," there is some risk that security can be compromised.

---

1. B. Lloyd, W. Simpson, "PPP Authentication Protocols," RFC 1334.

It is possible for hackers to monitor network packets and record a legitimate user's PAP log in sequence. They can then playback the log in at a later time, and gain access to the network. Since PAP has no time-out function, the hacker can use repeated trial-and-error attempts. Therefore, PAP is not a strong authentication method.

CHAP is a more robust authentication protocol. CHAP sends a "challenge" to the remote unit attempting to connect to the network. The remote unit responds with a calculated numerical value. The authentication device checks the response against its own calculation of the expected value. If the values match, the authentication is acknowledged; otherwise, the connection is terminated.

CHAP provides protection against log-in playback attacks, and trial-and-error attempts. The CHAP algorithm depends upon a "secret" known only to the authenticator and the remote access device. This "secret" is never sent over the link.

CHAP and PAP are good ways of ensuring that the correct remote device has dialed in to the network. Frequently, PAP and CHAP are included as internal protocols in the ISDN network devices. It should be remembered that both protocols authenticate the remote device, not the user. Therefore, they should always be used with some sort of login sequence.

Kerberos

Kerberos is an authentication protocol specifically developed for network security at the Massachusetts Institute of Technology. It uses an encrypted key that is passed to a Kerberos server for authentication purposes.

Kerberos is available in a number of shareware and commercial versions. However, it is rarely integrated into remote network devices. Kerberos has been designed to be used on TCP/IP networks. Generally, it does not support security access for other network protocols, such as IPX/SPX or AppleTalk.

Remote Authentication Dial-In User Service

Remote Authentication Dial-In User Service (Radius) is a propriety authentication server that can be used to provide remote access security. Some devices include or support access to Radius authentication servers.

TACACS

Terminal Access Controller Access Control System (TACACS) is another form of authentication. It uses the RFC 1492 access control protocol. Even though it is based on TCP/IP, a remote access user does not have to be connected to the network as an IP client to use TACACS.

Dynamic Password Authentication

Dynamic Password Authentication provides the user with a constantly changing password. Under this system, the user does not need to remember their password because it changes automatically and regularly. This leads to better security and it makes stealing a user's password far more difficult. It also can provide greater peace of mind for the remote user and the network staff.

There are several methods for providing Dynamic Password Authentication.

Security Cards

Security cards work by generating random and frequently changing numbers that can be used as passwords. The user either passes the card through a reader, or enters a sequence by keyboard as it appears on the card's LCD display. The random sequence is checked by a network device that is synchronized to the card.

Security cards are a good tool for authenticating the user. Since the password changes every few minutes, there is very little danger of stolen passwords. They do well with other forms of security, such as ICLID, call back, and PAP and CHAP security.

Like any security measure, security cards are not perfect. Stolen or broken cards are a concern. If the legitimate user loses the card, or if it is stolen, there is the same risk as someone stealing the keys to a house or car. Given the right set of circumstances, an unauthorized person can use the stolen card with a known account to gain access into the network.

Battery life and reliability are other concerns with security cards. Without a properly functioning card, the legitimate user cannot log into the network. This is more of an annoyance than a risk, but it is something that affects security card use.

It should also be noted that there have been some successful attempts to defeat the security algorithm incorporated into security cards.

Which Security Method is Best

It is obvious that one single method will not do it all. In reality, it is probably best to use several security mechanisms in conjunction with each other. For example, the network might use security cards to validate the user; CHAP authentication to validate the device; and ICLID to verify the correct number is connecting.

A final word of caution concerning security is in order. Some network device vendors are sloppy in how they treat security. For example, some devices default to no security when they are first installed or if they are reset. Unless the installers and users are both aware of this, it creates a security hole that can catch the network staff completely off guard. Therefore, it pays to be sure that any new network device, or any device that has been reset from its previous configuration, is not offering unauthorized outsiders the chance to get on your network.

One Final Thought

There is one final point to keep in mind. Placing a remote workstation on an enterprise network has the potential to expose the workstation to security risks as much as it exposes the network. This is particularly true if the workstation is configured to allow external users to attach to it.

Unexpected access to the remote workstation can occur when using TCP/IP applications like Telnet or FTP. It can also occur when the workstation supports peer-to-peer networking. For example, workstations running the Macintosh OS with file sharing turned on, when remotely connected, become accessible from anywhere on the network. The same is true of workstations running file sharing under Windows 95.

Remote users should be assisted by the network staff to assure that potential security holes on their machines are closed. This includes making sure that guest access is not allowed under Windows 95 or the Macintosh OS. Similarly, TCP/IP applications should have an appropriate host file created to prevent unauthorized access to the machine. This is particularly critical when the machine is connected to an ISP or an enterprise network with Internet access. There is no reason to expose the unsuspecting remote user to attacks from anywhere in the world.

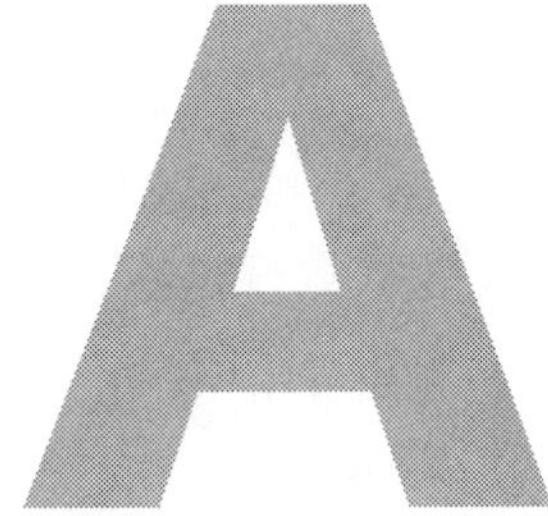

Remote LAN and ISDN Information Sources

This appendix includes a number of sources for remote LAN and ISDN information. Wherever possible, telephone numbers and World Wide Web site addresses are given.

Obviously, there are a significant number of sources available for ISDN and remote LAN access information. The listing in this appendix is not intended to be all-encompassing. Instead, consider it a starter kit. It will point you in the right direction, and at least get you started in your search for remote LAN access information.

The information is current as of this printing and as accurate as I could make it. However, many of these sources will no doubt change over time. Therefore, the accuracy of the telephone numbers, e-mail addresses, and web sites is not guaranteed.

ISDN Service Centers

There is a wealth of information about ISDN from a variety of sources. Many service providers have created ISDN service centers that are just a phone call away. ISDN centers are generally equipped to answer questions about ISDN in their regions, including availability and charges. Sometimes the centers also have information about ISDN equipment. The people staffing these centers are usually quite knowledgeable regarding ISDN services.

Ameritech	To order Home Professional & ISDN service call: 1-800-419-5400. To order Business Professional & ISDN service call: 1-800-417-9888. http://teamdata.aads.net/isdn/quote.htf
Bell Atlantic	To order or get information about Bell Atlantic's residential ISDN service, call the Bell Atlantic InfoSpeed center at 1-800-204-7332. You can also send an e-mail message to isdncin@bell-atl.com. General ISDN information is also available by calling 1-800-570-ISDN. http://www.bell-atl.com/customer/consumer/home.html
Bell South	To place an ISDN order, call 1- 800-858-9413 or 770-496-2925. For technical support: 1- 800-256-6923 or 770-496-2901 http://www.bst.bls.com/bbs/isdnintr.htm
NYNEX	Call the Nynex automated response system at 1-800-GET-ISDN for information about ISDN availability, pricing and applications. http://www.nynex.com/iixxxpg1.html
Pacific Bell	You can order ISDN from Pacific Bell by calling 1-800-4PB-ISDN, or by faxing your request to: 1-800-555-0886. http://www.pacbell.com/isdn/
Southwestern Bell Telephone	To find out more about Southwestern Bell's ISDN services, call 1-800-SWB-ISDN. http://www.sbc.com/swbell/shortsub/digiline.html
U S West	For residence & home office ISDN, call 800-898-9675. For small business ISDN requests, call 800-246-5226 http://www.uswest.com/isdn/index.html

ISDN Resources on the Internet

In addition to the Regional Bell Operating Companies (RBOCs) who maintain information pages on the Internet, the Internet features ISDN discussion groups and World Wide Web home pages dedicated to ISDN. Bellcore, the research arm of the seven RBOCs, also has a wealth of information available on the Internet.

Dan Kegel maintains a very popular and useful ISDN Web page. Be sure to check Dan's page out at http://alumni.caltech.edu/~dank/isdn/. It is one of the best sources for ISDN information, and it has links to a number of other ISDN Web pages.

The Usenet news group comp.dcom.isdn has a free-form open discussion concerning ISDN issues.

The ISDN FAQ (Frequently Asked Questions) has lots of information on the most often asked questions about ISDN service. It is available via anonymous FTP to host rtfm.mit.edu. Look in the directory /pub/usenet/news.answers/isdn-faq.

Some ISDN vendors provide information and support, as well, on the Internet. Many vendors have Web pages offering specific information on ISDN products. Here is but a short sample:

Terminal Adapters

http://www.3com.com/0files/nettechs/isdn.html
http://www.attns.com/er2f.htm
http://www.motorola.com/MIMS/ISG/Products/ISDN_Products.html
http://www.usr.com/Courier/imodem.html

ISDN Network Devices

http://branch.com/netexpress/netexpress.html
http://www.acc.com/
http://www.ascend.com/
http://www.baynetworks.com/
http://www.cisco.com/combinet/
http://www.cygnus.nb.ca/pri.html
http://www.digibd.com/
http://www.farallon.com/
http://www.gandalf.ca/
http://www.infoanalytic.com/isc/index.htm
http://www.intel.com/
http://www.microcom.com/isdn/isdn.htm
http://www.satusa.com/Planet1.html
http://www.shiva.com/
http://www.usr.com/
http://www.xircom.com/Products/bri.html

General ISDN Information

http://www.ccg4isdn.com/isdn/info.html
http://www.isdntek.com/isdntext.html
http://www.ocn.com/
http://www.sgi.com/
http://www.sun.com/
http://www.bellcore.com/ISDN/ISDN.html

Books about ISDN

Happily, there is no shortage of ISDN, networking and remote LAN access books. Just because you finished reading my book, there is no need to stop reading on the subject. Here is just a short sampling of titles about ISDN and remote LAN access:

ISDN, Gary C. Kessler, McGraw-Hill (ISBN 0-07-034242-3)

ISDN for Dummies, David Angell, IDG Books (ISBN 1-56884-331-3)

ISDN Solutions Guide, revised, Corporation for Open Systems (1995)

Remote LAN Connections, William Wong, M&T Books (ISBN 1-55851-438-4)

Sensible ISDN Data Applications, Jeffrey Neil Fritz, West Virginia
        University Press (ISBN 0-937058-341-9)

The ISDN Literacy Book, Gerald L. Hopkins, Addison-Wesley
        (ISBN 0-201-62979-8)

Using ISDN, James Y. Bruce, Que (ISBN 0-7897-0405-6)

ISDN User Groups

User groups can be a terrific source of information and encouragement. Some current ISDN user groups include:

- Asian ISDN Council
- European ISDN Users' Forum (EIUF)
- Indonesian ISDN & Internet User Forum
        http://www.idola.net.id/i3uf/
- North American ISDN Users' Forum (NIUF)
        http://www.niuf.nist.gov/misc/niuf.html
- Pacific Region ISDN/Data User Forum
- Southern African ISDN Forum
        http://www.saif.org.za/
- The California ISDN Users' Group
        http://www.ciug.org/
- The New York ISDN Users Group
        http://www.users.interport.net/~digital/index.html
- The Texas ISDN Users Group (TIUG)
        http://www.crimson.com/isdn/
- Washington (DC) ISDN User's Group

PPP RFCs

1764 S. Senum, "The PPP XNS IDP Control Protocol (XNSCP)."

1763 S. Senum, "The PPP Banyan Vines Control Protocol (BVCP)."

1762 S. Senum, "The PPP DECnet Phase IV Control Protocol (DNCP)."

1717 K. Sklower, B. Lloyd, G. McGregor, D. Carr, "The PPP Multilink Protocol (MP)."

1663 D. Rand, "PPP Reliable Transmission."

1662 W. Simpson, "PPP in HDLC-like Framing."

1661 W. Simpson, "The Point-to-Point Protocol (PPP)."

1638 F. Baker, R. Bowen, "PPP Bridging Control Protocol (BCP)."

1618 W. Simpson, "PPP over ISDN."

1570 W. Simpson, "PPP LCP Extensions."

1552 W. Simpson, "The PPP Internetwork Packet Exchange Control Protocol (IPXCP)."

1378 B. Parker, "The PPP AppleTalk Control Protocol (ATCP)."

1377 D. Katz, "The PPP OSI Network Layer Control Protocol (OSINLCP)."

1334 B. Lloyd, W. Simpson, "PPP Authentication Protocols."

1333 W. Simpson, "PPP Link Quality Monitoring."

1332 G. McGregor, "The PPP Internet Protocol Control Protocol (IPCP)."

10Base-T

An IEEE standard for Ethernet wiring over twisted-pair telephone cable.

100Base-TX

IEEE 802.3 standard for 100-Mbps networking over twisted-pair cable. 100Base-TX requires 2-pair Category 5 cable.

Address

A unique numeric identifier of a node on a local area network.

Address Resolution Protocol (ARP)

A protocol used to resolve a destination hardware MAC address from its known IP address.

Adapter

See Ethernet adapter card.

Alternate Mark Inversion (AMI)

An early framing code for ISDN and T1 circuits. AMI represents a 0 (zero) by the absence of a voltage, while a 1 (one; also called a mark) is represented by a positive or negative pulse. The polarity depends on whether the preceding 1 was negative or positive. That causes the marks to be inverted on an alternating basis. Therefore, the name *alternate* mark inversion. In many cases, AMI has been replaced by newer line codes such as 2B1Q and B8ZS.

AppleTalk

Protocols that allow Macintosh computers to communicate with printers, file servers, and other devices.

AppleTalk Remote Access (ARA)

A protocol that allows a remote Macintosh computer to dial in to an AppleTalk network over serial lines, such as ISDN or modems.

Application Program Interface (API)

A common interface that allows programmers to write higher-level code that accesses lower-level functions.

Asynchronous Transfer Mode (ATM)

ATM is an evolving service that promises very high speed connections. While ATM can be supported at T1 rates, its greatest advantage is found on multimode fiber at OC-3 (155 Mbps) rates. It also supports higher rates, such as OC-12 (622 Mbps) over single-mode fiber. ATM is a cell-switched technology based on the Broadband ISDN specification (B-ISDN).

Backbone

A network topology consisting of a single length of cable with multiple connection points.

Bandwidth On Demand Interoperability (BONDING)

A method used for aggregating B channels for greater bandwidth. Typically used during videoconferencing sessions.

Basic Rate Interface (BRI)

Basic Rate ISDN rate is a 2B+D service. It has two 64-kbps B (Bearer) channels, and one 16-kbps D (Delta or Data) channel. Each B channel can support simultaneous, independent, voice, video or data connections.

Bearer (B) Channel

The basic building block of ISDN. The B channel is a 64-kilobit-per-second (kbps) digital channel, designed to support voice, video or data.

Binary (or Bipolar) Eight Zero Suppression (B8ZS)

A data transmission format used for PRI and T1 services. B8ZS coding enables equipment to recognize an "all zeroes" condition in a data byte. A B8ZS code is substituted for the all-zero byte. The destination replaces the code with the all-zeroes byte.

Bit Error Rate Tests (BERT)

A series of tests that can determine the number of errors that occur in a line, over time.

Bootstrap Protocol (BootP)

A method described in IETF RFC 951 that provides a mechanism for dynamic addressing.

Bridge

A device that links two or more similar networks forming a single, larger network.

Bridge taps

Connections used for the inteconnection of telephone cables. When ISDN is installed, any bridge taps must be removed.

BRITE (BRI Terminal Extender)

Telephone network cards are used at central offices to extend ISDN over an ICS.

Broadband ISDN (B-ISDN)

A higher speed version of ISDN that forms the basis for an up-and-coming communications technology, called Asynchronous Transfer Mode.

California ISDN User's Group (CIUG)
> A regional ISDN user's group that has created interoperability bake-off sessions, where vendors can test compatibility between each other's WAN products in a neutral environment.

Central Office (CO)
> A building or facility where the telephone switch is located. The CO serves the local telephone customers.

Challenge-Handshake Authentication Protocol (CHAP)
> A protocol specified in IETF RFC 1334 that supports security over point-to-point links.

Circuit Switching
> A system in which an exclusive path exists between sender and receiver for the duration of the session or call.

Collision
> A situation that occurs when two devices on a network try to transmit at the exact same time. When this happens, their transmissions will bump into each other. When a collision occurs, both devices must retransmit the data.

Com port
> A PC serialized output port, typically using an RS-232-style connector. Used to support data communications outside the device. A newer version of the communications port uses the RS-422 standard.

Compression
> A method where file size is reduced, increasing the effective bandwidth of the link.

Connection oriented
> A method that exchanges information based on the establishment of physical connection. ATM and ISDN technologies use connection-oriented protocols.

Connectionless
> A method that allows data to be exchanged without first establishing a connection. LANs, such as Ethernet and Token Ring, use connectionless protocols. Many network protocols, such as IP and IPX, are connectionless.

Connector
> The hardware component of a device, such as a plug, which is used to attach it to another device.

Constant Bit Rate (CBR) Services
> *See* isochronous.

Contention
> A situation where there are more devices in the field that can connect to the network than there are network devices to receive the connections. Contention is based on the usually correct assumption that not everyone will want to be connected to the network devices at the same time.

Crossover cable
> A 10Base-T cable in which certain wires cross over within the cable, so that signals entering the cable on one pin exit on a different pin. A crossover cable can be used with some bridges

and routers to eliminate the need for a concentrator. This works if there is only one network device and a single computer on a remote 10Base-T network.

Customer Premise Equipment (CPE)

CPE is the telephone company's name for the equipment you own that is connected to the telephone network.

Demand Assigned Multiple Access (DAMA)

An out-of-band signaling system used for satellite connection. DAMA is compatible with ISDN and SS7 signaling.

Delta (D) channel

The D channel is a 16-kbps channel whose primary function is signaling between the central office telephone switch and the Customer Premise Equipment. The D channel is sometimes referred to as the data channel.

Device

Electronic equipment used on a network, such as a hub, router, workstation, or printer.

Device certification

In the United States, the Federal Communications Commission certifies devices in terms of their radio frequency (RF) emissions.

Driver

A program that controls the network hardware or implements the protocol stacks through which higher-level applications communicate with the network hardware.

Dynamic Host Configuration Protocol (DHCP)

A protocol developed by the Internet Engineering Task Force to handle dynamic network addressing. DHCP, which is an extended version of BootP, is described in RFC 1531.

Dynamic Password Authentication

This provides the user with a constantly changing password. Under this system, the user does not need to remember the password because it changes automatically and regularly.

Enterprise Data Network (EDN)

The EDN is typically a large internetwork, such as a corporate enterprise network, or the Internet.

Enterprise Network Data Interconnectivity Family (ENDIF)

ENDIF is a user's workshop under the North American ISDN Users' Forum. ENDIF has made a major contribution to remote LAN access by creating interoperability implementation agreements (IAs). These IAs have made it possible for multiple vendor's ISDN network products to interoperate together.

Ethernet

Protocols defining a type of local area network, characterized by a 10- or 100-megabit-per-second (Mbps) data rate. Ethernet networks can run over thicknet, thinnet, or twisted-pair wiring.

Ethernet adapter card

A component installed in a device that enables the device to connect to an Ethernet network. Network interface cards (NIC), with appropriate driver software, are considered to be Ethernet adapter cards.

EtherTalk

Apple Computer's protocol that allows an AppleTalk network to be connected by Ethernet cables.

Frame

The unit of transmission at the data link layer. A frame may include a header and/or a trailer, and a block of data.

Frame relay

A packet-switching technology that is derived from X.25, but operates much more efficiently. Frame relay performs fewer error checks and, therefore, offers much higher performance than X.25. Frame relay was designed to operate over digital networks. Frame relay was initially designed as a bearer service for ISDN.

Gateway

A device that translates protocols between two physical types of networks.

Group Workstations (GW)

A GW is a small group of networked workstations, such as might be found in a branch office or department.

H channel

The ISDN H channel offers high bandwidth connections ranging from 384-kbps (H0) through 135.168-Mbps (H4).

In-band signaling

A signaling system used for call management that steals some of the channel's bandwidth and redirects it to control call services.

Incoming Calling Line Identification (ICLID)

Also known as Calling Line ID, Caller ID, and Automatic Number Identification, ICLID provides the number of the calling party to the called party.

Individual Workstations (IW)

An IW is a single remote workstation or PC such as is typically used in telecommuting.

Institute of Electrical and Electronic Engineers (IEEE)

An international professional society that issues standards for networks and other electronics-related technologies.

Integrated Services Digital Network (ISDN)

A switched digital service that supports voice, video and data over a single telephone line.

Interexchange Carrier (IXC)

A United States national telephone company, such as AT&T, MCI or Sprint.

International Telecommunication Union—Telecommunications Sector (ITU-T)

The successor to International Telegraph and Telephone Consultative Committee (CCITT). An international body that sets world-wide telecommunications standards.

International Telegraph and Telephone Consultative Committee (CCITT)

An older international body that sets world-wide telecommunications standards.
See International Telephone Union-Telecommunications Sector (ITU-T).

Internet
> A world-wide network that connects millions of hosts and thousands of networks. The primary protocol used by the Internet is TCP/IP.

Internet Engineering Task Force (IETF)
> The IETF sets de facto standards for the Internet. These standards are called Requests For Comments (RFCs).

Internet Service Provider (ISP)
> Companies that provide dial-in Internet access for remote users.

Internetwork
> A network of networks, typically with many subnets or ancillary networks attached to it.

Interoffice Carrier System (ICS)
> A digital link that is established between telephone central offices.

ISDN Ordering Codes (IOCs)
> An attempt to simplify switch translations by creating a series of switch translation shortcuts or codes for ISDN equipment.

Isochronous Applications
> Time-sensitive applications, such as voice or video, that are intolerant of delays. Also known as Constant Bit Rate (CBR) services.

Local Access and Transport Areas (LATA)
> Localized telephone service areas, defined by the government after divestiture.

Local Area Network (LAN)
> A topology that allows multiple computers to connect to each other. Ethernet and Token Ring are two popular LAN topologies.

Local Exchange Carrier (LEC)
> The local telephone company.

Logical Channel Numbers (LCNs)
> Individual virtual channels on a common link. Terminal servers can take advantage of ISDN running on B Packet mode to set up multiple simultaneous LCNs for user access to common services.

Loopback
> A diagnostic test in which the transmitted signal is returned to the sending device after passing through a data communications link. The test allows a comparison of the returned signal with the original transmitted signal.

Media Access Control layer (MAC)
> Layer two in the OSI model. The MAC layer is concerned with transmitting information to the transmission medium. Bridging occurs on the MAC layer.

Megabits per second (Mbps)
> A measure of the rate of data transmission equal to a million bits per second.

Modem

A name derived from the combination of MOdulate-DEModulate. A modem is a device that uses a modulation-demodulation process to translate digital data to analog tones for transmission over an analog telephone network.

Multilink Point-to-Point (MP)

An extension of Point-to-Point Protocol that combines channels for greater bandwidth. Multilink is defined in IETF RFC 1717. Over ISDN, MP supports network connectivity using multiple B channels.

Narrowband ISDN

A form of ISDN. Basic Rate and Primary Rate ISDN are considered to be narrowband ISDN.

National ISDN (NI-x)

A specification that attempts to unify ISDN services. The first NI specifications are NI-1, NI-2, and NI-3, also known as NI-95.

National ISDN Council (NIC)

The National ISDN Council, along with Bellcore, is responsible for the development of National ISDN specifications.

Network Access Server

A device on an enterprise network, the Internet, or a LAN that allows remote users to access the network.

Network device

A bridge or router, typically that provides connections between networks.

Network layer

Layer 3 of the OSI reference model. Layer 3 is the layer at which routing occurs.

Network Operating System (NOS)

Computer code that controls the operation of a network system.

Network Terminator (NT1)

The NT1 primarily functions as part of the telephone network's central office telephone switch. However, the NT1 does provide limited information on the status of the ISDN lower-layer connection to the user.

Network topology

A physical arrangement of devices and cables in a network. Network topologies include backbone, star, and daisy chain.

Node

A single, addressable device on a network. Computers, networked printers, and routers are nodes.

North American ISDN Users' Forum (NIUF)

A user group charted and sponsored by the United States Department of Commerce through the National Institute of Standards and Technology. The NIUF has been the prime mover for the advancement and promotion of ISDN in North America.

Open Systems Interface (OSI)
An architecture that models network protocols into seven individual layers.

Operating System (OS)
Computer code that handles the low-level functions necessary to the operation of a PC.

Out-of-band signaling
A signaling system that handles call control in a completely separate network, resulting in higher user throughput and very rapid call set-up times.

Packet
A group of bits that has been formatted to be transmitted as a unit across a network.

Packet Assembler Dissembler (PAD)
A PAD takes individual packets and puts them on a common link. At the other end, the PAD takes data on the common link and creates individual packets again.

Packet Switching
An aggregated group of bits, called packets, that are individually addressed and sent from a source to a destination, typically over connectionless networks. Devices that operate on a packet-switching network must examine each packet to determine the appropriate forwarding action.

Password Authentication Protocol (PAP)
A security protocol for point-to-point links, as specified in RFC 1334.

Peer
The other end of the point-to-point link.

Pixels
Picture elements that are used to create a screen image on a computer monitor.

Plain-old-telephone-service (POTS)
The original telephone network was analog in nature. When the newer digital services first appeared, analog telephone services were given a new moniker: plain-old-telephone-service. POTS devices include standard telephones, answering machines, fax machines, and the ever-present modem.

Point-to-Point Protocol (PPP)
A protocol designed by the Internet Engineering Task Force to support virtually any network protocol over serial lines, such as ISDN or modems.

Port
An access point for data to enter, exit, or be repeated across a network; a hardware receptacle on a network device, such as a socket or jack, into which you can plug a connector.

Primary Rate Interface (PRI)
PRI in North America, has 23 B channels at 64 kbps each and one 64-kbps D channel. Each B channel can support simultaneous, independent, voice, video or data connections.

Protocol
A set of rules that allow computers to communicate.

Public Data Networks (PDN)

A PDN is a network, usually based on the X.75 protocol, that allows users to connect packet services to each other over a public network.

Quality of Service (QOS)

The grade of service provided by a given connection.

Regional Bell Operating Companies (RBOC)

Seven smaller "Baby Bell" companies that were created as a result of the 1984 divestiture of AT&T. There are seven RBOCs in the United States: NYNEX, Bell Atlantic, Ameritech, Bell South, Southwestern Bell, US West, and Pacific Telesis.

Repeater

A device that rebroadcasts a network signal, allowing it to travel for longer distances.

Request For Comments (RFCs)

A document used by the Internet Engineering Task Force to describe de facto standards for the Internet.

Reverse Address Resolution Protocol (RARP)

A method that allows a client to determine its IP network address.

RJ-11

A telephone-industry connector type, usually containing six pins. Analog devices and the ISDN U interface both use RJ-11 connectors.

RJ-45

A telephone-industry connector type, usually containing eight pins. Ethernet 10Base-T and the ISDN S/T interface both use RJ-45 connectors.

Router

A device that connects two or more networks. A router receives data from other network devices and retransmits the data to its proper destination over the most efficient path from one network to another.

Routing Table Maintenance Protocol (RTMP)

AppleTalk network updates sent out every ten to fifteen seconds. Used to exchange Apple-Talk routing tables.

Small Office/Home Office (SOHO)

A term applied to telecommuters and small offices that are remotely connected to an enterprise network, the Internet or a LAN.

Segment

Any single length of network cable between two nodes.

Segmentation

The process of breaking a packet into smaller units. Segmentation is used when sending a large packet over a network that can only support small packets. Segmentation is also used for inverse multiplexing techniques.

Sequencing
>The process of tagging packets or segments with numbers before transmission. This allows them to be sent in any order, and still be placed in the proper order at the receiving end. Frequently sequencing is used with segmentation to provide efficient packet transmission of multiple change links such as ISDN.

Serial Line IP (SLIP)
>A protocol designed to support network access over serial connections, such as modems or ISDN. SLIP supports just one protocol, TCP/IP.

Service Advertisement Protocol (SAP)
>A protocol used by Novell's NetWare network operating system. SAP messages advertise services and communicates between servers. SAPs carry information about what file servers are reachable on the network, and what services on those servers are available.

Service Profile Identifier (SPID)
>The SPID is used to identify the ISDN device to the network. It also identifies the service profiles (features) that are applied to a specific device or line.

Signaling System 7 (SS7)
>SS7 is responsible for a telephone network technology called out-of-band signaling.

Simple Network Management Protocol (SNMP)
>A protocol used for network management.

Spoofing
>A technique used to keep switched digital services from connecting networks when network update information needs to be transmitted to the remote side.

S/T Interface
>A six-wire (three-pair) ISDN interface. One wire pair is used for transmitted data, one pair for received data and one pair for power. The S/T interface is on the customer (user) side of the NT1.

Subscriber Line Carrier (SLC)
>A system used to extend analog and, sometimes, ISDN lines. SLC (pronounced *slick*) services are commonly used internally by the telephone carriers.

Switched 56
>One of the earliest switched digital services. It allowed digital calls to be placed between various locations.

Telephone switch
>Typically a large mainframe with many input/output ports. A digital telephone switch with special hardware and software is required to provide ISDN services.

Terminal Adapter (TA)
>A device that provides access from the PC com port to the outside world across an Integrated Services Digital Network. Terminal adapters get their name from their function of adapting the ISDN B channels to existing terminal equipment serial port standards, such as RS-232 and V.35.

Terminal End Point Identifier (TEI)
>The TEI is used with the SPID to identify the individual devices on the ISDN line.

Time-To-Live (TTL)

Time allocated by routers to packets that specifies how long they may remain on the network.

Training

A sequence of tones used to establish a communications link. Training usually involves negotiation between devices on both ends of the communications link. Training sequences are used for modems, inverse multiplexers, and many other communications devices.

Training time

The time it takes for a pair of devices to execute a training sequence and negotiate the parameters of the connection.

Translations

Information that is entered into a telephone switch. Translations tell the switch how the line must be set up to support the specific ISDN equipment on the line.

Two Bits One Quartenary (2B1Q)

A transmission code commonly used for ISDN BRIs. Two bits of data are mapped to one of four possible line voltage values.

U interface

The U interface is a two-wire (single-pair) connection from the Central Office. It is on the far (switch) side of the NT1.

Universal Asynchronous Receiver Transmitter (UART)

An integrated circuit chip that contains all the logic circuitry for the parallel-to-serial conversion required for signals to pass through the com port.

Unshielded Twisted-Pair (UTP)

A type of cable that is specified by 10Base-T in IEEE 802.3 using 22- or 24-gauge, solid copper wire with RJ-45 connectors.

Very Small Aperture Terminal (VSAT)

Equipment that uses transportable satellite link equipment and relatively small uplink/downlink dishes.

Wide Area Networks (WANs)

Extensions of local area networks that traverse building boundaries to give remote users access to corporate and Internet resources.

A

B

C

About the Author

Jeffrey N. Fritz is a Telecommunications Engineer with West Virginia University's Telecommunications and Network Services department where he is responsible for new technology development for WINnet, the West Virginia University enterprise network. He also oversees the daily planning, operations, and management of WINnet.

Jeff has played a key role in the implementation of Integrated Services Digital Network. Since 1988 he has directed the University's WINnet Network Applications Lab, a recognized leader in the development of ISDN and remote LAN access applications. Jeff is Chair Emeritus of the North American ISDN Users' Forum Enterprise Network Data Interconnectivity Family, and has also served as chair of the National Information Infrastructure Working Group.

Jeff is the author of *Sensible ISDN Data Applications*, published by West Virginia University Press. In addition, he regularly writes for publications such as *BYTE, Data Communications, Computerworld, Communications Week, Network World* and *Telecommunications*.

Jeff is a part-time instructor with the American Institute where he teaches the hands-on seminar and wrote the workbook for: Mastering and Implementing ISDN. He holds a Master's degree in Electrical Engineering.